Religion, Wealth and Poverty

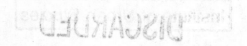

Religion,
Wealth
and
Poverty

James V. Schall

Canadian Cataloguing in Publication Data

Schall, James V.
Religion, wealth and poverty

Includes bibliographical references.
ISBN 0-88975-112-9
1. Economics - Religious aspects - Christianity.
I. Fraser Institute (Vancouver, B.C.) II. Title.
BR115.E3S32 1989   261.8'5   C89-091460-5

Printed in Singapore.

Contents

Foreword

This iconoclastic book trenchantly analyses numerous religious sacred cows, and finds them all wanting. Fr. Schall, a Jesuit Priest on the political science faculty of Georgetown University, views "social justice" as an attempt to wrest control of the economy from the citizen, and thereby strengthen the state; he lauds the profit motive as a great boon to the poor, and criticizes governmental welfare programmes as dependency creators. In his view, the poor are poor not because the rich are rich, but in spite of that fact. He sees an important role for religion as a wealth creating institution, but strenuously opposes the church's persistent opposition to democratic capitalism, the last best hope for the poor.

Michael Novak

Preface

Everyone recognizes a great deal of turmoil within the churches, turmoil that is reflective of ideological movements and tendencies in the culture at large. For the general public, the relatively sudden appearance of religion not primarily as worship or doctrine, but as social activism, has been not a little perplexing. Numerous sympathetic critics, many of the faithful, and interested observers sense that something is occurring with vast and unsettling implications for the well-being of the public order and for religion itself. They are not at all sure, however, that what is happening is itself in the best interests of religion or of the poor and outcast for whom it is said to be occurring.

A number of attempts to understand the origins and meaning of this politicized religious presence have been made in recent years. Paul Johnson, Michael Novak, James Hitchcock, E.O. Norman, George Weigel, Peter Berger, Anne Roche Muggeridge, Josef Ratzinger, Rodger Charles, S.J., Rael Jean Issacs, and Brian Benestad, among many others, have sought to trace the roots and implications of religion that presents itself mostly in political or economic terms.

From his very first address at Puebla in his first year as Pope, John Paul II has insisted that religion remain true to itself if it is to influence the civil order as it should. His insights have been too little understood because the way they are heard from a politicized religious standpoint makes his argument seem distant. In fact, it is in the direct line of the tradition that would limit the state and preserve the integrity of those things which religion teaches.

In *Religion, Wealth, and Poverty,* Father James V. Schall, S.J. analyses the issues of war and peace, wealth and poverty, spirituality and its relation to economic growth, charity and business, sharing and private property, liberality and initiative, and much more. He does so from a perspective that is new and refreshing, especially to the lay reader accustomed to receiving a strongly radical or even marxist perspective from academic or clerical intellectuals and media. Melding insights from the Bible, from Aristotle, and St. Thomas Aquinas, Father Schall reads like a breath of fresh air, not only because of his writing style, which is delightful, but even more so because of his scholarly insights, which are brilliantly iconoclastic, and because of his moral vision, which is in the tradition of that sanity of which G.K. Chesterton spoke so eloquently.

If anyone wants to see just how big a gap exists between the classical Christian perspective on human worth both for man himself and for the public order, over against so much radical clerical and academic writing purporting to provide methods and institutions for helping the weak of mankind, consider the following:

- **Defence.** Contrary to the often pacifistic notions of some U.S. bishops and other religious groups, weapons can and do play a positive role in society—in their capacity to deter what is even worse. True, on the assumption of universal good will, weapons would be unnecessary. But on that ground it would make sense to rid ourselves at once of doors, locks, fences, reinforced windows, caution for personal safety, body guards, and other protective necessities. Fr. Schall states: "Wars are caused by aggressors, not arms. Some people desire what *we* have. We can either give all of what we have to them or prevent them from taking it from us." (chapters 1, 19)

- **Hunger.** In an era when men can go to the moon, are capable of magnificent scientific and technological feats, and can achieve food abundance in many places, there is no excuse for starvation in any part of the world. There are explanations, however, and the biggest one is a political ideology of *dirigisme*. A basic premise in this philosophy is certain curious, positive rights, i.e., the so called "right to be fed." Not only false, this idea is dangerous as well. It is used as a stick to beat those who are capable of producing crops, for they must give them up, and an excuse for those who are unable to produce their own crops. And another false and pernicious idea is marxism. In the words of our author: "The best way to discover why Tanzania remains poor and depends on hand-outs is not to examine its soil or its rainfall, but to read the collected speeches of Mr. Julius Nyerere." (chapters 2,3)

- *Social justice.* This otherwise valid concept has been used as a veil for policies of forced income redistribution. "Justice" alone should never be used as the pretext for taking the honest earnings of a rich person and giving them to a poor one; indeed, it is not only dishonest to steal, it is also unjust. But the "social" hides all that, and seeks to render legitimate that which is illegitimate. The real issue, however, is "whether the actual control, production and distribution of wealth are in the hands of the citizenry, including the poor, or whether the citizens, especially the poor, are essentially reduced to objects of government 'care.'" (chapter 4)

- *Business.* We ought to take a cold, hard, and dispassionate look at how the clergy portrays the corporation from the pulpit and in the seminary classroom. The rich are rich, it is often said, because the poor are exploited by them, and the only way to change this imbalance is by ushering in a new society based on socialism. Profits, in particular, are demonized. "Religion is not presented as prayer, study, suffering or worship. Rather, its purpose is to defend 'human rights,' conceived mostly as praising certain left-wing dictators in the name of the Lord." (chapter 5)

- *Government.* In the natural order of things, the state has its place, but it is *not* to supplant the church in its historical role of ministering to the poor. Yet, unfortunately, this overemphasis on the state is precisely the aim of numerous ecclesiastics. But this view runs directly counter to the traditional Catholic notion of subsidiarity, according to which "while government was indeed legitimate and necessary, there ought to be very large areas of economic, cultural, religious, educational, and even political independence and autonomy." In particular, the family, the church, service clubs, business, labour, and all other actors in the voluntary sector, not the state, ought to have primary responsibility in fighting poverty. (chapter 6)

- *The poor.* The philosophy of "the preferential option for the poor" informed much of the discussion on their respective economies by both the U.S. and the Canadian Conference of Catholic Bishops. Although widely supported among religious persons, the concept skirts uncomfortably close to intellectual paternalism. "The poor, in spite of the rhetoric, cannot help themselves, but must be 'helped' according to some bureaucratic programme." However, "we do not really help the poor if we say we will take care of them no matter what." (chapter 7)

- *Charity.* Father Schall tells the poignant tale of the businessman who wanted to contribute half of his profits to the poor, and to encourage others to do likewise. Instead, without discouraging generosity, our author insists that "in general, the best way businessmen can help the poor is to provide for a growing, fair economy in which the vast majority of the population work for their own livings." (chapter 8)

- *Sharing.* Little children are commonly taught to "share," even by well-meaning people, and this activity is certainly encouraged in the religious community. Yet, Fr. Schall's iconoclasm is radical enough to permit a critique of even this hallowed tradition. The argument is that sharing implies ownership in common, a socialist premise which is only appropriate to small groups of people, such as the nuclear family, the kibbutz, the monastery, or indeed the Jesuit Order itself. Vastly preferable to sharing is "giving," which denotes something more than compassion or sharing, but is compatible with our cherished institutions of private property. (chapter 9)

- *Food and culture.* Most members of the "new class" of scholars, intellectuals, journalists, sociologists, and opinion leaders are highly disdainful of McDonalds and other representatives of the fast food industry. Not so Father Schall. For him, this is merely a prejudice against the food favoured by other cultures. Moreover, this form of bigotry is harmful: "One of the reasons for the extremes of the Irish potato famine, it is said, was because the Irish did not fish." (chapter 10)

- *Donations.* We have a responsibility not only to give for worthy purposes, but to ascertain that the money so donated is actually used for these good ends. Parishioners in North America are generous, but they fail to carry through on their obligation to make sure that the money they give for peace is not used for violence; that funds donated for religious purposes are not diverted to the promulgation of marxism. (chapter 11)

■ *Shoplifting.* Burglaries are commonly seen as a natural phenomenon. Store owners and insurance companies include a "theft premium" in their calculations, and conduct business as usual. We blame the victim, not the robber; i.e., it is a misdemeanour to leave ones car keys in the ignition. All this is evidence of a decline of religion and morality. (chapter 12)

■ *Productivity.* There is a rapidly growing rift between clergy and laity on the question of wealth production. The experience of the latter in actual productive activities has had almost no effect on organized American clericy. "We should not send our easily manipulated nuns and seminarians to slums and barrios to have them routinely return reciting canned ideology. Rather, if we think religion is really about nothing else than wealth creation, we should send them to places where men are rapidly learning to produce. To Hong Kong or Tokyo, not Lima or Dar-es-Salaam." (chapters 5, 13)

■ *Politicization.* The church is in danger of becoming just another economic or political lobby group. The Social Affairs Commission of the Canadian Conference of Catholic Bishops has sometimes trivialized the mysteries of Christianity by pretending that the faith supports this or that monetary or fiscal policy. Advocacy politics has been substituted for the essential elements of religion. (chapter 14.)

■ *Economic development.* The theoretically difficult doctrine of "human rights" has been used as an excuse for reducing economic liberty. And yet only free economies grow. They do so not because of their natural resources, but because of how "the individual, property, reward, work, and inventiveness are looked upon. When people are free to pursue their own goals within a truly limited, responsible state, there will be real development and liberty." (chapter 15)

■ *God and money.* Despite tens of thousands of Sunday school leaflets to the contrary, money is not necessarily an evil. True, it is possible to use the coin of the realm for idolatrous purposes and to promote evil designs, but pamphlets which loudly claim "You Cannot Serve Both God and Money" are highly simplistic. For one thing, they are incompatible with the parable of the talents. For another, the practice of passing the collection plate at Mass shows that money can be used for something worthwhile. (chapter 16)

■ *Economic gluttony.* The U.S. comprises but 6 percent of the world's population, and yet consumes some 40 percent of its resources. Although widely denounced in church circles as "economic imperialism," this statistic is reflective of differential productivity rates, not marxian "exploitation." North Americans consume more because they produce more, not because they take anything away from anyone else. (chapter 17)

■ *Virtue.* Some people define their virtue and even religiosity in terms of their concern for the poor. For such persons "the poor are never seen as lacking good initiative, or good judgement, or the will for ordinary hard work, but rather as the legitimation of organization for service." (chapters 18, 22)

■ *Political philosophy.* Political philosophy has lost the distinctively Catholic intellectual presence which once permeated it. Although the reasons for this shift are many and complex, the fact that religion has been perverted into secularism and marxism in the seminaries, divinity schools, and universities has played a large role. (chapters 20, 21)

■ *U.S. Bishops' Pastoral Letter on Economics.* This document seems to promote a more liberal or socialist agenda. Although there were widespread consultations with economists who reflected other points of view, the authors do not seem to realize how one-sided the final product is, nor how out of step it is with earlier Catholic teachings. (chapter 23)

■ *Sollicitudo Rei Socialis.* This is Pope John Paul II's statement on the economy, the poor and the relationship between the industrialized countries and the Third World. Father Schall is very much in accord with the goals of ending poverty and starvation, especially in the economically underdeveloped countries where these problems are most acute. However, he regrets the fact that the Holy Father did not sufficiently attend to the widely accepted means necessary to these ends: a work ethic, private property, and greater reliance on the free market. Fr. Schall also calls into question the document's apparent stance of moral and economic equivalence as between the Western nations which embody these values, and the Communist countries which do not. (chapter 24)

Father Schall's work is a strong challenge to liberation theology, the unholy alliance between marxism and religion. He ranges widely over many topics of vital importance to the religious community, and in his wake leaves untouched no sacred cow beloved of the forces of "progressivism" and ideology in religion and society. The Fraser Institute is pleased to publish the findings of this distinguished Jesuit scholar, but owing to his independence his views may or may not conform, severally or collectively, to the those of the members of the Institute.

Walter Block

ACKNOWLEDGEMENTS

For permission to reprint the following materials, the author wishes to give credit to the following journals: Chapter 1, *Hillsdale Review*, February, 1982; chapter 2, reprinted with permission from *Crisis* magazine, (1511 K Street N.W., #527, Washington, D.C. 20005), April, 1986; chapter 3, *Agribusiness Worldwide*, August, 1982; chapter 4, *Canadian Catholic Register*; chapter 5, *The Priest*, February, 1979, Our Sunday Visitor Press; chapter 6, *Homiletic and Pastoral Review*, June, 1983, pp. 25-29; chapter 8, *Vital Speeches*, July 15, 1982; chapter 9, *The Monitor* (San Francisco), December 24, 1982; chapter 10, *The Monitor*, 1978; chapter 11, *The Washington Star*, April 10, 1979; chapter 12, *The Monitor*, May 15, 1980; chapter 13, *The Monitor*, October 1, 1981; chapter 14, *Canadian Catholic Register*, March 12, 1983; chapter 15, *The Monitor*, July 21, 1983; chapter 16, *The Monitor*, October 24, 1983; chapter 17, *The Monitor*, October 6, 1983; chapter 18, courtesy of Business School, University of Illinois at Chicago, from *Free Enterprise, 15 Commentaries*; chapter 19, reprinted with permission from *Crisis* magazine, May, 1984; chapter 20, Center for Christian Studies, Notre Dame, Indiana, *Center Journal*, February, 1983; chapter 21, *Orbis*, Vol. 30, #3.

The author wishes in particular to thank Dr. Walter Block and the Fraser Institute, and Mr. Frederick W. Hill of Regina for their generous aid in this project.

ABOUT THE AUTHOR

James V. Schall, SJ, a native of Iowa, obtained an M.A. in philosophy from Gonzaga University in 1955, an M.A. in theology from the University of Santa Clara in 1964, and a Ph.D. in political philosophy from Georgetown University in 1960. Ordained as a Roman Catholic priest and a member of the Society of Jesus, Father Schall is a professor in the Department of Government at Georgetown University. He was a member of the Pontifical Commission on Justice and Peace in Rome, 1977-82, and formerly taught at Gregorian University, Rome, and the University of San Francisco. He is on the board of the National Council on the Humanities of the National Endowment for the Humanities.

Father Schall is a regular columnist for *Crisis* magazine and has contributed to scholarly, political, and theological journals in the United States, Canada, Europe, and Australia. He is the author of no less than 17 books, including *The Politics of Heaven and Hell: Christian Themes from Classical, Medieval and Modern Political Philosophy; Reason, Revelation and the Foundations of Political Philosophy; Liberation Theology; The Distinctiveness of Christianity; Another Sort of Learning; Redeeming the Time;* and *Christianity and Politics.* In addition, he has edited books on John Paul II, on G.K. Chesterton, and on the Pastorals of War of the German and French bishops.

Introduction

Around the questions of religion, wealth, and poverty there has grown a considerable literature and persistent controversy in recent years. Much of this controversy has been caused by the apparent conversion of certain formerly stable and non-ideological segments within religion itself to economic and political positions which explain themselves largely in terms of socialist or liberal theory. The intellectual roots of such analyses lie outside of, and contrast with, the sources of classical thought and revelation. Considerable reaction to this politicization exists. At its best, this critique of socialist or liberal positions seeks not just to "return" to the traditional sources but also to show how there is development within them to meet the widely recognized needs of mankind. This newer analysis promises more than the ideological positions have demonstrated that they can offer. At the same time, this newer philosophy of wealth and its production avoids the spiritual and political dangers which empirically occur in the ideological systems, even democratic ones, now practised in many parts of the world.

The questions about wealth and religion can be treated from many different aspects. In this book, I have tried to present more of a familiar, on-going commentary on the nature of wealth and wealth production, and how both relate to religion and public well-being. Hence, this examination is not intended to be a tract or treatise. Rather, I have used briefer, more pungent analyses and reflections which will serve to stress what the problems are, where they lead, their relation to the status of religion in the contemporary world, and how religion relates, at its worst and best, to questions of broad economic and political concern. I assume without too much question a realization that religion does affect our public good. Changes in religion's perception of its own role and nature will affect everyone, believers or not.

In these reflections, I have tried to emphasize again and again certain basic points. While we need perhaps longer and more incisive works, some of which I have included in the bibliography, we also need something less formal and more trenchant. Much of the difficulty for religion has arisen at the popular, not theoretical level. Each of these chapters was designed to say something about wealth, its production, and how it best serves its purpose. What we want for the poor is not ideology or loss of freedom, but a knowledge in the poor themselves of how not to be poor, and the existence of political and economic institutions from which all this knowledge can come forth and be put into practice. We need to respect the dignity and enterprise of everyone and to understand that human beings and social classes are not simply hostile to one another. This sense of the contribution of all, even the poor, is I think the central theme in classical and Christian thought about poverty. On the other hand, we have also learned in the modern world how not to be poor by being free and intelligent. Underneath this knowledge, however, is a struggle of vast proportions about the very nature of mankind and its relation to something beyond itself. Man does not, in fact, live by bread alone, a truth which is not intended to deny the goodness of bread. Ordinary discussions of wealth and poverty are, it seems to me, also religious and philosophical.

These arguments will be "minority" positions. I have not hesitated to state what I think is wrong and why, but I am mainly concerned with what is right. The dominant trends in religion and society are often otherwise than what I propose, but they are not the ones that really solve questions of poverty and wealth. In a period when both religion and politics are fervently discussing these questions, along with questions of war and peace, my remarks and reflections will serve, I hope, both to clear the air and focus thought on what is at issue, on what does aid the poor in freedom and in truth.

Chapter 1

Peace, War, Poverty; Some Myths People Swear By

To a peace rally at the United Nations Plaza, at the beginning of the Disarmament Conference in 1982, a Buddhist monk walked 3,000 miles from Los Angeles. There, too, a famous lady paediatrician said, "Give the American people a weapons freeze now." She did not say, however, "Give the Russian people a weapons freeze now." Whether a weapons freeze is a step toward freedom or a step to tyranny was not indicated. It might in fact be either. A 97 year old monk said, "This shows the world is about to be turned over and converted." A weapons freeze may indeed suggest that the world is "about to be turned over and converted," but to *what*, we wonder? There are some things to which we do not want to be converted. This is why we have weapons.

Weapons or Aggressors?

Many sincere people insist that wars are caused by weapons. A good woman, Margaret Thatcher, told the same United Nations Disarmament Conference that this was not so. Wars are caused by aggressors, not arms. A sign on Bush Street in San Francisco suggested that nuclear weapons cause "human needs" *not* to be met. But Plato said that human desires are infinite. Thus they will never be satisfied. Therefore, we should control our desires.

Some people, however, desire what *we* have. We can either give all of what we have to them or prevent them from taking it from us. Most people whose human needs are *not* met do *not* live in societies with nuclear weapons. And we should be very careful to know just who it is we appoint to "meet our human needs." The servile state comes in on the rhetorical wings of charity and kindness. Alas.

Bread and Knowledge

If nuclear weapons were to disappear tomorrow, most people would still have the same needs, mostly still unsatisfied. Weapons are not easily or directly transformable into bread. And man does not live by bread alone. The man who lives by bread alone is significantly below the angels. He who knows how to make weapons also knows how to bake bread. This is not a question of war, just talent. But will and talent are not interchangeable, even though we need talent to do some things we want to do well. Evil is not just ignorance. Ignorance knows neither how to make bread nor weapons. Knowledge is good. He who knows how to make the weapons also knows or can learn how to bake the bread. But he may not *will* to do so. Virtue is not exclusively knowledge.

Losing a war may be the basis for prosperity. But some wars are best not lost. It depends mostly on to whom you lose. Prosperity seems to disappear when one's neighbour learns how to be rich, even though both are objectively richer than before. Some people choose not to learn how to be rich. Poverty is the most relative concept in the history of the world. The richest of kings seems like a pauper now, while the poor have television sets and ways to prevent themselves from reproducing. The poor need beauty as much as and probably more than they need bread. The poor are not poor *because* the rich are rich. If the poor wish to be rich, they need the rich to imitate and emulate. This is why rich and poor need to be neighbours, not enemies. We need not choose to be rich, but if we do, we need to know how to become rich. This attempt takes sacrifice and savings. Prosperity also disappears when men forget what caused it in the first place. Poverty likewise comes about when men choose not to learn about keeping wealth. Rich societies have become very poor. The rich are not always the good. The poor are always with us, even if we are rich, and even evidently if we are good. The poor come to rich societies to learn how to be rich. They take the places of the children of the rich who do not learn or who do not exist.

Peace or Suicide?

Many think that if we rid ourselves of our weapons, there will be no wars. Our enemies think this too, which is why they prefer that we have no weapons while they keep theirs. Enemies also know that it is far easier for them if their adversaries *choose* not to arm themselves. Some people call this the *peace* movement. Others call it suicide. And if we have no weapons, will there not still be fists, rocks, and slings? The longbow was once an ultimate weapon. When European cities realized that their walls were useless against newly invented artillery, they kept them up as ornaments and gardens.

Other people believe that poverty is caused by weapons. Still others hold the opposite; that if we take the guns away from the ordinary citizenry, only criminals will be armed. The man who shot the President was acquitted. The man who shot the Pope seems to have had Bulgarian connections. The men who shot Anwar Sadat were executed. Some people doubt whether anything is worth fighting for. Others, especially those living in repressive societies against their wills, know this is not so. Some argue, "better red than dead." The reds do not argue this way. Others die escaping from societies that are already red. And yet others have no chance to escape to any place. Some sorts of life are not worth living. "Better a millstone tied to his neck and he be cast into the sea . . . " "Give me liberty or give me death." But do not kill the innocent. The innocent have become weapons to defeat the righteous. Must we live in the worst state to be moral?

War and Poverty

Fear of war and fear of poverty have become the main instruments to eliminate freedom for those who think that war and poverty are the worst evils. The reasons that cause men to fight are not the reasons that cause men to be poor, unless bread is also a weapon. C.S. Lewis wrote that neither war, nor poverty, nor death was the worst of evils. He who can think of nothing worse than war and death has not begun to think. Man lives by bread and by cake too, but he wonders about more.

Yet freedom cannot mean that "everything is permitted." Some things are simply not "permitted," even if they happen rather frequently and we see them every day in our midst. We live in a world in which evil is allowed. Human rights mean that some things are not "human" and other things are not "rights." A world in which evil can occur through human agency is a world in which something important can happen because of human initiative. It makes a difference what we choose and what we reject. Forgiveness means that there is something to be forgiven. We can only forgive what ought not to have happened. Every moment is therefore significant.

Some people hold that there can be good people in any sort of society, even in a corrupt one. Others maintain that individual goodness is a function of the social or natural environment. Some even say that the causes of war and crime lie not in poverty but in the will. Some poor people do evil. But many poor people do no evil, not because they are poor, but because they think something is wrong. Some rich people do good things. Most people seem to do a mixture of both, whatever their economic condition, society, or environment.

Dangerous Myths

Some myths are more dangerous than others. One dangerous myth is that if we *will* to stop making weapons, we will likewise *choose* to "cure" poverty. But poverty is not an illness. Poverty is alleviated by both knowledge of how to lessen it *and* the will to do so. Riches also involve work. Another myth is that if only we stop making weapons, we will remain free. Still another is that if we remain free, we will become rich. "Give me liberty or give me death" need not be the words of a rich man. They are more likely to be the words of a poor man who knows there are other things in the world besides riches, namely dangerous things. War societies can be poor societies.

3

The poor often attack the poor. Many rich societies do not go to war, neither do they aid the poor. Many poor societies are poor because they select to govern or misgovern themselves in a way that produces poverty. Societies which believe that somebody else exploited them will remain poor until they exploit somebody else. With this mentality, such societies will never become rich by learning for themselves how to produce wealth. Wrong ideas are the final source of poverty. Many rich societies are rich because of someone else's efforts or invention. Oil is not wealth without an economy which engenders and generates riches. Neither will oil be wealth when someone produces a substitute for it. Henry Ford was Saudi Arabia's greatest benefactor.

The Lethal Will

All the atomic plants ever built have killed far, far fewer humans than the bicycle or the penknife. Abolish the bicycle? The most lethal weapon known to man is the human will. That does not mean that we should destroy our wills. But we can change our minds.

Poor societies can be just societies with discipline, so can rich and middle class societies with self-discipline. Poor societies can lack freedom but have bread, even steaks. Rich societies usually have little poverty. But they need not have freedom, and there are many sorts of misery. Slaves often eat well. Some rich societies, however, have many poor people. They may also have enough freedom and talent for the poor to become rich and the rich to become poor. The poor do not want wealth given to them. They prefer to earn it.

If we turn our weapons into ploughshares, we may not choose to plough. If we turn our ploughshares into weapons, we may not need to fight. But then again, we may. Aristotle said that sometimes it is less than human *not* to be brave. Never to fight can mean that nothing is worth fighting for, a very shallow life. Weakness can be innocent. Chosen weakness can invite aggression. Never having to fight may mean being ready to fight. Eternal vigilance is the price of liberty. Mere survival is *not* another name for peace. It is, however, another name for slavery. Cowards survive. Run, run, run away . . . Some things should frighten us.

The Boer War

In 1929, G.K. Chesterton wrote an essay on Hilaire Belloc in which he described their first meeting. When they were both young journalists they had taken a particularly unpopular position on the Boer war while it was going on in South Africa. Neither opposed this war on pacifist grounds, namely on the theory that it was wrong to fight for anything. Nor did they oppose it on the grounds that it was wrong for little peoples to fight for their own freedom. Both were pro-Boer. They thought it was right for a small people to fight against an invader, even if the imperialists were, as both of them were, English. Chesterton went on, "We disliked cosmopolitan war; and it was hard to say whether we more despised those who praised war for the gain of money, or those who blamed war for the loss of it."

These last words stick—those who "blamed" war for the loss of money. Wealth can always be reproduced, if we know how to produce it in the first place. Witness Japan. If the only reason we blame war is because it loses our money, do we praise it because it gains wealth? Men keep fighting wars because they know that the theory that war is caused by poverty is false. Margaret Thatcher said that the British fought in the Falklands because of a principle. Men ought to find a better way than war, to be sure. But it does not follow that they have yet found this better way. Augustine remains. And it is quite possible to imagine a worse way, one that is actually called "peace." This would imply that nothing is worth fighting for. Avoid death at all costs, including principle.

The Nuclear Freezers

This logic is what the "nuclear freezers" and such folks do not understand. This is why we ought to know how those who want to convert us envisage the world *before* we decide to follow them. Walking 3,000 miles from Los Angeles to New York proves nothing about war or peace. But it's a long, long way to Tipperary. War is not caused by poverty or weapons. Nor is peace "caused" by wealth or empty hands. If we do not have something to live for, we will have nothing to die for. If we have nothing worth dying for, it does not really matter much whether we live or die. *Carpe diem.* Eat, drink, and be merry, for tomorrow we may still be alive.

Four wars were going on in recent years, not counting Lebanon and Grenada, none of them nuclear, none except Grenada judged to be just or unjust by the clergy. A newspaper report also said, "A solar flare so huge that scientific instruments couldn't measure it shot from the Sun's surface, releasing more energy than the Earth uses in a year." When the sun reabsorbs the earth, will nature be unjust? If we blow ourselves up, will we have more profound questions to ask than if we die in our beds one by one?

The foundation myth in *The Republic* of Plato suggests we should believe that we live in a just order and do what is best for us when all is ordered to the good. At the beginning of *Acts*, it says, "Why stand you there looking up?" The myths we swear by tell us what we are.

5

Chapter 2

On the Causes of Hunger

"Space exploration is another area of virtually unlimited potential," Arthur C. Clarke explained to us. "Almost anything imaginable that people want to accomplish could be done in the next century, with the exception of interstellar flight—and even there we could build probes to get to the nearer stars in a few decades."[1] Thus we live in an age in which we are told on good grounds that there is almost nothing we cannot do if we want to—fly to the stars, eliminate poverty, do all our business at home, feed all the hungry. Few still accept the notion of automatic progress as preached in the last century, though most of us suspect that our potentiality is far greater than we usually comprehend. Our acknowledged finiteness ought not to dictate an overly narrow view of our possibilities.

Indeed, it might well be argued that what we "can" do is a function of our understanding of the world. The reason things do not go right can often be explained by a theory about the world itself or man's place or powers in it. We cannot improve either ourselves or the world if we believe that the world does not exist, or if we hold that we "must" do what we in fact "do," or that no correspondence exists between our minds, our hands, and the world outside of us. And if we believe, implicitly or explicitly, that the world or something in it is "evil," then clearly we ought not to "do" anything except escape from it or destroy it.

We are, furthermore, aware that what we might be "able" to do may not actually get done. That is to say, our capacity to do things must be accomplished in terms of our willed goals, according to which, as Aristotle taught us, we praise or blame one another for the goals themselves and for the means we choose to reach them. Many things that ought to be done will not be accomplished either because we cannot agree on how to do them, if we have already learned how to do them, or because the chosen goal conflicts with other perhaps more fundamental ends. We remain finite, however much we "might" accomplish. We must, in other words, actually learn what we can do by experiment, mistake, and reflection. Or else we must be taught by someone else who already knows. We must be humble enough to learn. We must be generous enough to teach.

Knowledge and Growth

"The accumulation of experience is now focusing, for the first time in human history, on the industry of knowledge itself as the prime sector of growth," George Gilder wrote.

The rise of the knowledge industries is the most promising development in the history of economics. For knowledge and experience are the real capital of human progress—the true source of the productivity of human effort. Knowledge is the power to create, the prime fruit of the commercial imagination.[2]

Henri Pirenne, writing a half century earlier, began to describe this process by which men first learned how to be productive, to exchange, to invent instruments of credit and account, to put into circulation foods, clothing, and machines that had never existed before.[3]

Our dignity is thus both given to us and learned by us. The "power" to create is given in our free, rational nature with which we are born. The actual making or discovering of something new, we must learn by experience and risk. Yet we also disagree about what human life is worth, what it is about. Political societies are ultimately built on these differences. The classics called them "regimes," and these are not indifferent measurements. Agreed goals or coerced ones can only be reached or known by the people in these regimes if they conform to the theories or options defining the particular political constitution in question. Often then some things do not come to be—the alleviation of hunger is one of these—*because* the way to accomplish them conflicts with the regime's picture of what "must be" in this or that polity.

Defining Hunger

At first sight "hunger" seems to be easy enough both to define and perhaps to eliminate. Yet mothers who speak of their growing seventeen year old sons as "always being hungry" are not speaking the same language as those who attempt to define some sort of minimal, necessary diet, however this may be delineated culturally. Much of the argument about actual starvation and hunger is really a debate about statistical calculations, often used for identifiably ideological purposes. To whose "advantage" do descriptions of starvation, ones that make it very widespread or ones that eliminate it altogether, really work? No discussion of hunger statistics is adequate without a very hard, critical look at the origins of the statistics about hunger themselves and the organizations generating or using them. This includes the United Nations' calculations above all.

Widely quoted data that starvation had ended in China during Mao's rule were directly related to the idea that Mao's society was somehow a model of perfect human organization. This surprising view was held in certain Christian religious circles at the time. Such statistics had little to do with the facts of starvation themselves. Moreover, we must constantly distinguish between random catastrophic hunger situations, caused by unique natural or political upheaval, like Stalin's starvation of the Ukrainians in the 1930s, and abiding ones that persist over generations. Efforts to relieve the former are generally quite different from efforts to relieve the latter. Likewise, we must remember that our understanding of and ability to produce adequate nutrition are themselves subject to progress and learning, and probably regression as well. Using current standards, once upon a time, everyone was either starving or badly undernourished.

A Right to Food?

Some would also argue that "to be fed" is a "human right," however much a certain absolutism may lurk in that apparently innocuous phrase. On the other hand, one of the signs of a free, developed society is that a very small percentage of its population is needed to produce adequate, abundant food for itself and others. Moreover, in the history of most developed nations there was a point when its own food producers both learned how to grow more and how to profit from this increased knowledge. The very success of farming means fewer farmers in the long run. Keeping them down on the farm may thus be very bad policy. Medard Gable, a research assistant of Buckminster Fuller, stated the situation well:

> Everyone who graces this planet with his presence deserves all the food his body needs to function optimally. Food for life should be a birthright, not an earned right. Billions of humans should not have to work their lives away for food and suffer the consequences if they are not successful.
>
> The entire resources of…Earth are for and can meet, if used and reused wisely, the regenerative life support needs of 100 percent of humanity…The world's total production of cereals, roots, pulses, fruits, nuts, vegetables, meats, fish, milk and eggs is enough to supply every child, woman, and man with over 2.3 kilograms (5 pounds) of food per day. A well nourished human being can be taken care of with under 0.6 kilograms dry weight of the right combinations of the above foods, plus water. The present state of human knowledge is such that this condition cannot only be improved, but maintained on a continuously sustaining basis for all generations to come if we husband and midwife our resources as well as we know how.[4]

If this "right" to be fed is uncritically accepted it can easily become a tool for refashioning society for purposes other than food. It can be used to control a people, so that there is no political unrest. Food is also politics. This fact is not a defect in either food or politics.

Let me be clear. The "right to be fed" can be turned into a formula to blame those who know how to produce food for the condition of those who do not. When this sort of thinking takes place, those who do not know how to produce adequate food (or more often, who are unwilling to learn because of commitment to various ideologies which denigrate private property, profits, and individual initiative) see themselves exempt from any duty to make their own peoples adequate producers and distributors. Adequate food supplies then become "what is owed" rather than what is produced.

Hunger and Ideology

The hunger problem will never really be solved until those political regimes where hunger largely occurs over a long period of time become sufficient producers of their own food. Solzhenitsyn said that a regime can deliberately keep food in short, rationed supply to control the people for other ends. Except through commerce no one will ever be able to have enough food unless he learns to produce his own. But to do this, someone else may have to teach him to produce, or even invent something not yet in existence.

"One question... is never posed about the Third World: the question of the political responsibility of the Third World governments for the economic underdevelopment of poor countries," Jean-François Revel remarked.

> Many of the economic maladies of the Third World are related to politics...Nkrumah in Ghana, Nyerere in Tanzania, Touré in Guinea plunged their respective countries into decline by stupid administration or policies motivated only by ideology...
>
> These considerations aren't meant to overlook the purely economic aspect of the problem of poverty or the necessity of North-South cooperation. They are meant to recall that economic assistance and technology don't suffice if the governments that receive them are badly governed. The movement of "less-developed" countries to a "more developed" stage presupposes the acceptance of political responsibility.[5]

The major causes of hunger are almost always related to the quality of the governmental regime and its theory about how mankind is to be organized where there is (or is not) hunger. Ideology, in fact, is the main cause of hunger, along with, as P.T. Bauer noted, certain attitudes to work, reward, and order.[6] The relation of religion and moral practice to wealth producing is much closer than we are normally willing to admit. Certain doctrines and beliefs will guarantee continuing poverty.

Government Failure

While showing that farmers in poor countries do respond to new ways of production, if given a chance, Theodore Schultz in his Nobel Prize lecture on "The Economics of Being Poor," put the situation quite well:

> Future historians will no doubt be puzzled by the extent to which economic incentives were impaired during recent decades. The dominant intellectual view is antagonistic to agricultural incentives, and the prevailing economic policies deprecate the function of producer incentives. For lack of incentives the unrealized economic potential of agriculture in many low-income countries is large... For want of profitable incentives, farmers have not made the necessary investments, including the purchase of superior inputs. Interventions by governments are currently the major cause of the lack of optimum economic incentives.[7]

Even if there is a natural or isolated political disaster in a given country or area involving famine, effective relief is usually impeded not by lack of adequate external supplies and gifts, but by governmental inefficiency or corruption. Recurrent famines have been a "normal" part of the history of every century except perhaps our own. We easily forget this.

Modern agriculture and transportation, together with *ideas* about generosity and obligation, have been combined to eliminate local famines throughout the globe that result from drought, floods, insects, poor techniques, or politics. Today it is safe to say that famines have practically disappeared, apart from those which are politically induced or exacerbated. Every famine in recent decades has been followed by angry protestation that foreign relief was not delivered due to incompetence or governmental interference at some internal or external level. Many parts of the world (not all) do respond generously to particular disasters. What is not so clear is that this generous response may disrupt the working structures of the place in need of aid. Further, the aid may not be allowed because of ideologies which see in this relief a challenge to the society in need of assistance. Some people refuse to admit they are in need because that involves an admission that the cause of the need was the theory upon which the society is based.

No Reason for Hunger

The politics of hunger, then, can be looked upon from a number of angles. There is no reason for anyone to be hungry if the normal means and methods of production and transportation are allowed to function. We continue to produce more food each year, as Julian Simon has shown, in spite of the vested industry of the doomsday ecology schools, whose basic agenda usually has goals other than merely meeting human hunger.[8] Some people claim that starvation is widespread in order to implement certain population control theories and to install societal coercion to support them. Others use "hunger ideology" as a method to destabilize functioning economies and impose on them marxist-socialist forms of rule.

Reviewing Suzanne Toton's book *World Hunger: The Responsibility of Christian Education*, Francis X. Maier wrote:

> The theme here is that feeding the hungry is merely pallia-tive, not substantive. What we really need is to dismember and restructure the entire Western economic system which allegedly ensures poverty, and, through it, hunger.
>
> This sort of analysis, to put it mildly, is open to some debate. But after a while you just get weary; it's as if the author and reader came from different planets. Toton believes, as a matter of religious faith, that wealth creates poverty. It's an error that's impregnable in its singularity.[9]

We might aptly name these views the "restructure-the-world-to-feed-the-poor—only-in-socialist-systems" school or the "control-humans-to-feed-them" school. Both are major sources of the absolutist mind in the modern world, a mind which allows nothing but its own narrow ideology to rule. By severely limiting human horizons and potentials, these people seek to gain absolute control of the human population, its coming into being and its final organization.

Perhaps the main source of confusion about hunger, however, concerns the classic distinction between justice and charity, between state and voluntary organizations. We seem to live in a period in which the public rhetoric of justice has embraced and subordinated to itself the ends and motives of charity. This absorption tends to make political and economic questions superior to personal and spiritual ones, let alone those relating to a transcendent end.

This perspective has likewise tended to neglect a fundamental under-standing of human finiteness which requires men and women to learn and relearn how to relate properly to Earth. This neglect has led to a thesis which would attribute remaining human ills such as hunger or disorder to existing political institutions. From here, it is but a short step to the ideological theme that the reordering of man's societies is the solution to all human ills.

Changing Society

No doubt it is true that inefficient or corrupt government is the explanation for a large part of the hunger remaining in the world. It is likewise the case that we know in general how to go about alleviating hunger. Certainly there are ways to attempt the productive task which will not work or which will lead to political systems with far greater problems than hunger.

The greatest of tyrannies are by no means those which suffer most from hunger. Tyrants buy grain from Canada so they can produce weapons at home, while keeping the peasants in tow. Where charity is allowed, we can expect that from these generous resources we will be able to meet the individual crises that do arise. After all, institutions themselves cannot be unjust since only individual human beings can be just or unjust. There can, of course, be better or worse regimes. But just because there may possibly be a better form of rule, it does not follow that regimes are best changed immediately or that any change will be for the better.

A society which in its political formation seeks to arrogate all those means which historically emerged from the impulses of individual charity and generosity, can only end up by claiming total control over all phases of life. Failure to understand this has led much religious thinking about poverty and hunger to the brink of the totalitarian state in God's name. In the end the real causes of hunger deserve a fair hearing.

Chapter 3

From Poverty to Productivity: The Religious Factor

With considerable truth we can say today that ideology is the main cause of poverty. More and more both religion and politics, insofar as they reflect ideology, tend to strengthen and prolong the grip of poverty. What we believe then is the main cause of whether we have or have not. What we hold about the world, man's place in it, what he is capable of doing, with what incentives, for what reasons—these questions more than any others decide whether an individual or people will be rich or poor.

There are once fertile countries which suddenly fall into poverty because of a change of religion or politics. As well there are once sterile areas now flourishing through the efforts of new peoples with new religious or political ideas. The main reason the poor countries of the world remain poor is because of their ideologies. The best way to discover why Tanzania, for example, remains poor and depends on handouts is not to examine its soil or its rainfall, but to read the collected speeches of Mr. Julius Nyerere. He may be a very good man, but he chose the wrong theoretical ideology to explain his country's poverty to itself. He gave some of these speeches to religious groups which have spread the doctrine widely. And this has promoted coercion—with poverty as the inevitable result.

Food Self-sufficiency

Thus, if we think that adequate diets are both possible and important, we need to have a world-view which allows them to come into being. We must reach each individual person through human agency, preferably not by coercion. On the other hand, the "demand" for a "right" to good diets or proper recreation, both noble goals in one sense, can become in practice a tool with which to impose an absolute state on an unaware people. In this way the demand undermines the attainment of the goal.

Thus current movements for food self-sufficiency often sound quite lofty, but they are frequently suspect. Indeed, the very elusive statistics about world hunger are among the world's most politicized calculations. They are almost never free of ideological overtones. Too often they bear the hidden and unexamined thesis that the poor are poor because the rich are rich. Or worse, that the hungry are not fed because the satiated have exploited them. Ironically, the best way to starve the poor would be for the rich of the world to stop eating, to stop being rich.

Once these erroneous doctrines about poverty and hunger are accepted as principles, then peoples, classes, and individuals must be seen as intrinsically at odds with each other. Hatred becomes justified as a matter of social or moral "necessity." Religious notions about concern, charity, and benevolence are then subtly transformed into terms of revolution and violence; these are even seen as "spiritual" tools.

Narrow Theories

The single most important concept that needs emphasis for any serious understanding of poverty and its causes is that wealth is produced not taken away from someone else. The world is not a zero-sum game in which the advantage of some must inevitably be the loss of others. This latter notion is true only if our narrow theories of wealth and poverty make it so. Rather we need a view of the world that looks upon innovation and growth as something new, something added, something more, not as something exploited, pilfered, or taken away unjustly.

Poverty is the original state of men and nations. We need to know not so much why the poor are poor, but why some are not still poor. The answer to this latter question is as much philosophical and religious as economic and practical. The possibilities of the latter, economics and practical effort, depend on the former, religion and thought. Whatever may be said on the grounds of tolerance or scepticism about the different religions, philosophies, and ideologies at work in the world, what cannot be said is that the structure of their beliefs and ideas makes no difference to how we live and achieve.

Thus the passage from poverty to productivity is prevented not just by lack of work, science, reward, or innovation, but mainly by ideas about work, science, reward, and innovation. If we do not begin here, we will not understand why the poor are poor or how they can be otherwise.

Chapter 4

What Is True Social Justice?

"Social justice," in one sense, can be looked upon as the order of distribution of the goods of a regime; this distribution itself is based upon the production of goods and services. Thus we can speak of different kinds of justice according to the differing sorts of regimes, wherein the latter are distinguished according to the varying visions they have of themselves and their purposes. An oligarchy pursues, in its distribution of wealth and honours, in its arrangements of offices, the purpose of gaining and protecting wealth in its own sake. Wealth making, of course, is not wrong. Indeed, it is the necessary condition for our rendering "aid" to the poor. Many current ideological positions simply do not understand how wealth comes to be in the first place. Still when wealth making is erected into the be-all and end-all of society, it distorts human life within it.

If we want to change an oligarchy, however, we do need to envision another sort of justice. Since wealth getting is not the worst conceivable distortion of a regime, it is possible to change it to something worse in the noble name of "improvement." It might result in some sort of tyranny, so that an oligarchy is likely to be better, even for the poor, than a future tyranny. And if we should strive to create and distribute wealth in freedom, there would still be many different, mostly just, ways to do so.

Freedom

The freer we are, the more ways are available to us to accomplish things we ought and want to accomplish. In general, the more we place freedom at the centre of our ideas about justice, the more likelihood we will have to achieve what is in fact just. On the other hand, we must be able to recognize a tyranny or ideology when we see one. This recognition is more difficult than most are willing to admit. This is why truth can never be divorced from freedom. Sobering as it is, almost all tyrannies in this century were imposed in the name of improvement, in the name of "justice," often with the consent of the governed, and often with the consent of religion.

The central internal problem of social justice is whether the actual control, production, and distribution of wealth is in the hands of citizenry, including the poor, individual persons, families, and voluntary groups, or whether the citizens, especially the poor, are essentially reduced to objects of government "care." In the latter case, poverty becomes the main rationale for increased government control over society. As the Israeli scholar Yair Aharoni wrote, "A new social order has evolved that started with a reliance by citizens on government for the solution to certain economic, social, and cultural problems and has grown to include pressures on government to mitigate almost every risk any individual might be asked to bear."[10] We cannot deny that government has some basic positive function, but the problem is how to keep government economically viable, and limited, while promoting the initiative and freedom of persons and families.[11]

Revelation

Christianity is not a revelation about politics or economics. This is not a defect in revelation, but its recognition that we have our own limited capacities. Not everything needs to be revealed. The great British historian, Christopher Dawson, wrote in 1934, in words still valid today, that Christians

> should remember that it is not the business of the Church to do the same things as the state—to build a Kingdom like the other Kingdoms of men, only better; nor to create a regime of earthly peace and justice. The Church exists to be the light of the world, and if it fulfils this function, the world is transformed in spite of all the obstacles that human powers place in its way.[12]

For increasing numbers of critics, a half century later, it is beginning to look like Christians are joining the camps of those who claim they are producing a "kingdom like other kingdoms, only better." The test of religion more and more seems to be one of embracing the "right sort of politics," wherein certain institutions or movements are identified, in spite of empirical evidence and spiritual warnings, with the essentials of the faith.

Christianity rather is a revelation about what politics and economics is *not*. In this it allows, indeed, insists that questions of justice be resolved by experience, reason, law, and invention. "What is the use of discussing man's abstract right to food or medicine?" Edmund Burke asked. "The question is upon the method of procuring and administering them. In that deliberation I shall always advise to call in the aid of the farmer and the physician, rather than the professor of metaphysics."[13] These remain wise words two hundred years later.

Ideology and Poverty

The main cause of poverty in the world today remains ideological; it can be the wrong "metaphysics," or political choice of leaders of the poor about what caused their condition, or it can be the failure to grasp what it is farmers do, what makes them produce. Mankind had to discover as part of its dignity what good and liveable arrangements of the economic and civil order are. Some regimes are worse than others, hence the classification of them into various kinds of regimes of "justice." There is not usually just one correct or certain way to do things. That Germans, Japanese, Canadians, Brazilians, or Italians do things differently is generally a good, not a bad thing. And this is true even though the manner in which each society conceives its purposes, its under-standings about life's meaning, will be classified as good, better, best, or bad, worse, or awful. Some people try to get out of some regimes; many try to get into others. This flow is usually a reliable sign of the location of "just" regimes, even if they are not the best.

From ancient times, it was recognized that an abstract description of what might be "best" could be extremely dangerous to people. In more modern times, man began to wonder why noble ideas about justice so often led in practice to various forms of tyranny, while still retaining the language of justice. On the whole, "justice" language is not the language of revelation, even though ideas of righteousness seem to be related to politics. So attractive is the language of justice that even the great tyrants insist on using it, and on preventing any affirmation that their regime is not just.

Importance of Justice

In his encyclical, *Dives in Misericordia*, John Paul II recounted the importance of justice to the modern world. He went on:

> And yet, it would be difficult not to notice that very often programs which start from the idea of justice and which ought to assist its fulfillment among individuals, groups, and human societies, in practice suffer from distortions. Al-though they continue to appeal to the ideal of justice, never-theless, experience shows that other negative forces have gained the upper hand over justice, such as spite, hatred and even cruelty.[14]

The first thing we can do for true social justice is, therefore, spiritual, beginning with prayer, self-knowledge, mercy, sacraments, and meditation.

This religious context remains the first duty of religion to society, what society has a right in justice to expect from its spiritual resources. This principle is what John Paul II meant at Puebla in Mexico when he said that the Church does not need "to have recourse to ideological systems in order to love, defend, and collaborate in the liberation of man." (III.2) From religion's own spiritual depository it already finds inspiration for acting "in favour of brotherhood, justice, and peace." In a sense it is true that if we want to think about justice, we do well to begin to think about—and acquire—mercy, the self-awareness of what we and our friends in this world really are, namely persons created and redeemed at a great price.

Chapter 5

Horizons for Productivity

"The belief that the prosperity of particular individuals, groups, or countries," P.T. Bauer wrote, "accounts for the poverty or material backwardness of others is almost always invalid." [15] Anyone who has followed religious trends today cannot help but be astonished by the radicalized beliefs and activities passing for faith in even the most staid of ecclesiastical enclaves.

Thus religious men and women of all denominations lobbying in the halls of Congress for the poor have become folk heros in certain fashionable circles. If for no other reason, business especially, but the whole society in general, ought to take a cold, dispassionate look at how theologians in pulpits and seminary classrooms are zealously explaining corporate activities.

Seemingly business in the newer catechism has replaced "original sin" as the cause of evil in the world. "Profits" have shoved aside certain classical cuss words as being unmentionable in polite company. This seems doubly ironic when we are beginning to have a better look at all of this, thanks to Roger Heckel (1978, 1980, 1981), Michael Novak (1982), and George Gilder (1980) among others.

Trendier than Thou

Many spiritual training programmes to mould young men and women in convents and seminaries consequently include a heavy dose of working with the poor, itself worthy enough, no doubt. As well, there is an even heavier dosage of tinged explanatory propaganda about why the poor are poor. Practically all national meetings of priests, religious superiors, ministers, and even bishops feature a weighty diet of this material. The older idea of a religious house, that of a big brick institution out on an isolated hill overlooking say, Spokane, the kind I went to, is definitely out.

On the contrary, today, spirituality is to travel to, for example, Guernavaca, Mexico—with its proper centre for language and social studies founded on the theme of "Yankee, Why Did You Come?"—to "feel" how the poor really suffer or, second best, to some local inner city slum.

Religion is not, for the most part, presented as prayer, study, obscurity, separation, suffering, or worship. Rather, its purpose is to defend "human rights," conceived mostly as condemning dictators and exploiters in the name of the Lord.

In the West (and South), however, the impetus for this radicalized version of Christianity is the alleviation of poverty. But poverty in this context is no longer what it was for a Francis of Assisi. Francis gave up riches to become poor. Riches were dangerous, as ascetical Greek, Christian, and Jewish tradition always suspected, whereas the very premises of modern socialism are to make everyone rich. If we really loved the poor, we would, in the older spirit, tell them to stay the way they are!

Faith and Justice

There was an action programme in California, which, with no hint of historical irony, was called "Companions for Justice." This group was a successor, it seems, to a similar "Horizons for Justice" programme, a six week live-in and training experience for priests and seminarians. It "seeks to change hearts by providing concrete, personal experience with those peoples whose lives are marred by poverty...." "Marred" by poverty? How different from Francis, who did not use the poor to learn from but chose to be poor. The modern poor will still want to know whether these "changed hearts" actually know much about what to do about their poverty.

The very words "justice" and "faith" have, by a strange dialectic, replaced "charity," "liberty," and "humility." This change is something the enemies of Christianity have been officially trying to accomplish for 2,000 years. And "faith" is reduced mostly to "justice," which, in turn, is itself something whose curious description is quite familiar to anyone knowledgeable at all about modern political and economic thought.

The implications of this movement ought not to go without critical public reflection. Are we still dealing with religion here or with its subtle transformation into a very tenuous thing, quite at odds with the tenets of classical religious thought?

A Litany

What is taught in many religious circles today? Mostly this:

- The poor are poor *because* the rich are rich.
- The poor are getting poorer because the percentage gap between the rich and poor is slightly increasing.
- The rich are rich because they *exploit* the poor.

- The only way to change this is to alter the *consciousness* of the exploited people to be "aware" of their condition to become angry or even violent.

- A new order based on political, socialist-oriented principles *must* be instituted soon to redistribute worldly power and wealth.

- This process is called "justice" and has practically co-opted any other meaning of the word.

By carefully following this religious pedagogy, the net result would be to guarantee that the poor remain forever poor. Therefore, a permanent absolutist society would have to be established everywhere to assure forcible redistribution of what is left. Then we would have to prevent coercively this system from being called anything but "socialism with Liberty and without Violence." No wonder religion has often been suspected of harbouring totalitarian tendencies!

The real objection to this mentality is that it will not work for the end professed, the one that justifies its means, the abolition of poverty. Paradoxically, the only countries or institutions not studied carefully or visited by these religious analysts are those in which poverty is rapidly being reduced. Just to be certain they will not be carefully examined, these places are called "fascist," still a cuss word even worse than "profit."

Thus the really interesting problem in the modern world is not so much why the poor are poor, but, rather, why not everyone is poor? Exploitation theory simply does not begin to explain this. Consequently, there ought to be a programme called not "Companions for Justice" for highly educated clergy to mingle briefly with the poor, but one called, to use my colleague Joseph Zrinyi's marvellous term, "Horizons for Productivity."

Go East Young Man

What we ought to be doing is not sending our easily manipulated nuns, college students, and seminarians to slums and barrios to have them routinely return reciting canned ideology in the name of faith without a clue about the difference. Rather, we should send them, if we think religion really is about nothing else, to places where men, indeed, are rapidly learning to produce, to Hong Kong or Tokyo, rather than to Lima or Dar-es-Salaam.

Instead of heavily laden socialist type theological texts, our young ought at least to have a look at W. Beckerman or W. Gaylin, to know of Norman Macrae, Irving Kristol, *The Next 200 Years*, Julian Simon, Paul Johnson, P.T. Bauer, and *The Economist*. For an early reflection on faith and justice, instead of *Marx and the Bible*, they might try Barrington Moore's *Reflections on the Causes of Human Misery and Certain Proposals to Alleviate It*, or Jacques Ellul's

Betrayal of the West, or Igor Shafarevich's *The Socialist Phenomenon,* which is also a meditation on the will to death.

Then with some really new ideas and horizons, concerned religious people might actually have something to tell the poor. In any case the problem of poverty, like slavery, will not ultimately be solved by political action disguised as spirituality, nor by religion masquerading as modernization.

Until we study why men came to be productive in the first place, until we stop preaching doctrines that prevent any real progress from even beginning, the message of religion in the modern world will be seen by the real poor as twofold in its betrayal of them:

- The God of their ultimate destiny will have been taken away from them by making faith into politics.

- Meanwhile, they will find themselves locked up in non-productive systems which merely "redistribute" static economic goods and then proclaim there is no "distortion."

Such a religion is, indeed, the opiate of the people.

They do not deserve it.

Chapter 6

The All-caring State

Noble ideas and lofty principles often lead to highly unwelcome consequences, while very tacky and oddly shaped experiences frequently get things done. One of the strengths of the clergy used to be that it had a lot of practical experience; this made it sceptical of cure-all ideas. Somehow it sensed that the worst tyrannies were erected in the name of the most noble goals.

There are two dangers in expecting too much. One is a sort of paralysis which achieves nothing at all. The other consists of overturning the world in the vain hope of reaching perfection. Since Plato, proponents of this latter strand of thought have toyed with the idea that the location of this responsibility is the state. Religion, in some sense, was what protected us from this sort of political assumption. It long stood steadfast against the idea that all would be well if only we granted the state the power and responsibility to make all things well.

Within the past few years, certain ecclesiastics and other religious leaders have been appearing regularly before state legislatures or congressional committees. They typically testify that religion is not capable of alleviating problems in the areas of housing, welfare, food sufficiency, or education on a voluntary basis. For the first time in 50 years, the government itself has officially wondered whether or not the real problem is that it claimed the capacity to do too much. And now religion finds itself unprepared or even theoretically unwilling to admit that the state ought not to do almost everything.

From an historical point of view, one can wonder if this is not a loss of faith in both state and church. However, it does seem to confirm Leo Strauss's suggestion that the modern state does bear within itself religious objectives and expectations without the religious resources to implement them. Paradoxically, what seems new is that religion itself no longer seems to have its own religious sources to carry them out either.

The State Supplants the Church

Auxiliary Bishop Joseph Sullivan of Brooklyn, for example, stated before a House Budget Committee Task Force that the voluntary agencies are already overworked, while government has the major responsibility to see that all needs are met. "From a practical standpoint," Bishop Sullivan remarked, "it is simply not within the realm of possibility to suggest that the voluntary sector can replace major and necessary government programs." The key word, perhaps, was "replace." Evidently, in this approach, the natural order is for the government to administer major and necessary programmes. There was no hint of any experience that such programmes may themselves be the cause of the problems in the first place.

Meanwhile, before the House Committee on Banking, Finance, and Urban Affairs, Auxiliary Bishop James Lyke of Cleveland held that:

> While the charitable activity of religious institutions is increasing and will continue to increase, it cannot and should not substitute for the essential responsibility that government has to play in meeting basic human needs. The harsh reality of our present economic system is that without substantial and effective government intervention, people will go without shelter. We believe that the federal government has the ultimate responsibility to see that this does not happen.[16]

Again one wonders whether this governmental role is merely a substitutional one or one rooted in a belief that government ought to be the provider of housing. Furthermore, this view says nothing about the vested interests of government bureaucracies to control housing markets, nor does it state a preferred principle according to which housing ought to be provided by the people themselves through the marketplace.

Ecumenical

The most ambitious statement was ecumenical, coming from Rev. Daniel F. Hoye, then General Secretary of the United States Catholic Conference, Rabbi Bernard Mandelbaum, Dr. Claire Randall, Dr. Ronald Sider, and Foy Valentine, the latter three from Protestant organizations. Using the Constitutional phrase that it is the government's role to "promote the general welfare" in the broadest possible sense, their statement (March 31, 1982) repeated the now almost doctrinal thesis that government should be the provider of basic human needs without ever indicating the implications of this thesis either in political experience or in the American tradition of governmental rule. Indeed, this statement argues that charity should be restricted to a very narrow area for what is left over, if anything, after the government provides everything else. In fact for the government to suggest what charity ought to do is seen as a violation of church and state. The notion that charity is some sort of residue over and above justice is very unusual.

> Made in the image of God, the human person is endowed with a special dignity, a dignity which is protected by a fundamental set of basic human rights, not dependent on

charity alone. Among these rights are the right to those basic necessities which are required for proper human development—adequate income, food, clothing, shelter, medical care, employment and basic social services...Government must fulfill its responsibility to ensure that the basic needs of all citizens are met...Furthermore, we believe it is our duty to remind the government of its fundamental obligation to social justice—its responsibility to ensure that no citizen goes without the basic necessities for a dignified and decent human life.

Needless to say, we have here a political theory that would yield, in the name of human rights, all power to the state.

Subsidiarity

In modern times, the Catholic Church, under the general concept of subsidiarity, has stood for a certain notion in social philosophy. This is the view that while government was indeed legitimate and necessary, there ought to be very large areas of economic, cultural, religious, educational, and even political independence and autonomy. These areas should have their own sources and institutions. The so-called "voluntary" society was seen to be a normal, even preferred arena for most everyday human activities. The family in particular had its own justifications, rights, and independence. The family and voluntary organizations needed economic and political capacities to defend themselves, including property or its moral equivalent. The Christian distinction between the things of God and Caesar suggested the idea of a limited state wherein Caesar did not control everything, especially the most important things. The legitimacy of Caesar was not to be an excuse for handing all of society over to him.

Recently, this whole tradition has been transformed, even perverted. Religious institutions now tend to downplay the voluntary aspect of society, which from a spiritual aspect is its most important side. Formerly it was the state which was more likely to try to take over other voluntary organizations, including the family. Today, it almost seems that the democratic state would like to get out of the business of running so many things, only to find itself urged to persist by religion on the grounds of the general welfare. Ironically, this means that the state has a moral duty to provide and guarantee just about everything.

"Human Rights"

Economic recession in particular can obscure what is happening. It makes this widening of state power palatable. *The Wall Street Journal*, in an article on European economic pessimism, cited a Dutch construction worker lamenting,

"The world is saturated—there's no buying power anymore," with a German machine fitter adding, "Nobody has any solutions any more" (May 10, 1982). Such contexts suggest a return to the "human rights" position which tries to justify the idea that it is the state that is responsible for everything; it must guarantee not only the general conditions of justice and law, but just about anything that people might want.

Religious sources have embraced without much questioning a kind of "rights inflation." This over-emphasis magnifies the expectations of the people, who are subtly told that they are less than human if they do not possess from the state a whole host of "rights." These include a right to leisure, food, housing, work, and to a wondrous list of other things, the provision for which is consigned to the state as its primary moral duty. *To be* comes to be identified with *to be taken care of*. That such rights cost money, especially when they are to be provided by the state, never seems to have been stressed by the proponents of this sort of approach. Yet not only is cost a factor, almost always greater when the state becomes involved in their provision, but the unattended and unexpected result is that by a process of "concern" and "care," we are left with a state which has no reason *not* to control everything. This too is ignored.

Loss of Vitality

The traditional bodies that have served the function of limiting the state, of warning of its overreaching tendencies, have themselves lost most of their spiritual vitality. They do not even claim to have "any solutions anymore," except to turn problems over to the state under a political theory which aggrandizes it. We are dealing here not so much with an aggrandizement on the part of the state, which itself has an inkling of what is going on, but a bankruptcy in the moral and religious area. The modern church is too often willing to initiate little and is content to recommend to the state the duty of providing whatever the public wants.

This in turn brings us back to the central problem. Religion traditionally claimed as its sphere of competence the study of what we ought to want and whether our wants are themselves disordered. This kind of discourse, except in certain areas of political theory, where we are beginning to hear talk of virtue again, has almost totally disappeared from religious conversations. It is replaced by bishops, clerics, and seminary professors, who testify to the various legislative, administrative, and judicial bodies that the state ought to do most of the care and providing. Citizenship becomes the right to receive from, not the freedom to do.

An Objection

In his book, *What Are Human Rights?*, Maurice Cranston wrote:

> The traditional human rights are political and civil rights such as the right to life, liberty, and a fair trial. What are now being put forward as universal human rights are economic and social rights, such as the right to unemployment insurance, old-age pensions, medical services and holidays with pay. There is both a philosophical and a political objection to this. The philosophical objection is that the new theory of human rights does not make sense. The political objection is that the circulation of a confused notion of human rights hinders the effective protection of what are correctly seen as human rights.[17]

Anyone who follows the ins and outs of the human rights discussion must be struck by the accuracy of this insight. We are busy replacing the concept of human rights basic to our political freedom and protection with an understanding of "rights" that gives all power and control to the state in the name of these very rights themselves, which are rather privileges and results of largely voluntary activities.

This "totalitarian" view of modern natural rights theory, in other words, is now appearing almost without opposition in some of the churches. What we can best hope for, in this eventuality, is that the clergy returns to its primary task. This task would be one of not encouraging the state to solve our problems by rather one-sided political activism and narrow political options but rather of reminding the people of their own personal resources, which are not exclusively political. When these latter are brought to bear, they have the effect of properly defining the state by limiting our desires and activating our initiatives. No doubt the state need not be our "enemy," but who is to save us when even the clergy seems to suggest it is our salvation?

Chapter 7

Religion and Wealth

Socio-religious philosophy has recently been dominated by a phrase of abstractly impeccable credentials, which is nevertheless highly unfortunate. This phrase is variously rendered as "option for the poor," or "choice for the dispossessed," or "preference for the deprived." It has both religious and secular overtones and interpretations. Its secular component is that we live in a value-free, relativist world in which no intellectual order can be discerned. There is nothing that would indicate any absolute truth of either metaphysics, social policy, or personal life. So the "option for the poor" perspective gives a sense of seriousness to a system and to lives that by definition lack any ultimate value. In a world which has little sense of transcendence, what substitutes for the divinity turns out to be some form of the human collectivity. This is itself taken as a kind of inner-worldly mysticism, usually based on the group rather than the individual human being.

Within this collectivity, moreover, meaning is given by identifying the most tragic problems and formulating a theory about how to meet them. This approach involves reintroducing a covert theory of good and evil, this time not based on any sort of commandment or natural law deriving from what man is, but from the terms of the ideological analysis of poverty and wealth. This too is why this position is so lethal. It is now possible to identify the "causes" of evil, in political terms, with some individual or group of individuals who, presumably, bring about the poverty itself, and not with sin, *the* great distortion of the human condition.

This result means that there is moral justification to eliminate these people who cause such defined evil simply because they fall within the theory's analytical definition of what is the cause of poverty, that is, of evil. In the old Christian tradition, individuals may or may not commit evil, but they were not evil themselves. One of the major reasons for the violence associated with modern ideologies is precisely the position which permits us to identify individuals or groups or nations as the causes of evil. We miss the deeper meaning of current discussions of poverty and wealth formation if we do not perceive this level of intellectual discourse contained within it.

Blessed Are the Poor

The religious component of the phrase, "options for the poor," suggests that Yahweh loves the poor. The poor are blessed so that there is some divine sanction or sign directing our energies and our policies toward the weak or least privileged. The poor were not taken to be absolutely innocent or irresponsible, so that they became objects of someone else's care. Indeed, the religious tradition held that the poor had a spiritual advantage over the rich. In a way, even though the rich were not in themselves evil or wicked, still, given a choice, we ought to choose to be poor if we are concerned about our relation with God. Nevertheless, the rich could be holy and good.

The notion of "option for the poor," however, has some serious problems connected with it if it is not carefully considered. The first problem is the intellectual paternalism contained within its framework, which urges us to care for or to be concerned about the poor. Here the religious person (or ideologue) becomes the one who fulfils this role and acquires a sense of self-satisfaction, while the poor become the "objects" of care.

The second problem is that the way to aid the poor involves choice on the part of the directors of society. The poor again, in spite of the rhetoric, cannot help themselves but must be helped according to a bureaucratic programme. The classical discussion of the middle class state seems almost totally forgotten. The final point is the suspicion that there is something wrong about being poor, that the poor somehow are less human because of their economic status. One often gets the impression from those who so urgently advocate political measures to aid the poor that they believe that they are almost creating human beings rather than dealing with those already here. There are after all a surprising number of "new heavens and new earths" in revolutionary literature.

Those who "work for the poor" are, therefore, engaged in a process of radically "making man to be man." What men, women, and children are from nature is defective. It is thus necessary to replace this cosmic inadequacy, to change the very being, the very species of man to conform to other, new, man-made norms. The "option for the poor" in this sense becomes cast in the language of radical liberty, of new worlds, of new metaphysics, in this vale of tears.

The Fact of Poverty

What response can we make to this intellectual initiative? In the first place the poor are not poor as a result of the wealth of the rich. In the beginning of the modern era, even two hundred years ago, almost everyone was poor. The real question is, why is not everyone now poor? The answer is that some men have learned how to produce wealth. If this had not been discovered, learned, and passed on, everyone would continue to be poor.

Furthermore, the very learning how *not* to be poor, which is not known by instinct or revelation, is a risk or an adventure which gives mankind some real opportunity to discover things by and for themselves. The fact of poverty in history is not itself a sign of the non-existence of God or the perversity of men or nature. The only hope the poor have of not being poor is the example of the rich, or their own self-discovery of the same methods of wealth accumulation. These discoveries can successfully determine what will and what will not work to become not poor. This approach alone respects the basic dignity of both the poor and the rich. It reaffirms their basic human inter-relationship.

Burying Talent

In the New Testament, it says that the poor will always be with us, which is psychologically true. There will always be someone richer than we are in one way or another even if we are quite well off. So the New Testament reprimanded the man with but one talent, the poorest in fact, not because he only had one talent and not five or ten but because he buried his one talent. He could at least have put it out at interest to make it minimally productive.

The poor, in other words, if we respect their real dignity, can be the causes of their own poverty. There is something insulting about continually telling the poor that their problems are somebody else's fault. We do not really help the poor if we say we will take care of them no matter what. We are interested in the multiplication of being not its collapse into sterile unity. The New Testament recommends general honesty in trade, not stealing, and paying taxes, even by miraculous means, but also that we not build our houses on sand lest they be washed away.

One recent winter, on the Monterey Bay beaches near my brother's home in California, many very expensive homes, built on sand, were washed away. I saw them. In retrospect many blamed the government for letting people build on sand; a few blamed themselves for being so unforeseeing, and some blamed the structure of the world. Everyone's insurance went up. It is not just the poor who have building problems.

Aristotle suggested that there will be a wide range between great wealth and extreme poverty. Healthy society tries to have most people live in their own homes with their own property, acquired by their own energies. Most people should fall some place in between the extremes of rich and poor.

The virtues of humility and moderation were designed to prevent us from placing too much emphasis on our not having what others have whether by their work or talents or luck or even corruption. Our dignity does not depend on what we have but on what we are. But we ought normally to have something, and we ought to promote those systems that allow for and encourage the production and creation of new wealth, which is the only real solution.

Ultimate Resource

Finally, the ultimate resource is not oil and coal or land but the human brain. We have no idea just how rich we are or can be with the cosmos and the minds we have been given. The record of almost every scarcity in the modern world is that the very lack of something was the cause of the discovery of future abundance. We do not usually learn how to be richer if we are content with what we have. So we need a system which encourages us to invent, experiment, change, take risks, use our brains.

With social theories which are based rather on the idea that all "getting" is a "taking away" from someone else, we must live in an armed camp. But this alternative does not arise from the world itself but from our mistaken theories. What I want to suggest here is quite simple. The main problem of poverty and wealth today, both religious and secular, is intellectual.

If we do not think properly, we will not do what we need to do to achieve the goals of abundance and freedom. And this achievement is what should be the risk of our creation and the promise of our human relationship with one another. The only "option for the poor" worth caring about is the one that incorporates true knowledge of how wealth is produced and innovatively distributed. Without that knowledge we will all end up being poor and blaming each other for our lot. Life is more than riches and poverty. Once we know this, we can begin to think about riches and poverty in a more profound manner, one which offers some hope of achieving those moderate yet splendidly abundant possibilities which surely are the gifts of earth and mind.

Chapter 8

From Compassion to Coercion: The Strange Paths of Contemporary Religious Politics

In the 1960s, when Black Panther Elridge Cleaver spoke at the University of California, he was consistently greeted with cheers and adulation. On his return a couple of years ago (1982), however, now rather repentant and with a new religious orientation, he was booed and jeered. To such a charged, hostile reception, especially where academic freedom ought to reign, Cleaver remarked philosophically, "When you come to Berkeley, you have to be prepared for just about everything."

Academics no doubt are easily tempted into thinking they are competent in all spheres and on all subjects. A clerical academic may suspect in addition that what he does not know by his own capacities will conveniently be revealed to him from on high. But do not count on it. The perhaps apocryphal story was told in the old days of a young Jesuit arriving on campus only to be assigned to teach "torts" in Fall Semester Law School. His only comment was, "I'll be glad to, what are torts anyhow?" Apparently, they do not make even Jesuits like that any more. In any case, the philosophical distance from nothing to everything to something cannot be traversed except by a creator, as Stanley Jaki suggested some years ago.[18]

One Thing at a Time

I am sceptical enough, however, to think that anyone who actually claims to be prepared for everything is, in fact, more likely to be prepared for nothing in particular. Since we can only be conveniently shown one thing at a time—life, someone once quipped, is just a succession of "one damned thing after another," which may explain why we are in time and not eternity—the real way to prepare for everything, which seems somehow to be our ultimate destiny, is to take one thing at a time. Reality may indeed be made to conform to our peculiar condition. By beginning with something very real, very particular, with a baby, say, rather than with all humanity, or with a small plot of ground rather than the common possession of the whole earth, we can best prepare for everything.

Thus more can be said for owning, say, a quarter section in Pocahontas County, Iowa, than for belonging to an organization in which everything is owned in common. Now I do come from Pocahontas County, Iowa, where I grew up amidst talk of quarter, half, and full sections of land. And I do belong to the Society of Jesus in which everything is owned communally. I live in a completely voluntary, socialist society, which means roughly that I do not want everyone else to dwell in such circumstances, however apt they may or may not be for me.

Mine and thine are categories which protect and foster most of the worthwhile things of our human condition. Voluntary socialisms typical of the monastic tradition, which the Church has wisely never advocated for everyone, can only be healthy if they are exceptions, if they are not the coerced rule for everyone. Rather they should be a free norm for a few, designed to witness to something higher than the world itself, something to which all are also called, even in the legitimate world of mine and thine.

Cannot Know In Advance

Life will seem more whole, more concrete, when we chart very carefully where especially noble and spiritual ideas lead, and establish whether they turn out to be as exalted in practice as they sounded in theory. We cannot deduce how the world works merely by reflecting on it in our own minds, as Stanley Jaki pointed out in his *The Road of Science and the Ways to God*. Something is "out there" for us to learn, something which we must use our minds to discover. We cannot know in advance what we ought to be shown or be thankful for.

The man after whom America was named, one Amerigo Vespucci, the Italian cartographer, was also a dealer in spices. In this latter less exalted, but no less metaphysical capacity, Vespucci was recently named the Patron of International Pickle Week. At first sight this may seem to be no momentous piece of information to anyone this side of Ronald McDonald or we avid fans of pastrami on rye. But think on it, as the Vice-President of this pickle celebration gravely remarked, we should be thankful that our country was named after the said Italian gentleman's first rather than his last name. "Otherwise, we would be living in the United States of Vespucci" and singing "Vespucci the Beautiful" and "God Bless Vespucci." In other words, we should count our blessings, while salvation does seem to begin in such little things as what's in a name.

Collectivity

Yet since Vespucci, in the course of human events, is no less improbable a name than, say, "Missouri," let alone "Pickle" or even "Pocahontas," for that matter, let us assume that we all are indeed prepared for just about everything. Let us suppose that we are in fact liberally educated but that we retain our fondness for unusual places, unusual names, unusual events, for that indeed constitutes the actual context of the lives of most of us. We are each non-repeatable beings, sent forth into a world which more and more is inclined to treat us as members of some class, category, or collectivity.

I like to state this problem in the following manner: We now claim our existence to be composed of "rights" granted by the state, whereas we actually exist in a truth grounded in liberty, which alone can consign to the state anything it has or does. Joseph P. Duggan remarked that our human development, at bottom, "has to do with the meaning, aspirations, and worth of every individual".[19]

The central issue is whether this meaning, aspiration, and worth of each individual has any grounding outside the rights-granting, public-caring definitions of the state itself. In other words, does the individual have any meaning transcendent to the state, any given reality that limits government? I ask this in the context of the history of political theory which suggests that the single institution most likely to claim all power over men is this very civil community. Once men, explicitly or implicitly, no longer believe in anything higher than the state, it is absolutely logical that the polity replaces the divinity in describing and establishing what constitutes the essential outlines, the essential "rights," by which we will or will not allow anyone to exist.

Group Culpability

My thesis here is that we are caught not in a crisis of "evil" but in a crisis of "goodness." Our very virtues as we have come to define them are coercing, if not actually "killing," us, in a world wherein our vices have become not personal but primarily political. Moral culpability now falls not on the individual but on the group. We are in the process of losing that central idea of our culture, namely, that the person grounds and defines all societal reality, no matter how it be conceived.

As an example let me recount this incident, I think a typical one. Not too long ago, two men and three juveniles, all blacks, were arrested for conducting a campaign of terror against Southeast Asian refugees in the Hunter's Point District of San Francisco. During previous months, it seemed, there had been numerous assaults against Southeast Asians, the most serious one leading to the arrest, was against the property and family of a Mr. Heung Kwong, who apparently had yelled at the youth to get away from his car parked in front of his apartment. The young men came back a short time later, shot his windows out, wounded his son, and finally tossed a Molotov cocktail into his apartment.

These seem to be the bare facts of the case as recounted in the *San Francisco Chronicle* (June 1, 1982). The Kwong family lived in a public housing project, which was recently rehabilitated by the City's Housing Authority, whereas the nearby black section was not refinished as soon. What interested me in this incident, however, was not the idea that racism is not an exclusively white phenomenon, nor as Aristotle said at the end of the *Ethics*, that most human cities will have problems controlling their young men. It was rather the reaction of the arresting police officer, who told the reporter, "These incidents stem from jealousy. It does appear that the (Southeast Asian) refugees have preference in housing."

Let us suppose for a moment that this preference is a fact, which may be justified on humanitarian, foreign policy, economic, cultural, or construction grounds. What is disconcerting is that this sociological reason about housing is, without any apparent awareness about its dubiousness in the mind of either the reporter or the officer, given to explain a specific, violent attack with bullets and Molotov cocktails on an individual family. Evidently the Kwong family in particular were attacked only because they were members of an identifiable class or group of people judged to be "guilty" of some corporate injustice. Except for yelling to protect his property, which is presumably a virtue, Mr. Kwong did nothing to those youths who shot at him. There was nothing personal in it at all that would excuse or mitigate a given act on the classical defences of ignorance or passion. Jealousy was mentioned, but it was not personal jealousy, directed at anyone in particular. Mr. Kwong's next door Vietnamese neighbours would have served the same purpose.

Injustice

Logically, no doubt, the men should have tossed the Molotov cocktail into the Housing Authority Offices, if the real cause of the problem was its decision to rehabilitate the Southeast Asian neighbourhood before the black one. Yet we must wonder, since when does such a political reason justify violent attacks on a particular human family for no other reason than that they are members of a group?

What we have here, in other words, is a philosophical problem. We see what happens when we are no longer, in our spontaneous thinking or in our public policy, concerned with real individuals like Mr. Kwong, who are in need of civil order. We are concerned rather with abstract presuppositions that allow and justify terror to particular human persons, because some theory explains why violence "must" happen. We have an explicit determinism at work here which reduces the responsibility for the action of human beings, which reduces human life to a series of necessary mechanical responses.

In order that no one shall be accused of violent crime, we must deprive everyone of his individuality. Whether the actual youths who shot up the Kwong's apartment had any such sophisticated notions in their minds other than getting even is not even mentioned. Interpretations, not facts, count. And the personal motives of the youths themselves are irrelevant anyhow, since in a good part of public life today, in spite of our much vaunted individualism, concrete persons no longer exist; except, that is, as incidental exemplars of static sociological categories into which everything must fit to have any legal standing.

The Legal System

Thus beginning at least with the unborn, we hold that what counts is not extra-mental existence but legal existence. What does not exist legally, does not exist at all. The real battles are being fought over control of the legal defining processes. The group we belong to becomes more important than our individual existence. It takes a keen mind to call Hitler's genocide what it was, while calling legal abortion a benefit to humanity and the furtherance of "human rights." The notion of a natural existence and a civility based on it, is replaced by an ideological definition of which groups are allowed to exist and what makes them act.

Thus when some poor person's house is not rehabilitated before his poor neighbour's, it is sociologically required that he shoot up his neighbour's house. "Who is my neighbour?" thus automatically becomes a political question. The man doing the shooting is justified because what causes "crime" is bad housing, or, at least, relative standing in the replacement of bad housing. Worse, this process is effected not by the citizens as part of their own enterprise but on the basis of the priorities of the state.

Happily, many people in far worse housing situations do not set fire to their neighbour's home. This restraint is because they think, as individuals and in principle, that it is simply wrong to burn up any individual neighbour's house. However, this seems not to have occurred to the arresting officer or to the reporter recounting the case. In seeking to justify or to excuse a violent act, we thus end up by depersonalizing both the victims and the attackers. "Society," in this case the Housing Authority, becomes the cause of our civil ills and *a pari* of our civil "goods." For according to the same article, "although San Francisco has some 7,000 federally subsidized housing units, there is always a lengthy waiting list for apartments." As some wise economic wit once remarked, if a good thing is underpriced, it will always be oversold. There is also the point that the very existence of the Housing Authority raises questions about whether it may not itself in fact create more housing problems than it solves.

Personal Dignity

By seeking to reform the world rather than ourselves, by placing the problem in our houses rather than in our wills, we no longer seek first to convert ourselves. We must judge it wrong to fire bomb a neighbour no matter what sort of house he lives in, or what sort we live in. We no longer seem to believe in a core personal dignity capable of being addressed by moral argument or grace. We are only perfect if our environment or society or our genes are perfect as defined by law. But this can change. Our demand for benevolent and compassionate explanations has never been greater.

Yet, to achieve this delicate balance, we deprive ourselves of individual autonomy, while we place only those restrictions on our collectivities that enable them to care for us completely without our recognizing what this implies. There is, as Joseph Sobran remarked, a positive industry of making us all "victims" of society. In this way a benevolent government can take care of us, can protect us, by compassionately organizing us in order to take over our well-being.[20] By a strange turn of irony, secularized Christian ideas have become responsible for handing more and more categories of people over to the state. The government needs morally to justify the growth of its internal organisms, while the people allow it because they no longer seem to have the moral or doctrinal energy to believe that they ought first to take care of themselves. This result, at bottom, may be a failure of religion to believe in itself.

Thus we gallantly strive to achieve the classic natural and, more especially, Christian virtues, such as charity and mercy. We do so under the guise of corporate compassion and benevolence. We do this not in the name of ethics or religion but in the name of an all-caring state subject to no definition of what is to be cared for but the state's own criteria. I prefer to argue, on the other hand, the very opposite thesis. "Faith" has sometimes become a tool to promote what are, on careful analysis, certain selected objectives of a predominantly ideological thesis, ones inimical to both religion and politics. Yet they are ones which often have their origins and justifications in a misplaced Christian dogma that suggests that we ought first to do good, wherein "good" is practically defined as what can only be achieved in grace.

What I want to suggest, is that almost unknowingly we are trying to accomplish Christian ends by political means. We do so in such a way that we have placed these ends under our own, not divine guidance. And in so doing we not only corrupt religion but we remove those limits which enable politics to remain only politics and not some worldly substitute for religion.

The Least of the Brethren

To indicate further the drift of my argument, let me cite in rapid succession three short passages—the first from the *Gospel of Matthew*, the second from the Soviet mathematician Igor Shafarevich's penetrating book, *The Socialist Phenomenon*, and the third from southern novelist Walker Percy's *Love in the Ruins*. When put together, they will, I hope, better indicate what I have in mind:

1)   Then the virtuous will say to him in reply: 'Lord, when did we see you hungry and feed you; or thirsty and give you drink? When did we see you a stranger and make you welcome?'...And the King will answer, 'I tell you solemnly, in so far as you did this to the least of these brothers of mine, you did it to me' (*Matthew*, 25: 37-40).

2)   It is to Christianity that socialism owes its concept of an historical goal, the idea of the sinfulness of the world, its coming end and last judgment...The existence of certain related elements in Christianity and socialism is indicated, for example, by the phenomenon of the monastery, which seems to realize socialist principles within Christianity (e.g., the abolition of private property and of marriage). It would be extremely important to discover aspects shared by Christianity and socialism, to trace how the Christian concepts are redirected within socialism and ultimately turn into a denial of the fundamentals of Christianity (for example, when God's judgment over the world is reinterpreted as the judgment of the 'elect' over their enemies...)[21]

3)   Leroy, like Ellen, believes that right is right and in doing right. You're a doctor, so do what a doctor is supposed to do. Doctors cure sick people.

The terror comes from piteousness, from good gone wrong and not knowing it, from Southern sweetness and cruelty. God why do I stay here? In Louisiana people still stop and help strangers. Better to live in New York where life is simple, every man's your enemy, and you walk with your eyes straight ahead.

In the dark mirror there is a dim, hollow-eyed Spanish Christ. The pox is spreading on his chest...It is the new Christ, the spotted Christ, the maculate Christ, the sinful Christ. The old Christ died for our sins and it didn't work, we were not reconciled. The new Christ shall reconcile man with his sins.[22]

The least of the brethren, Christian concepts becoming the denial of Christianity, the final Christ reconciling man *with* his sins rather than having him repent them, not by converting individual men and women but by changing the definition of evil—if we reflect on these remarkable passages, we see that we begin with a desire to do what can only be accomplished in grace. We end up seeking to do the very same things by ourselves. Then we notice that in the name of benevolence and compassion, we begin to call good what tradition called evil. We did not notice why the good went wrong, as Walker Percy noted, so we could only call what we did "good," because we thought we could accomplish by our own civil processes what the revelational tradition held was the result of ways that were not our ways.

Limited Government

Chesterton put it well in his essay on "The Book of Job":

> When once people have begun to believe that prosperity is the reward of virtue, their next calamity is obvious. If prosperity is regarded as the reward of virtue, it will be regarded as the symptom of virtue. Men will leave off the heavy task of making good men successful. They will adopt the easier tasks of making our successful men good.[23]

We ought to strive to make good men successful also, and the great confusion in recent religion is how to do this. But if we decide that whoever is successful is for that reason good, if we do not try to locate the good in itself, we have overturned any standard of good based on human nature that would by its own existence limit the state. In former times, the word "successful" usually had economic overtones, such that goodness and riches were identified, as in early Calvinism. Today, it appears rather that successful refers to a recipient of corporate and political redistribution guaranteed in terms of compassion and benevolence, along with those paid for providing these public services.

We have, consequently, relocated both the good Samaritan—"Who is my neighbour?"—and the Last Judgment—"Lord, when did we see you hungry and feed you?" Now these are primarily civil goals, defined by "rights" and public policy, themselves subject to no prior natural law criterion. They are not personal goals or initiatives defined by liberality and charity. Indeed, public charity and compassion make personal religious virtue unnecessary, even threatening. Walker Percy was right. Private virtue is dangerous. It is best to walk with our eyes straight ahead.

The sick, the young, the poor, the homeless, are now mainly categories to be administered to by organizations of the state or to be placed under their control. The entrenched privileges of the administrators and workers in these "caring" industries are key questions of public policy. Thus we give "eternal" reward in the only way civil society can reward eternally, that is, by what it in fact honours, fosters, and protects. The inspirations and goals of Scripture have been reworked to conform to modes of activity once thought proper only for the individual. This result explains, in part, why those doctrines which define human worth in non-political terms—specifically, the divinity of Christ and personal resurrection—are under such fire today in politicized theological circles. The transformation of utopia or paradise into politics is not entirely accidental.

Real Subversion

Phyllis McGinley once wrote a poem entitled, "Subversive Reflections," which went like this:

> *If wit engendered worthy deed*
> *And only the good were gay,*
> *Bad company would seldom lead*
> *The innocent astray.*
> *Toward primrose pastures few would stir*
> *In search of light and colour*
> *Were virtuous people merrier*
> *Or the naughty people duller?*[24]

The quaint notion that virtue is dull and naughtiness merry is, I suppose, commonplace. After all, even the Good Shepherd went out after the one Lost Sheep, while the Prodigal Son remains a sort of folk hero. Still, if Phyllis McGinley's subversive reflections seem rather odd today, it is because we are so much more aware that what is really subversive in our public order is not vice or naughtiness, which at times seems like the law of the land, if not the established religion, but virtue itself as it was always understood in ethical and Judaeo-Christian reflections. Socrates was killed because truth was disruptive of the given political order in Athens.

What is currently behind the effort to interpret all Christian notions in terms of politics appears to be merely a subtle way to tame the radicalness of revelation, so that it conforms in its own language to what the state is willing to coerce, usually following some secular or marxist criterion of the good. In truly Christian terms, the radicals are not radical at all, but conformists to current ideologies.

Ordering the Soul

In a recent lecture, Russell Kirk worried that even the churches no longer know what virtue means. He remarked:

> What the Church always has been meant to do really is to offer a pattern for ordering the soul of the believer, and to open a window on the transcendent realm of being...
>
> Now the churches of America ought to do far more good work toward the renewal of virtue among persons than they are actually performing nowadays...I do not mean that the Church should be censorious as it was in Scotland in Knox's day...I do mean that the Church ought to address itself less to prudential considerations of the hour's politics—at which business the Church usually demonstrates its incompetence—and much more at showing the pertinence of the

> theological virtues to our present discontents, private and public.
>
> ...Most graduates of seminaries seem incapable today of discussing virtue, or particular virtues, with much historical or philosophical insight. For the moment, we must not look to institutional Christianity for rousing moral virtue...If it is to come alive again, probably it must be revised by some other power.[25]

These surely are not encouraging words. They intimate that Christians themselves identify their efforts with contemporary political notions. These notions are usually formulated from certain ideological modifications of doctrine common in religious spheres. Religion at times seems to function as a support for established forms brought into power by political means. This too is why both marxism and many non-theist versions of liberalism are beginning to look upon religion as an eventual means to implement and solidify, if not justify, their own goals. Religion is not so much the opium of the people but a way to reach the masses with ideological visions.

Charity

Not too long ago, I had a phone call from a gentleman who told me that he was a successful businessman. He was very much concerned to help the poor and needy. He felt his wealth was given to him for this purpose. His net profit each year over and above his income was perhaps $50,000, of which as a matter of principle, he gave roughly one half each year to various orphanages or other good works. He did not in any way publicize his generosity, nor reflect too much on the nature of a society that would allow such generosity to occur. He wanted to organize a group of similarly minded businessmen and women who would voluntarily follow his own spiritual initiatives with regard to the use of earned wealth. This effort would be good for business, for the poor, for society, and for his soul. I was, of course, much touched by this sincere desire to aid those who need extra help, as well as with the sense of responsibility which wealth gave this man.

Yet I was somewhat sceptical from another angle about this worthy idea. In general, the best way business can help the poor is to provide for a growing, fair economy in which the vast majority of the population work for their own living. Without a growing, free economy, each person finds it difficult to take care of himself and his family. The type of aid to the poor this gentleman had in mind was not directed primarily to this question but to the poor who, as Scripture said, "will always be with us," for one reason or another. The major effort of business and government ought to be directed to the vast majority of those able to care for themselves, not neglecting those who cannot.

The Private Sphere

I have often suggested that anyone giving money to a university, a school, a church, a hospital, or any sort of good work ought to make sure that his gift is both addressed to the purpose for which it was intended and that its intentions not be perverted. There are strong movements beginning in our culture which seek to prevent any gift giving except for public purposes defined exclusively by the state. These are movements, in other words, which seek to deny the very idea of the private, the non-political.

So I undertook to tell the kind gentleman that he should at least be aware that the understanding of wealth, its production, and usage was a very controversial and misunderstood item in many areas of academia and religion today. What if he were to give his gift to some parish in, say, Nicaragua, only to find out that the good pastor used the welcome cash to establish a printing press in order to instruct the flock on the bliss of religious marxism, or even to supply weapons to "worthy" causes? Or what if he found out that the group he was supporting taught from the pulpit that all wealth belonged to the state, that it was merely exploitation, so that in giving half his income the man was merely returning ill-gotten goods, making reparations? Would he then be so enthusiastic about his project? The man seemed quite aware of such problems. But he wished to practice the classic Judaeo-Christian teaching about wealth, that it ought to be freely given when it was gained by legitimate human enterprise after the man's own life was first provided for. The taking care of our own remains the basis of our helping others. Unfortunately, we live in a world wherein the state "volunteers" to take care of our own while we are asked to care for the poor of other continents.

Good Intentions

I have called this chapter "From Compassion To Coercion," in part to emphasize the fact that it is not our *intentions* alone that decide whether a policy or a private act will work or not. Most of the good intentions in our society do seem to stem from either Greek-Roman or Judaeo-Christian inspirations. However, what happens to these intentions and inspirations to care for the poor, house the homeless, clothe the naked, protect human life, when they become not acts of personal virtue or grace achieved in freedom, but policies of the state? We know, of course, what happens, to the unborn. At a recent court case involving a Princeton University student caught plagiarizing in an examination, the Judge said, "I wish Princeton viewed this matter with greater humanity...I can't, however, mandate compassion."[26]

Theoretically, the courts should mandate justice. They have to leave compassion and humaneness largely to the broad sphere of life wherein not every virtue or fault is a responsibility of state legislation. But when compassion, benevolence, and humaneness become objects of law, they become justifications for the state to control all sides of life, not in the name of virtue, not even as usurpation, but almost with the approval of a people who want to be so controlled.

What we really need is some way to reclaim the virtues, natural and religious, from the state which now operates these increasingly expensive take care tasks by its own methods. Russell Kirk was right to wonder where we might find a new source of virtue in our society. In the end the only way to reduce the power of the state is to reclaim private and religious virtue for the individual and those voluntary organizations which he forms by his free initiatives, such as the gentleman suggested for the poor. If we do not do this, increasingly there will be only the state.

Compassion to Coercion

The most important public issue today, in other words, is that our religion and our ethics again start preaching and teaching about what we can do ourselves by the initiatives and graces that come to each of us. Otherwise, our passage from compassion to coercion will be steady and irreversible.

Flannery O'Connor once remarked that "the novelist with Christian concerns will find in modern life distortions which are repugnant to him and the problem will be to make these appear as distortions to an audience which is used to seeing them as natural."[27] The greatest political distortion of our time is to grant to the state the caring, compassionate, benevolent function, which seems now natural for it to have. We ought to wonder, however, why this function so often seems to end up being in fact coercive rather than benevolent in its effect. The answer seems to be that we cannot institutionalize as organisms of the state what ought to arise in freedom and grace, what ought to be exercised by persons to persons rather than by groups or classes.

The Princeton judge was right when he said that he could not mandate compassion, though he betrayed the same dangerous mentality when he hinted that Princeton University could. Where the state mandates compassion, ultimately it turns out to be coercion. By a strange path of religious politics this latter result now seems to be advocated in the name of the public good. Unhappily, this is done by religion itself, which claims it cannot exercise the compassionate functions. We have become victims to be taken care of by the state. The poor, always with us, have become secular legitimizers of the modern coercive state, wherein what exists is subject only to what manages to make itself legal. The decline of religion is the rise of the state.

Chapter 9

On Sharing and Giving

I had a friend in San Francisco who used to share everything with everybody, especially me. We did not go to lunch. We "shared" it. "I'd like to share this pickle with you." "I'd love to share some thoughts on the Poet MacDougal." "I'd like you to share a few moments with my cousin Hector." It used to drive me nuts, but I could never quite figure out why.

Now I am no stranger to the Aristotelian theory of knowledge. I know that if each of fifty people knows something of this chair or that El Greco, there are not suddenly fifty chairs or one person.

The more spiritual a thing is, the more it can be ours without itself becoming less. In contrast, if I want a cold glass of beer to assist me in watching the Redskins, the 49ers, or the Georgetown basketball team, the beer must disappear in me, not you. Elementary, right?

Anyhow, brace yourself for the worst. Thanks to a friend in Maryland, who "shares" with me a subscription of *The Chesterton Review*—that delightful journal from, of all places, not Beaconsfield, but Saskatoon, Saskatchewan—I think I am on to the answer of what bothers me.

Individual Differences

Of course, I am not totally against sharing. No, Sir. When we were boys, I never really minded "sharing" my brothers' ice creams, after I had just finished mine. This happy state lasted until they got bigger than I.

Certainly, we share things, especially things we don't own, like the Jefferson Memorial. It is just that they are not the highest things. The highest things we possess, or they possess us, yet without consuming or destroying or subsuming us.

The highest things, like God, make us more particular. This is why I am not a pantheist or a Buddhist. In the everlasting, I want there to be me and you, or perhaps "you all," if our souls pass through the Southland, as the lovely "Ballad of the Rebel Soldier" goes.

In the August 1981 issue of *The Chesterton Review* an essay Chesterton wrote for *The New Age* on January 4, 1908, on "Why I Am Not a Socialist," was reprinted. This is another one of those disturbing metaphysical essays which suggest that Chesterton would have invented Christianity were it not already invented when he came along. He would have called it "sanity," but what's in a word?

I had a friend who, I suspect, did the same thing, even though that's heresy, strictly speaking. But today, as in Chesterton's time, the only real "heretics" worth their salt in the public order are the orthodox believers. They seem to be the only ones not conforming to prevailing mores. But this may be a grace, that is, a delight.

'Tis Nobler to Give than to Share

As to "sharing," I have always held the unorthodox view that it is more difficult to receive than to give. Scripture sometimes seems to say the opposite, sort of. It says it is more "blessed," but my point is about the Third Person in the Trinity, not the Second or the First.

Pride, the ultimate deformity, means essentially that we cannot receive anything from anybody, that the only world we will live in is our own. In Hell, they share, but they don't give or take. This is why prideful people are so boring. They cannot admire new stars or new babies, because they did not make them.

"I greatly prefer the pleasure of giving and receiving," Chesterton wrote.

> Giving is not the same as sharing: giving is the opposite of sharing. Sharing is based on the idea that there is no property, or at least no personal property. But giving a thing to another man is as much based on personal property as keeping it to yourself.

Chesterton went on to say what Aristotle once said to Plato, that he would rather have his own beat-up hat than share a thousand brand new ones with just anybody. Hats, Chesterton thought, were as unique as fingerprints.

Give and Take

What we really want to know, then, is "What we would have if we could get it?" Of this, a friend wrote:

> Have you ever noticed that after you really tell God that you don't care what happens and that He's won the war of wills, that you get what you wanted but then you discover that it is no longer what you want or the way that you wanted it? Mark Twain says there is a solemn warning in this moral, or a solemn moral in this warning, but no matter.[28]

Here is how Chesterton put this point, and no one, I think, has put it better:

> And if I were a poet writing an Utopia, if I were a magician waving a wand, if I were a God making a Planet, I would

deliberately make it a world of give and take, rather than a world of sharing.

I do not wish Jones and Brown to share the same cigar box; I do not want it as an ideal; I do not want it as a very remote ideal; I do not want it at all.

I want Jones by one mystical and godlike act to give a cigar to Brown, and Brown by another mystical and godlike act to give a cigar to Jones.

Thus it seems to me instead of one act of fellowship (of which the memory would slowly fade) we should have a continual play and energy of new acts of fellowship keeping up the circulation of society.

Now I have read some tons or square miles of Socialist eloquence in my time, but it is literally true that I have never seen any serious allusion to or clear consciousness of this creative altruism of personal giving.

For instance, in the many Utopian pictures of comrades feasting together, I do not remember one that had the note of hospitality, of the difference between host and guest and the difference between one house and another.

No one brings up the port that his father laid down; no one is proud of the pears grown in his own garden. In the less non-conformist Utopians there is, indeed, the recognition of traditional human liquor; but I am not speaking of drink but of that yet nobler thing, "standing drink."

The world is made up of givers and receivers, while those who merely share, I suspect, remain locked up in a very little world in which everything belongs to everyone else and nothing to each.

Religion as Private Property

In the world God created, however, the mystical world of our particular existence, everything is intended to belong to me, including God. This is the substance of the Christian revelation. And when you give away something that really belongs to you, you begin to discover that even you do not belong to you. You belong to him who gave you. And they say that in the Trinity, the three persons "share" the same divine nature. I'll buy that, but only if it means what orthodoxy says it means, that God only appears to us as Father, Son, and Spirit, definite persons who do not blend into each other in one big confusion.

In the meantime, I often go to my brother's place in Aptos or in Reno for ice cream, *his* ice cream. He gives and I receive it. We do not "share" it. And that is the highest order of things among brothers.

Chapter 10

The Problem of Starvation in the World Today

The problem of who, if anybody, is starving in the world, and why, is both a complex and controversial one. After considerable study of the matter, I am inclined to believe that most people who are hungry—the very definition of which is largely cultural—are so because of ideology. Actually, there is a fair amount of agreement that the earth is quite capable of supporting practically any number of people we might think up if food production were the sole criterion.

Indeed, Norman Macrae in *The Economist* of London, one of the few really sensible writers in this whole area, held that we could easily produce a glut on the international food market so great it would dwarf all other issues. The Ganges Valley in India, the Yangtze in China, the Mississippi Valley in the Midwest, and even the smaller San Joaquin Valley in California can by themselves come fairly close to supplying the world's basic food needs if farmed with the intensity and skill of the Dutch or Japanese. What causes insufficient food production are fundamentally the theories, values, and ideologies that interfere with or fail to foster those means of achieving the planet's capacity in this area. Some seem even to welcome starvation in order to prove their theories.

Not by Bread Alone

Once this potential is granted, endless arguments ensue over which ideology or value harms or helps. Such controversy will continue to go on since man, the political animal, is really more interested in power than in food. And I suspect that most people who talk of food are really quite interested in power. There are not a few people who have vested ideological interests in starving people. Man does not live by bread alone, as one rather famous person once put it. And this was said not to play down power, but to remind us that full stomachs are in some ways more unsettling than empty ones.

Most men subsist and prosper because of two general kinds of grain—rice and wheat. Corn, maize, oats, and barley can of course be added, but most of these reach us through meat, something that is by no means fully necessary. In fact, I would suspect that it will not be long before the meat cycle of our eating will be mostly bypassed. It is beginning to look as if a good deal of "agriculture" itself can be bypassed through direct manufacture. The basic, the only "natural" resource even on the earth, we should again realize, is the human brain.

Generally, North Americans tend to eat their wheat in the form of bread in its various varieties from hot dog buns to doughnuts. Admittedly, bread can be very good. This is unfortunate since wheat in the form of what Italians call pasta is a far more wonderful way to eat it.

However, since Italians eat happily both bread and pasta, no exclusive choice need be made. And like everything else worthwhile, there is good pasta and bad pasta. There is bad pasta in the United States. I have had too much, though we are improving. In all my years in Italy, I hardly ever had any bad pasta.

Pasta Theory

Even though there are many legends about the origin of pasta in Italy, mostly connected with China where they presumably eat rice, the now practically universal custom of eating a big bowl of fettuccine or a wonderful lasagna or rigatoni with all the various sauces to put on top is a thing of less than a hundred years, even in Italy. Indeed, it was the invention of various machines to cut and dry and package pasta that made it the widespread first dish it is in Italy, where, if the Communists take over, the one thing we can be sure they won't touch will be the pasta asciutta, at least not until they ruin agriculture in general, as they invariably do.

In spite of its simplicity, pasta can and does appear in almost six hundred different forms, lengths, and shapes. Basically, there is pasta stretched out long into the shape of a cord or tube, pasta bent or lined, and pasta in ribbons or sheets. Onto this marvellous concoction, or in it, you can put any kind of sauce, butter, oil, or meat. The variety is almost infinite, though usually you also want some good parmigiano cheese.

The authentic Italian pasta is usually so much better than others because it is made of a proper proportion of hard and soft wheat. There are two styles of cooking it also—the so-called cold boil (15-20o C.) used in Sicily, Liguria, and the Abruzzi, and the hot boil (40-100o C.) used in the Neapolitan tradition. When pasta is done properly, it should be chewy with a kind of bounce to it. I have always found it strange that the various cuts and shapes of pasta, even when made from exactly the same dough, could taste so different. But it seems a happy fact that such is the case.

Food and Culture

The story of pasta has a lesson for the human race. The regions of Italy only gradually learned to eat each other's foods, and this slowness was due more than anything to political and economic reasons. There are more than just a few instances on record in which people have been hungry because they did not like wheat or rice or corn. This was not a question of availability, but of taste. One of the reasons for the extremes of the Irish potato famine seems to have been because the Irish did not fish. Most Europeans still won't eat corn-on-the-cob, for instance, a form of blissful ignorance. The learning to eat and develop other peoples' foods is part of the process by which we create our capacity to provide for all.

There is more economics in this process than we are usually given to realize since our effective demand for what we need or want is what stimulates someone else to meet that demand. I sometimes think that the fast food industry which developed in recent decades, McDonald's and its imitators, with its combination of mass market, individual ownership, and controlled product excellence, is one of the great potential solutions to any remaining hunger question. But this method could work only if it were allowed to be used in all societies, which is again a political question.

Food is a very cultural thing, to be sure. Food ought to be more of a spiritual enterprise than a biological one. This is why the meal together is such an important part of our being. Yet achieving a broad and adequate production and distribution depends very much on economic attitudes and political forms. Starvation today is, as I have suggested, almost invariably a function of attitudes or ideologies that restrict effective food production or distribution in the name of some power goal.

In any case, pasta, especially in its most wonderful form, spaghetti, is one of the world's great pleasures which we all should have the chance to enjoy. Belloc in *The Path to Rome* told of walking exhausted (this was in 1902) into a small town in northern Italy and ordering with various signs and words pasta with cheese and tomato. Then the waiter brought him "that spaghetti so treated, which is a dish for a king, a cosmopolitan traitor, an oppressor of the poor, a usurer, or any other rich man, but there is no spaghetti in the place where such men will go, whereas these peasants will continue to enjoy it in heaven."[29]

Chapter 11

Know What Your Giving Will Do

No one, presumably, doubts that it is more blessed to give than to receive, though we ought to praise receiving. But is it so blessed to give if the receiver takes what you give and uses it for a cause you quite disagree with, a cause in fact quite dangerous or immoral? Are you still so blessed? Or have you merely been had?

You can only live in a world in which generosity is possible if you likewise live in a world wherein it can be abused.

Baltimore, a couple of years ago, was up in arms over a priest fund raiser, most of whose solicited funds evidently never made it to the cause for which they were requested. They went mostly to support the organization organized to solicit the funds, as it were. Costly self-perpetuation.

Not a few cynical types think this sort of thing happens on a much grander scale in another city not so far from Baltimore. In their view, this is almost the nature of modern bureaucracy, ecclesiastical or civil. But, in any case, was the priest the only one guilty? What about the giver?

Careless Giving

In these days, I think, the greatest causes of corruption arise not from stealing, nor from fraud, not from the crooks in general, acknowledged or otherwise, nor even from the Mafia, but rather from the generous givers who do not clearly realize the exact purposes for which the money or the time they contribute is being used. North Americans, to be sure, are recognized as a basically generous people, as everyone from de Tocqueville to Solzhenitsyn has acknowledged. Belloc said we were the world's least materialistic people because we looked on goods as things to be used or given away, not just to be hoarded and kept. But, we are often said to be "generous to a fault." This fault may be killing us.

Billions of dollars are made available each year to be given away. Our tax laws encourage this giving, and it is healthy that we can give things away privately, rather than through the government for its political distribution. We have even invented institutions to give away what we give away, institutions corresponding to other inventions designed to take what we have given away. (The chief benefactors of these processes are usually called "professors.")

We prefer, however, a society in which the government is not the sole "giver." We have very unpleasant names for societies in which governmental apparatuses make this latter claim to be as its sole giving agencies. We suspect that our freedom is connected with our capacity to give something of ourselves and for purposes we ourselves think fit.

Misuse of Funds

A serious moral problem today, a problem paradoxically most acute for the churches, the corporations, and the universities, is the question of to what ideological use their generously given funds are put. Stephen Chapman wrote in *The New Republic*, "Not only has the World Council of Churches no way to see that its funds are spent only for non-violent purposes, it has no interest in doing so."[30] The ideological use of church funds, in the meantime, has become one of the key problems about the credibility of religion in recent years.

Anyone familiar with a similar kind of anti-business and anti-democratic propaganda emanating from numerous Catholic sources will be equally disturbed. This propaganda is all financed mostly by people of good will, by pious Christians who trust.

So, if it is blessed to give, it is much more blessed to know to whom we give, to know what the receivers plan to do with our cash. C. Lowell Harriss of Columbia wrote: "Current general demands for 'social responsibility' do not yield clear specifications of what a company should do. Business officials have an obligation to put rational content into the alleged 'responsibility' before acquiescing to the demands."[31]

Charitable Social Responsibility

Churches, universities, foundations, even governments have an obligation to be what they are. When their expenditures of privately solicited funds are used for purposes contrary to their public beliefs and goals, no one has an obligation to bankroll them. Moreover, they themselves have a duty to be accountable in that what they receive is used for purposes known to and approved by the giver.

Giving is a noble quality. This is why it is so easily corrupted. To suspect that more disruption in our society today comes from the good givers than from the forcible takers seems bizarre. But this is too often the case. Or, to put it the other way around, ideas will corrupt us if we do not know what ideas are.

In our society, the "givers," pious though they be, too frequently contribute funds to the "takers" who specialize in ideas and movements that, in effect, make giving impossible. Charity was never intended to mock intelligence. If you do not know, do not give. Or conversely, give but know—in detail.

Chapter 12

Burglaries without Burglars

A friend of mine owns a department store in California. He used to tell me that a proprietor, even after taking all the precautions, must calculate that shoplifting is a regular, not negligible item and must be accounted for carefully if a business is to survive. This loss appears as part of the cost to the consumer, who bears the burden of such moral violation.

A 1980 survey on the decline of morality in Great Britain, long a law-abiding society, noted that "shoplifting costs an estimated 500 million pounds ($1.15 billion) a year."[32] A friend of mine in Maryland told me that his house had been robbed five times in a year. It is no longer possible to report such losses, as it only raises the insurance rates, while it is certain that the police have little concern for such small-time operations.

The Census Department prepared for the Justice Department a report based on 60,000 interviews across the country on "The Cost of Negligence: Losses from Preventable Household Burglaries" (March 1, 1980). According to this report, almost one-half of the burglaries in the United States could have been prevented by locking doors and windows. Sixty-two percent of burglaries were not reported to the police, and burglars seemed not to rob the poor but the rich—which seems rather obvious.

Blame the Victim

Yet the tenor of this report somehow seemed odd to me. Burglaries seemed to be looked upon as a kind of natural phenomenon which was inevitable. If there was any culpability, it was not in the burglar but in the one from whom something was filched.

The thesis seemed to be that there were indeed burglaries without burglars, only the "burgled." These latter, in fact, were exercising a bad influence on society by leaving their garages unlocked.

Such logic leads to the conclusion that if no one had anything to steal, or if everything were locked up, there would be no burglaries. Many can, no doubt, still remember small American towns wherein no one ever locked his doors. People could do this because of certain basic moral expectations.

The first expectation was that the citizenry could trust each other, that stealing was considered wrong and not an automatic mechanism produced by the mere sight of an unlocked door. Today by contrast home and plant protection equipment and devices are one of the big growth industries.

No Free Will

This kind of thinking about the crime of stealing is quite common. It is indicative of views of human nature which are coming to be accepted as a fact of our society and of our nature.

This view would hold that many, if not most people, are not free in their actions. They behave as they must. When certain classes of objects are placed before them, it is necessary that they act in a certain way. Since they must so respond, such as the burglar before the unlocked door, it is not pertinent that we seek out thieves and try to correct or punish them. Human beings cannot be expected to achieve a higher standard from within themselves. They can only be channelled by external conditions.

Therefore, we preach the locking of doors and not police and criminal justice proceedings to constrain, or moral exhortation to reform the robber. He is what he is. He is a fact.

Thus it becomes a misdemeanour to leave your keys in your car. The person who sees the keys is only doing what he must do. This laxity about keys makes it "cruel" and "unusual" to attempt to find and punish the crime doer. He in fact does nothing in the classical sense. He only "reacts" or "behaves" or "responds."

Today, the word "behaviour" seems rather to mean the setting in motion of certain predictable reactions over which we have no control and therefore no responsibility.

Such thinking, I suspect, lies at the heart of a good many robberies. No sane Christian has ever doubted that men are tempted to steal. That is, after all, why there was a commandment in the first place.

Thou Shalt Not Steal

But at least stealing usually has the dignity of being a free human action. If, however, we tell ourselves that burglars are not the causes of burglaries, the average sensible robber will logically conclude that such actions are expected of him. Therefore, he will feel quite free to increase his clandestine activities against open windows. He will not be accused of fault if someone leaves his door unlocked.

Thus the television or bicycle of the neighbour is rightfully the burglar's. There needs to be no restitution. There arises a whole industry engaged in selling off stolen goods and a whole insurance industry which foots the bills.

The disappearance of the burglar, however, foreshadows the disappearance of the burgled. The person is reabsorbed into the mechanism. So the next time you are burgled, don't call the police. Call the Census Bureau and tell them how many windows you left open. Then you can call the police and turn yourself in.

Chapter 13

Healthy Materialism

According to some scholars, there are economic laws, ethical laws of reason, and revelation, the discovery of which is a part of the human enterprise. The violation of these laws leads, even with the best of intentions, both to immorality and poverty. According to others, however, there are as many "economics" as there are tenured professors to concoct them. In this view, a person chooses his economics as he chooses his pickles and beans at a picnic potluck.

This later perspective is often a kind of sophisticated scepticism. It bases freedom on the non-existence of any objective order or at least on our inability to know it. The former is a belief in an order of things open to the human intellect and will. The second view is mostly liberalism, which has been the dominant view, in one form or another, in the schools in recent decades. The first is typical of conservatism, based today largely on a careful analysis of the cost, performance, and ideological direction of existing liberal policies.

Socialism is one form of liberal theory, arrived at, however, by rejecting chaos and scepticism. It opts for an ideological economics which seeks to impose an abstract form on a people to conform them to the noble-sounding ends of the humanly conceived vision. In this context, what is the place of religion? The role of religion has been recognized in economics at least since Max Weber, R.H. Tawney, and Amintore Fanfani. Still, outside of certain valuable hints in Maritain's *Reflections on America,* there has been strikingly little serious religious effort to understand the nature of how and why wealth is actually produced or distributed. For some authors who have more recently tried to correct this inattention, see Novak (1986) and Gilder (1981).

Liberation Theology

It is now almost dogma that human liberation, a word too often designed to substitute for the Christian idea of salvation, necessarily means some kind of socialism. In many Christian circles, this view is held much more firmly than any of the older theological doctrines. As a matter of fact, several of these doctrines have had to be dropped or modified to keep the socialist ideologies in their purity.

We have a great need, no doubt, for precise, incisive attention to all sides of the ethical and religious values in economics and politics. But we need one not constrained by liberal or socialist, not to suggest marxist, presuppositions. In one sense, the very origins of modern economics lie in the secularization of this same Christian idea of salvation. This is a theme that has partly been recounted by J.B. Bury and Carl Becker, and recently updated by Robert Nisbet's *History of the Idea of Progress*.

Undoubtedly the greatest and most subtle threat to religion, particularly Christianity, in the modern world is the widespread, massive, even brilliant effort to make it an ideological tool. Religion, including Catholicism, has been much less resistant to this sort of phenomenon than anyone might otherwise have anticipated. At this stage, it is not clear that this effort will not be largely successful.

Creating versus Redistributing

Christian social thought has not adequately examined in its own terms what is in fact its greatest asset: the question of how and why wealth is produced in the first place. The alleviation of poverty, the main theme of so much religious anguish, is not the same as equitable distribution of wealth. Indeed, the latter may well be what prevents the former. The distribution of wealth is mostly an ideological question in modern form.

We can make everyone relatively rich, but not equally rich. Yet there is an enormous religious (and secular) literature on distribution, written almost as if it were possible to talk about distribution in isolation from the question of how wealth is produced. Once this most dangerous thesis is accepted as a religious proposition, it is but a short step to accept as "natural" the idea—rejected out of hand in classic Christian statements like *Rerum Novarum*—that classes are intrinsically hostile to one another.

The burden of this transformed Christian theology will then have to be that of justifying class struggle as a tool, supposedly, to aid the poor, once this notion of ideological distribution is accepted as true. The religious literature will then be filled with quaint notions of a theology of violence, structural reform, and social sin, among the most dangerous ideas Christian personalism has ever encountered.

Risk and Freedom

The stakes in all this are very high. It is beginning to look like there is a rapidly growing rift between clergy and laity on the question of wealth production. Here, the experience of the laity in the actual productive fields has had almost no influence on the organs of American clericy. The irony of this is that we know today largely how to pass from poverty to wealth. It is not done by imposing socialist ideologies in Vietnam, Central America, Africa, or any other place, with or without the aid of religious zeal.

The countries and cultures rapidly learning the secrets of wealth production are becoming the world's most advanced societies. Detroit is desperately imitating the Japanese, not vice versa. Christianity has been speaking in a very ambiguous way in recent years. On the one hand it warns against materialism and lack of freedom; on the other, it demands poverty relief without a change of religion or cultural values.

The fact is that a healthy materialism is part of what the Incarnation taught us. Risk and freedom are parts of the very process of alleviating poverty. Growth in variety and distinctness is intrinsic to growth itself. Religion, in other words, remains in dire need of relearning about religion and economics.

Chapter 14

Economic and Religious Orders

Insights into the nature and extent of the current religious confusions are becoming more frequent and more pointed. Essentially, there is agreement that what is quintessentially the Christian faith is not being taught to the faithful (or anybody else) in either schools, the media, universities, seminaries, pulpits, or even some episcopal statements. What substitutes for the essential elements of religion is largely advocacy politics, itself not entirely or even mainly grounded in Christian thought. The result has been, among ordinary people, a loss in the perceptions of the faith and their corresponding replacement by a social analysis decorated in theological garb that is essentially indistinguishable from certain political ideologies.

Brian Benestad's book, *In Pursuit of a Just Social Order*, carefully detailed this process in the U.S. Catholic Conference during the years 1966-80. Ellen Wilson, one of the most incisive young writers on Catholic affairs, wrote that at the practical level where it counts, young men and women are not being taught that specific body of doctrine or guided in the practices that go with it.[33] Students in good Catholic programmes, she wrote, are simply "religious illiterates." The bishops have talked a good deal, she said, about their responsibility to provide moral guidance to U.S. Catholics on the "great" issues such as nuclear war or capitalism. But meanwhile in religion classes, a little girl asks her "who Jesus Christ was."

Just Another Lobby

The Church has a great stake in not presenting itself as just another economic or political lobby. Unfortunately, it sometimes conceives its main purpose to concoct "alternative" policies, to be a sort of ecclesiastical "shadow cabinet," waiting to explain how the world could be better run if it just voted for these practical policies.

In this context, the Statement of the Social Affairs Commission of the Canadian Bishops has received special attention. George F. Will, the perceptive columnist, gave the document close scrutiny in *The Washington Post*; "Canada's bishops say their criticism of Trudeau's tax and budget policies is 'inspired' by the Gospel. They make much of the fact that Jesus' mission was to bring 'good news to the poor,' and the fact that Jesus 'was himself a worker.'" From such facts they bring Canada's economic policy to judgment.

> There is no surer trivialization of the mysteries of Christianity than the pretense that the faith, properly scrutinized, supports this or that fiscal and monetary policy. But this is axiomatic: clergy become vocal about headline-grabbing controversies of social policy when they lose confidence in their ability to speak convincingly about such untrendy subjects as sin and salvation (January 30, 1983).

We would, of course, like to think such comments to be exaggerated. But on reading the document itself, they seem if anything, too mild.[34]

The document affirmed that "our concern about the economy is not based on any specific political option." Yet, the spirit seemed highly biased in favour of a very radicalized view of society. Key words like the following are hardly neutral in origin: "alternative economic vision," "dominant economic model," "self-reliant models," "new industrial strategies," "monopoly control of prices," "Darwinian theories." The attesting idea that economists (or theologians) actually know how to cure inflation exactly or slow growth in every case, so that some conspiracy prevents politics from bringing in the perfect order, is highly suspect.

Salvation and Economics

Eugene Poirier, a Canadian Jesuit economist, recently wrote some incisive lines that are relevant to this issue:

> It is extremely important to keep the problem of justice in the civil order, as distinguished from the religious order, clear to avoid the confusion too often created by modern day discussions of faith and justice, which fail to distinguish adequately between justice as the revealed holiness and sanctity of God and justice as a social virtue. The religious order, especially in divine revelation, is founded on an authority of service based on charity (love of God and neighbour) which knows no minimal standards, no sanctions, and no penalties, but only the mercy and compassion of one who gives his own life that others may live eternally.[35]

The economic order ought not to be confused for the direct object of religious attention but it should be seen in its own reality, with its own norms. The danger of confusing these two realms is again to elevate the power of the state so that it is expected to do what can only come from higher motivations. The restriction of religion to its own sphere is, at the same time, a freedom for it and for society in trying to work out its economic problems. Otherwise we again seem to make salvation a product of our economic theories.

Chapter 15

The Right to Develop

The Foundation for Democratic Education brought out the second volume of its collection of Addresses by the U.S. Delegation to the U.N. Commission on Human Rights in Geneva (*Rethinking Human Rights*, 1983). This collection is a series of brief, pointed addresses given mostly by Michael Novak and Richard Schifter on this often confused topic. They are unique because they avoid the sort of statist ideology in which this otherwise noble topic is so often cast today, especially in the United Nations and in many academic circles.

The best book to extend the argument in these addresses would be Joseph Sobran's *Single Issues*, which concisely shows how and why so much rhetoric on human rights ends up in radical ideology and totalitarian states.

So often exhortations on human rights in practice result in making them instruments to destroy personal, familial, and group liberties. This is done through complete state control offered in the name of "compassion." What is confusing about the issue of "human rights" today is that the phrase is used by every movement and ideology. Everybody is for human rights, which in practice means that both absolutism and freedom are propagated in the name of human rights.

Generally, there is a totalitarian and a democratic version of human rights which both use practically identical language. Since the totalitarian version is so widespread and dangerous, perhaps we should drop the term "human rights" and stick to a vocabulary of freedom and experience.

Personal Dignity

However, the phrase seems too valuable to give up, while the actual history of the notion reveals it to be a function of personal dignity. The hallmark of the totalitarian version is that the state defines, grants, and secures all rights according to its own self-constructed criteria. This version is why most of our pro-abortion movements are "totalitarian" in this precise sense; they establish the civil law as the definer of human life, not the life itself.

The democratic version of rights grounds them in the personhood, freedom, and value of each existing person from his actual beginning. This person has a destiny and worth that transcends the state, which thereby is the servant of the person.

These addresses of Novak and Schifter range over a wide area of subjects from Israel to Salvador and self-determination. In part they were designed to reverse the thirty year trend at the United Nations of never officially protesting any real rights violations in marxist countries.

But the address that seemed especially outstanding to me was Novak's on "The Right to Development." Paradoxically, in no area is there more confusion and dangerous ideology, often parading as religious concern, than in the field which tries to explain why the poor are poor. The hallmark of a classical ideological answer is always, as we have seen, "because the rich are rich."

Almost the very opposite is in fact true. The only hope for the poor not being poor is the lesson to be learned from the developed countries about how wealth is in fact produced and innovatively distributed. This history and the dimensions of this problem must be grasped.

A Sorry Record

"There are today almost 800 million persons living in absolute poverty, many of them children," Novak remarked.

> Mr. Chairman, in the year 1800, fewer than 200 years ago, 800 million comprised the entire population of this entire planet. Nearly all of them lived in absolute poverty, with a life expectancy of about 20 years. Most died as children.
>
> The miracle of development, Mr. Chairman, is that there are now, today, more than 3.5 billion persons alive who do not live in absolute poverty. Our task is to extend that number until it includes every human being on earth.
>
> Development is a fact... And it is also a process which must be speedily brought to its completion.

What was refreshing about Novak's address was its willingness to confront head-on the statist development myths and prejudices. These myths are the real causes of our remaining political and economic underdevelopment on this planet.

What Novak initially did was to point out that development is not so much an abstract right, implying that somebody else owes us something because of our condition, but rather an obligation following from real, tested ways of producing what removes absolute poverty, namely, wealth. The fact is that many people are poor in highly endowed areas of the world, while others live in places seemingly abandoned by nature, yet are rich.

What is the difference? In almost every case the difference has to do with how the individual, property, reward, work, and inventiveness are looked upon. The statist view of economic and social rights is often used today to control and tyrannize whole populations in the name of ideological justice, that is, what is defined by the state.

The Top 30

If we look about the world today, Novak noted, we will discover that real prosperity exists in only about 30 of the world's 160 nations. These 30 have mostly non-statist views of man. They concentrate on individual and personal responsibilities not collective rights. For them, the state is a servant, not an answer.

When the opposite is the case, when the state owns the property, schools, bureaucracies, farms, and industry, not to mention the newspapers and T.V., not only is there little prosperity, there is even less personal freedom and personal dignity. Each individual, indeed, ought to be what he can be; each is a social being. "The rights and powers of social groups derive from the consent of the individuals who comprise them." When individuals are free to pursue their own goals within a truly limited, responsible state, there will be real development and liberty.

If for political, religious, or moral reasons people do not act, there will be little development. The state in desperation will increase absolute control. Thus it will continue to marshal the little available wealth and fail to call forth the personal incentive that alone can produce more wealth.

Three great ideas especially have changed our times, Novak observed:

> Individual solidarity, through free association, and inventive liberty. When these ideas are embodied in institutions and the daily habit of life, entire peoples experience growth both in the domain of rights, and in the domain of economic and social development.
>
> Where these ideas are absent, one often sees power and might, but all too little liberty, all too little bread, all too little individual happiness. Against these three ideas, the counter-revolution of naked power chokes whole peoples in militarism, secret police, and endless waiting in lines.[36]

The surest way of ending up in an absolute state then is to locate the cause of development in a state theory which assumes all rights under its own definition and control.

Chapter 16

Both God and Money

One Monday morning in a Carmelite Monastery Chapel still filled with incense, Blessed Sacrament exposed, I distractedly noticed on the pew in front of me one of those parish announcement folders on which is printed a message about the day's readings. This particular one was published by The Liturgical Press, for the Twenty-Fifth Sunday in Ordinary Time.

In large green letters, there were three statements on the folder, each followed by brief explanations in brown ink. The green statements read: "You Cannot Serve Both God and Money," "Where There Is Money, There Is Menace," and "A Weapon of War." While each of these statements might be true if carefully presented, none seemed to give a balanced view of the nature of money.

This suspicion was further illustrated by a very large drawing taking up much of the rest of the large page. It showed a rather anguished male (naturally) kneeling and prostrate on the steps of an altar on which was etched the "$" sign where the "IHS" (or "IRS") usually is found. Behind the altar was a large ornamental backdrop where a sacred painting usually is, only this time it was a reprint of the United States one dollar bill.

The Root of All Evil

The explanatory readings pointed out that Luke 16:14, the God and mammon passage, had several translations for Jesus' teaching about wealth, each rather pejorative. Money was said to need "redemption." It is but a man-made means to regulate human relationships. The main reason why money is "tainted" or "elusive" is because it can become an idol which can replace "God in our devotion and service."

Finally we were told that idolatry was not money's only danger. For money could serve as a weapon against others. I suppose this meant something more than throwing half-dollars at someone we do not like. Money, it turned out, is also as much a problem for corporations and other collectivities as for individuals. Money has become a "matter of life and death," so that we cannot remain "indifferent" to it.

Simplistic Analysis

Obviously, we ought not to presume that the back of a Sunday morning church bulletin will contain a complete instruction on a Christian's view of wealth. Money can become an idol, no doubt. Aristotle had suggested that money could easily deflect us from seeing worth in things themselves, that it was a distraction and a danger.

Many indeed think that Catholicism in particular followed Aristotle too closely in this teaching on money. As a result it became a major cause for failure of Catholic countries to enter the modern industrial world. The idea that money can have a moral use, that it can also be abused, that it enables us to do many more immoral things than we might were we poorer, these are valid ideas.

Yet money can also enable us to do many good things we would otherwise leave undone. The refusal to make money, even if disguised as religious virtue, can be an injustice to others. A father and a mother cannot just abandon any attempt to produce an adequate home environment for themselves and their children on the grounds that Christ would prefer that they did not make their mortgage payments.

Scripture also tells us that we have talents and these talents are diverse; some have more, some less. This is a fact not an evil. Interestingly, in the parable, the person who is chastised is the one who refused to put his talents to productive purposes.

Something Worthwhile

Wealth is not just something locked in the ground. Most metals were simply there in the earth until we learned to use them. Wealth production and wealth distribution are ways of serving God. Not every attempt to produce new wealth works. This means that our efforts to improve our lot will often fail.

Part of the drama and risk of human life is that we must learn how to produce a sufficiency and an abundance of what we need. The created world is somehow open for us to use our brains and talents. But, as in all things, we can indeed use our wealth for many purposes which are evil.

Money does reveal the drama of our freedom in a most graphic manner. Religion has historically spoken more about the possible abuses of money than about its proper uses and especially about its creation in the first place.

Many claim to be scandalized by the practice of taking up collections of money at Mass or other religious services. Yet this is really a lesson about the use of money. The symbolic teaching is that money can be used for something worthwhile. Not all money is, after all, hush money.

The church no doubt can and does waste some of the money it receives, as can everyone else. The service of wealth creation and distribution, however, is a real one, the real hope of the poor. This idea ought always to be counterbalanced against the symbols of wealth as idolatry or mammon found all too often in religious literature and Sunday morning leaflets.

Chapter 17

On Wealth Consumption

A letter to the editor of *The Monitor* caught my eye because it repeated a statement I have seen a thousand times in almost exactly the same words. It read: "We in the U.S. are some six percent of the world's population, consuming some 40 percent of the world's resources..."[37] This sort of statement will, almost invariably, go on to talk about "colonies," to imply that other nations are kept "forcibly" in tow by the six percent one way or another.

"Economic imperialism" is a common term used in this context. This economic system, it is held, keeps up (unjustly) higher Western standards of living. (Japan, of course, is also unjust because it successfully imitated and improved on Western economic prosperity).

At first sight this seems to be a question of simple mathematics, the kind you can do without a computer. Anyone can deduce ethics from facts—the 6 percent and the 40 percent. In a "perfectly just world" (the kind that does not exist, to be sure), the 6 percent would naturally consume 6 percent and the 40 percent would consume 40 percent. Any third grader can figure it out, right?

Simplistic Economics

Wrong. There is almost no correlation between population percentage, consumption statistics, and political or economic judgements about comparative wealth and, more especially, its causes. For example, *The Economist* of London (August 27, 1983) pointed out that "the American government and seven other rich western countries pay for nearly two thirds of the UNESCO budget." This suggests rather that the poor countries are exploiting the rich!

In a famous essay on the Third World, Peter Berger noted the doubt about whether the great colonial powers, such as France or Britain "in fact profited more from their colonies than they put into them."[38] Statistics rooted in a static world picture almost always completely misunderstand what produces and distributes wealth. Such is the risk of having one's thought locked into a static world view—the 6 percent and the 40 percent model. If the six percent who produce such a large percentage of wealth should discontinue to do so, the remaining 94 percent would be the first to be poorer and would, in addition, lose the concept of how to become richer.

Lenin and Marx

Ideas about how 6 percent "exploit" 94 percent are usually, if probed deeply enough, grounded in Lenin's book *Imperialism*. This book was a skillful attempt to explain why Marx's original economic predictions about the growing pauperization of the working classes in industrialized societies did not work as they were supposed to.

When they follow the right models, Third World countries are in fact actually taking over many of the tasks of production formerly associated with the industrial revolution. Industrialized societies are moving into areas of wealth production that never existed before.

The real problem is whether for internal political reasons North American governments might cling to jobs even their own people will not do, and so fall into stagnation. Or rather will they, along with the Europeans and Japanese, contribute to produce ideas and things which can alone meet the potential of all men, including the poor.

John Naisbitt in his *Megatrends* put it this way:

As Third World countries take over many industrial tasks, the United States must be prepared to take the lead in the innovative new tasks of the future—or face the prosect of being a Great Britain, whose steel and automobile companies are merely disguised widespread-employment programs.

All the while, as we tread water, unwilling to choose the winning businesses of the future and unable to let go of the losers, Japan and the "new Japans" of the Third World are free to eclipse our lead.[39]

We do not live in a static world because of the nature of the human mind, the first and last resource. The principal thing that can prevent increased wealth for everyone is not some limit on resources but confused ideas about wealth production, especially that notion which says that poverty is caused because the rich exploit.

Equal Poverty

Wealth will inevitably be distributed unevenly, but not unjustly, because not everyone wants the same things. This diversity is the result of a freedom that causes the energies which lead to wealth production in the first place. Indeed, the idea that we have "finite resources," all to be placed under political control for "just" distribution to everyone equally, is the major intellectual premise required before national or world-wide poverty can be imposed on everyone. We should not be so naive as to think that no one wants to make this imposition.

This result, I suppose, inevitably brings up the socialism-capitalism question, a question so confused especially in religious circles. I like the remark of Joseph Epstein in his "The Education of an Anti-Capitalist":

> The passion of the anti-capitalist is for justice over freedom. In this view, without justice there can be no real freedom. I once believed this, but the events of the past two decades have caused me to believe otherwise. Of the few political thoughts in which I have serious confidence, one is that justice has the best chance of being attained where freedom is the greatest.
>
> For all that can be said against it—that it can be inhumane, that it can encourage greed, that it is no respecter of tradition—capitalism, of all the known economic forms, does the most to maximize freedom; and it does respect and reward discipline and effort, which remain the best known ways—perhaps the only known ways—to attain those freedoms most worth having.[40]

Thus, the relation of population and consumption percentages cannot stand by itself. It has little economic significance. Factors of newness, freedom, and production must be included. The true enemies of the poor are those ideas that will keep them so, ideas like the 6 percent and the 40 percent, which at the same time deny them freedom and opportunity.

Chapter 18

Religion, Virtue and Economics

Most prognosticators bold enough to grapple with questions about the nature and future of modern economic systems centre their attention on a few key observations. This approach hinges on the ability to identify and evaluate from among the myriad influences that might come to bear, those centripetal forces likely to exert the greatest influence on the shape of the future. In this context it seems almost inevitable that those ideas successfully forged and sustained in the pits of ideological struggle will be among such forces. I want to focus on a theme, both time-honoured and current, that is being tested in such a struggle.

It is a plain fact that capitalism is characterized by inequality in the distribution of wealth and income. Moreover, some disparity seems to be a deeply embedded feature of the widely recognized capacity of capitalist systems as unsurpassed creators of material wealth. As well they improve the lot (absolutely if not always relatively) of practically all who make their way within them. I leave aside the important point that no large-scale economic system ever known has been without similar disparities. Nor will I take up the issue that such disparities, in terms of real wealth, may be even greater and more firmly embedded in systems proclaiming their fealty to equality. The issue at hand is the fact that capitalist societies are marked by inequality in the distribution of worldly goods. The extent of such inequality obviously varies among such societies but we are still at a stage of development where some or often many at the lower end of the distribution are widely and generally regarded as poor.

Electricity and Poverty

One of the most serious implications of this fact is that we are often led to promote policies to help the poor which instead harm them. The idea sometimes comes packaged in a beguilingly simple cover that can be easily perceived as "straight thinking." *The New Yorker* magazine, which likes to package its straight thinking in a special department, once used its space to display some folksy wisdom from a district manager of a Florida electric utility. "For a quarter of a century, he [the manager] has worked for the power company and he maintains that the best way for a home owner to reduce his electric bill is to economize on electricity."

Fair enough. Humour often clarifies. But just as often it oversimplifies. A reduction in the demand for electricity may well increase costs to the economizer. And it should be remembered that before recent times no one spent a dime on electricity. Our ancestors were the perfect electricity economizers. But they were not better off for having extra funds to spend elsewhere. Those funds were not yet even created. We may be poorer if the electric company raises our bills, but we are hardly richer it we have no electricity in the first place. To state the matter somewhat differently, the worst way to economize on electricity, and perhaps the best way to keep costs high, is to prevent new modes of electricity production from being demanded, discovered, and delivered.

Source of Wealth

Just as belief in a simple straight line between "less use" and "better off" can be grossly misleading, so too the simple straight line between poor and rich can mislead. Indeed, it could be maintained that belief in the latter relationship, overtly or covertly, is itself one of the main causes of poverty, something that prevents us from getting at the real causes of wealth production. To be sure, in some carefully defined cases the rich do abuse the poor. Yet the fact is that the main reason the poor are not poorer, the major reason the poor also have a chance of becoming richer, is that the enterprising and innovative, both rich and poor, have learned how to create wealth, have learned how it is possible to pass from poverty to wealth through work, thought, organization, risk, and competition, in societies that do not prevent such activities or their rewards. The worst thing that can be done to the poor—something compassionate and religious people instinctively advocate—is to use political power to seize wealth from the "haves" and hand it to the "have nots." To do this on any significant scale is to cause wealth simply to disappear in the name of equality, in the name of no one having more, since more is always presumed to be a sign of exploitation. The most likely result would be a community of shared misery rather than a society of creative giving and receiving. In the latter, "more" comes to exist from inventiveness and creative effort rather than from someone else's already existing possessions.

The static concept of the world, upon which exploitation theory depends so heavily, presumes that all possible wealth already exists as a sort of natural given, so that morality means cautiously parcelling it out (usually under some state control) to present and future generations. Future and "possible" mankind become as important as actual living persons. The result for those living in the present is a parsimonious existence ruled by an absolute state guided by a "compassionate" bureaucracy, which devotes its time to preventing any person from having more than his due according to the controlling ideology. Belloc's depiction of the "Servile State" provides an appropriate picture of this ideal of compassionate caring.

Loving Poverty

Secretly, I suspect, religious people often love poverty. Apparently, in some deeply felt fashion, it justifies their existence, at least in this world. "I work for the poor" often takes on the aura of the older "Credo in Unum Deum," the "I Believe in God." Certain strands of liberalism and socialism, like secular brands of mysticism from the Enlightenment, are often even more enamoured of poverty. Perhaps this is so because poverty becomes for some the last refuge for meaning in a world devoid of natural purpose or supernatural presence. "The poor you have always with you" of Scripture is translated, roughly, into the necessity for elaborate bureaucracies to care for the poor, since they cannot take care of themselves. This result, in turn, justifies caring industries more and more divested of close relationship to the objects of care. For both religious and secular worldly enthusiasts then the attention directed toward the poor authenticates programmes, actions, structures, and reforms, all presumably to relieve poverty, but only according to a stipulated pattern usually framed in ideological terms. Consequently, by a series of curious intellectual reversals the poor are never seen as lacking good initiative, or good judgement, or the will for ordinary hard work, but rather as the legitimation of organization for service.

Finally, when all else fails, the poor are to be denied existence itself, since it is cruel to bring a poor child into the world. "Not to be" is then considered existentially better than to be poor. Joseph Sobran put it well:

> Even as enlightened voices sternly urge us to take responsibility for unseen strangers, they soothingly release us from responsibility to our own children. If these two positions seem inconsistent, they can be politically harmonized: We can discharge our duties for "compassion" through politics, while the state relieves us of our nearer duties. Since this form of "compassion" is brokered by the tax-collecting and wealth-distributing state, the reasonable inference is that what we are headed for is the totally politicized society in which relations among citizens replace relations of kinship. [41]

This politicization of all of life erases the distinction between private and public, between mine and thine. By an ironic twist, as Sobran went on, we arrive at that condition for the masses which even Plato envisioned only for the guardians:

To put it simply, we are required to love, and provide for, our neighbour and our neighbour's neighbour, and our neighbour's neighbour's neighbour, but not our own sons and daughters. This has quite literally given a new meaning to the word "compassion," which now implies a strangely politicized form of love; a highly unnatural love, at the expense of the more natural kinds.

The Poverty Vow

Poverty, to be sure, has a religious as well as an economic meaning. The "vow" or "virtue" of poverty was never conceived against a background of penury but against a background of absolute or relative wealth. Indeed, the religious meaning of poverty—even in its secularized versions—is a function of its economic meaning. The early Benedictine monasteries devoted primarily to prayer and work were among the real originators of the idea of wealth accumulation and capital, since work produced wealth and for monks wealth had to be spent for beauty or charity or more capital. A universal vow of poverty such as members of religious orders take would, however, signify a one-sidedness about the worth and meaning of physical creation, the very being of which leaves it open to improvement by the human mind through the human hand, as Aristotle already saw. If nobody has anything, nothing can be freely given up, a problem at the root of all communal property theories however elaborated. And if nothing can be given up, the sacrificial element in the vow of religious poverty becomes meaningless. Likewise, if we have nothing, we cannot reveal our characters in the use of our wealth and goods, as Aristotle also pointed out.

On the other hand, poverty when it is undertaken on a voluntary basis is often claimed to be a sign of a willingness to "share"—itself, as we have seen, a most curious concept—the lot of the poor. The poor in this context are assumed not to want to be rich but to prefer a world in which everyone is equally poor or at least everyone appears to be equally poor. The poor who want to get rid of their poverty, however, are not interested in imitators who tell them symbolically that it is all right to be where they are, especially religious people whose ambition for their own selves is never to be anything but poor. The actual poor are rather interested in those who have learned how not to be poor. The voluntary poor should know this. Those who sacrifice their lives to teach wealth making, in addition to what is beyond it, are the ones whom the poor most respect. Religious poverty, at its best, was never intended to witness to a concept of civilization wherein wealth was not produced, nor to one in which only the state controls wealth. Rather, it was intended to witness to higher things, to remind us of the actual place of the things of this world for both poor and rich within an overall scheme.

Religious Poverty

Poverty in the religious sense was not meant to deny the worth of things but rather to suggest that worldly goods, however defined or accumulated, even by monks, are not by themselves adequate to satisfy the human spirit. Poverty in this specialized sense is a virtue, symbolic of a higher value without which our kind would be locked into the narrowest type of existence. But poverty is meaningless if not voluntary—which is why the poor can be graced even in their poverty, why they live worthwhile lives even if their income be less than the poverty level. Human worth and the level of income are not related on a one-to-one basis—something well worth being reminded of once in a while. Poverty might best indicate a sacrifice of what otherwise might be. But it can also mean a failure to learn how to improve the world. Man is a craft endowed animal who can order the physical creation and its riches to his purposes, who ought indeed to do so. Not every system or economic idea will produce wealth. What is most needed is an understanding of why riches come to be in the first place.

Ironically governments, especially governments of poorer peoples, by their lack of understanding of poverty or of economic growth can be the causes of poverty. In another dimension, it is quite possible to imagine societies in which there is no poverty but no freedom or virtue either. The virtuous are not necessarily the rich or the poor, but those who, rich or poor, have chosen the right things in their lives. The rich are not necessarily evil, though like the poor, they can be. The environment of the rich may indeed be very little conducive to virtue, which is why religious people often prefer poverty. This view suggests that there is no alterative to virtue as the proper way to live amidst either wealth or poverty.

The latter conclusion, too, represents the logical outcome of what Leo Strauss called "the modern project," which presupposed that abundance could substitute for virtue. Poverty, in other words, as a religious concept ought to witness to the transience even of abundance. But abundance at its best is a natural result of man's relationship to the world when he uses his mind and his hand. Not every idea or technique produces abundance or wealth, but it is good that these latter come about. Yet abundance by itself does not result in virtue. It may in fact exist both in unfreedom and in dissipation.

Economics then leads back to the question of *quid sit homo*, what is it that man is for, what is he about? And the answer to this sort of question, as Aristotle saw, requires both an openness to our practical lives and to questions that the world itself cannot finally answer. An economics that dogmatically closes off this latter sort of the question is a tyranny, one that fails to arrive at abundance, or even if it does, fails to allow any freedom. Poverty, abundance, and virtue remain the context of our thinking about what our wealth, or its lack, is for in relation to humankind and the destiny of each person within it. "Straight thinking" then remains a worthy goal even in a world in which there are economizers of such things as electricity and no easy solutions.

Chapter 19

On War and Poverty

Glancing through some newspapers stacked haphazardly on a grand piano in San Francisco, I came across an article by a fellow clergyman in *The Voice*, from nearby Oakland (February 27, 1984), which featured the following observation in boldface on page three: "The well-documented facts are that defense spending is crippling the global economy." On reading this, I muttered to myself: "Well-Documented Propaganda!" Why "propaganda" and not "facts" is worth some consideration.

The implication of the boldface statement, of course, was that poverty is *caused* by arms spending, that if only swords are melted into ploughshares, there will be no poverty. My own suspicions are that poverty and swords are not particularly related, or if they are, that the most probable relationship between them is that the knowledge of how to make swords can at least suggest ways to create wealth and vice versa. There will not likely be one without the other, or at least not for long. The only peoples who have vast wealth without the swords, say the Japanese, depend upon someone else's arms, while the Japanese have already proved that they know quite well how to make the swords. But without someone else's arms to allow them to act prosperously, there would be no Japanese wealth. Nor would there be any if the Japanese did not learn how to produce wealth in the first place and will to expend their energies to do so.

Arms and Wealth

Interestingly, Alexander Solzhenitsyn advised the Japanese that since they could no longer rely upon their allies, they would have to prepare to defend themselves and look for more reliable comrades elsewhere, precisely among those who actually know what it means to have no arms.

> A quick survey of the western world reveals that Japan does not have any absolutely trustworthy allies. But that does not mean it has none anywhere in the world. On the contrary, there are a great multitude of such allies; there are more of them, in fact, than of anyone else. They are the peoples

oppressed by communism on four continents (Address in
National Review, December 9, 1983).

This position might suggest that the relation between arms and wealth may be
more negative than we might be willing to acknowledge, namely, that arms can
be used in the name of those ideologies which prevent others from becoming
wealthy. The energies of those systems that produce wealth among individuals
and the energies of those powers which use coercion to keep control over the
unwilling poor flow in drastically different directions. Both the Chinese and
the Soviets seem to be realizing this as we approach the 21st century.

This connection between the sword and poverty is a very popular doctrine.
It bears many hidden assumptions, and is repeated in some fashion or another
by almost every political and religious leader of good (or bad) will in the world.
Still let me affirm that these remarks do not arise out of an unconcern for the
plight of the poor of the world, however this poverty be calculated. They stem
rather from a much deeper respect for them than that which often seems
manifest in the swords-ploughshares problematic. To put it bluntly, if we spend
our time pursuing the notion that arms cause poverty, we will in all likelihood
end up promoting the very poverty we are concerned to alleviate. We will
prevent there being any space in which wealth can be produced in freedom, and
freedom in truth is, after all, wealth's final purpose.

Guidance of the Rich

Often too we hear it claimed that the poor of the world prefer to live in a well-fed
tyranny than in constrained liberty. Since there is considerable evidence that
the poor vote with their feet whenever they can escape from a well-fed tyranny,
I think this notion is something of an insult to the intelligence of the poor. The
poor essentially do not want the artificial sympathy of those who identify with
their lot, yet who have not a clue about how to improve it. Rather they seek the
guidance of the rich, the instructions of those who know how to be richer. This
latter endeavour is in no way helped by the famous "exploitation" thesis, which
would argue that the reason the poor are poor is because the rich are rich. The
rich are rich rather because they know how to be productive, because they have
the discipline, values, energies, opportunities, talents, and desires to be something other than poor. This experience is the real service those religions and
philosophies which know about the world, can perform for the poor. The last
thing the poor need is a religion or an ethic that suggests to them that their
poverty is due to the limitation of world resources, or to the moral failure of
others. Keeping the poor in poverty is the consequence of those tyrannies which
claim that poverty arises from the exploitation of man by man. Wealth is, for
the most part, created, not taken away.

Creating Wealth

Poverty, of course, does not normally "arise." It is what is originally there. What is *not* poverty is what must arise. The great compliment the Creator gave to man was that of *not* informing him about how to do everything. Wealth is something that will be there if man learns how to create and distribute it. If he cannot or will not or may not learn this, he will remain poor. Wealth creation is not merely a question of good luck or fortune, though these things also exist in this universe. It is rather largely a question of discovering, risking, learning, trying, discarding, tinkering, and directing one's energies in a definite way that, as the saying goes, "works." If anyone for personal or ideological reasons is unable or unwilling to learn such things, themselves learned and passed on by some of our predecessors and contemporaries to us, the only way he will become rich is to contrive to take it from those who have learned how not to be poor. The same capacities that can produce weapons can produce all sorts of wealth. Thus to deny ourselves the capacity to make our weapons is tantamount to choosing permanent poverty, while leaving ourselves open to those who have a theory of wealth getting based on taking it, not earning it, with sufficient weaponry and strong enough wills to carry their theories out.

No Zero Sum Game

Poverty is not caused by arms. Even if we should somehow solve the war problem, we will not *ipso facto* solve the poverty problem. The world is not a sort of narrowly limited pot from which, if you have something, you must have taken it from someone else. Poverty, moreover, has never been considered the ultimate in moral evil. Indeed, most religious traditions have held that the poor were far nearer to God than the rich. This preference did not mean, however, that religion should exert all its energies to prevent men from becoming richer, however much it should exert its energies to teach the poor that their particular human lives are worthy even if they have little or nothing. Conversely, the occasions and opportunities for war might well be greater as people become richer, so that in practice to advocate that the poor be guided to become richer would at the same time be a multiplication of the occasions of war.

Some people maintain that we have strife and dissensions in the world because of the distribution of property; that if only there was some sort of communal ownership, we would solve all our problems. Aristotle observed:

> Such legislation (for common property) may have a specious
> appearance of benevolence; men readily listen to it, and are
> easily induced to believe that in some wonderful manner
> everybody will become everybody's friend, especially when
> someone is heard denouncing the evils now existing in states,
> suits about contracts, convictions for perjury, flatteries of
> rich men and the like, which are said to arise out of the

possession of private property. These evils, however, are due
to a very different cause—the wickedness of human nature.
(1263b15-23)

My suspicions are, in other words, that the attribution of war to problems
of property arrangement, usually related in the rhetoric of this subject, would
deflect men and societies from a serious consideration of what might in fact be
at the bottom of their problems.

The Benefits of Defence

Moreover, we forget the "positive" side of arms, as it were, namely their
function in allowing a civil space. Here is an area with frontiers or boundaries
in which we might learn to pursue what is a suitable life for some part of
mankind, even if others will not or cannot live in a similar space. Our ability to
recognize that not every societal system works for freedom or wealth or
production assumes that we must live in a world that is quite imperfect in many
ways. In it, men disagree on what is important in the most radical way. Too
zealous a pursuit of arms as *the* enemy of human beings easily results in opening
mankind to its worst enemies, who are usually unlikely to be worried about
poverty except as a means of civil control. Adequate and sufficient arms may
in this sense be the reason why we can have an economy at all in which we can
learn how to make men wealthier.

No doubt, it would be silly to maintain that there is no illegitimate use of
arms or that the sole reason people are not better off is their failure to learn how
to be rich. Aristotle's remark about human wickedness is enough to make us
wary of this position. On the other hand, the world is not a sparse place. Indeed,
the real temptation of the modern intellectual seems to be an unwillingness to
believe and learn about how much has been given to us in the form of our
intelligence and our hands as the primary resources and tools in this universe.

Moral, Religious Roots

From this point of view, then, we can take another look at the arms and poverty
issue. We suggest that the real cause of why the poor are not better off is moral
and religious. Perhaps by constantly suggesting that poverty is caused by
structure and not something internal to the order of spirit, we prevent the poor
from being anything else but poor. For when all is said and done, envy and
greed do exist in us, both if we are rich and if we are poor but also if we are
anything in between. One of the great slanders against the poor is that they have
no vices, that they are not like the rest of us because of their poverty. The case
that can be made for sympathy for the poor ought not therefore to be based on
a theory of exploitation or a societal arrangement that in essence denies that the
poor have any value or dignity or freedom of their own.

The primary reason the poor remain poor is because of the theories which their political leaders and distant sympathizers have so often chosen to explain their poverty to them. The surest guarantee that the poor will remain poor and without freedom is the theory that says that wealth is taken and not created, a thesis that appears in a variety of guises among us. We fail to understand why we have arms and how this is at its best, related to helping, not hindering, the poor, because the knowledge of wealth production is a product of freedom. If we continue down this path of confusing war and poverty, we will end up preventing further growth in wealth, which is alone the great hope of the poor who want, by their own energies and efforts, to become not poor.

Faulty Logic

No doubt, it can be said of all arms that they are wasted. It is a commonplace to say that the best weapon is the one that is never used. From this truism we are tempted to conclude that the original weapon therefore ought not to have existed in the first place. But this position is to forget Aristotle and the fact that many of the things that are wrong, though not all, can be prevented. Once we understand this caution, we can say that weapons are indeed useless and prevent a better deployment of world resources and energies. In saying this, however, we mean to imply that the human condition ought in some sense to be other than it is. But this proposed otherness can be healthy only so long as we do not lapse into a kind of utopianism which, when it speaks of arms and poverty, adamantly believes that the realities of wickedness and greed can be eliminated easily by some ideological formula or deft political move.

Arms might indeed be a "waste." But if we wish to be free human beings, no amount of wealth could ever compensate for our inability to be free and to speak the truth.

What seems clear, finally, is that the poor understand this position. They realize that their ability to become something other than poor is directly related to the existence of spaces in this world in which men can act freely. To be sure, this awareness does not mean that free men and women will act generously, but this too needs some teaching, some discipline, some space in which such notions as generosity and charity can achieve normal existence. Some 'facts' can, indeed, be used for 'propaganda'. Arms in some sense exist in order that there be at least some regimes in which the latter be not identified with the former.

89

Chapter 20

Political Philosophy and Christianity

Four books dealing more or less directly with Catholic social thought have been published, each of which is acutely critical of the direction much of this thought has been taking in the past decades. All of them appreciate the central tradition of Catholic social thought and theological doctrine. Each in its own way flies in the face of the prevailing winds of current theological mood because each suspects that classic orthodoxy is really the key to the proper understanding of things. These books are: Rodger Charles, S.J., *The Social Teaching of Vatican II* (San Francisco: Ignatius Press 1982); James Hitchcock, *What Is Secular Humanism?* (Ann Arbor: Servant Publications, 1982); Thomas Molnar, *Politics and the State* (Chicago: Franciscan Herald Press 1982); and Brian Benestad, *The Pursuit of a Just Social Order: Policy Statements of the U.S. Catholic Bishops (1966-80)* (Washington: Ethics and Public Policy Center 1982).

In addition to these four, of course, Michael Novak's *Freedom with Justice* (San Francisco: Harper & Row 1984), along with his *The Spirit of Democratic Capitalism* (New York: Simon and Schuster 1982), ought to be mentioned. Likewise, I am very impressed with Thomas West's books on Cicero and Socrates and his lecture "Philosophy and Politics," which he gave at the University of Dallas (September 24, 1982). If we add to this list E.B.F. Midgley's work and John Finnis's *Natural Law and Natural Right* from England, with Germain Grisez's moral theology and Henry Veatch's work on the natural law, we can see that we are in fact in one of the more fertile periods of Catholic social teaching.[42] There is an unfortunate tendency to argue that Novak's work in particular is somehow outside the central line of Catholic social thought,[43] but I think that in its general thrust, particularly regarding the unique nature of modern productive economies, it is within its own lines an original and needed expansion of this teaching.[44]

Yet, this welcome ferment has made little impact on the hierarchy, in the seminaries, or in the universities, which may suggest that the centres of thought are no longer to be found in these institutions. Moreover, the controverted nuclear war question has apparently put everything up for grabs, from Augustine to Hobbes, from freedom to security, so that we seem to be witnessing a crisis of political philosophy. The serious intellectual confusion of the abortion issue with the war issue has further indicated how much we need clarification in these areas.

Bishops' Politics

I intend here to concentrate on Brian Benestad's book, which has had a profound impact upon our perception of how bishops in fact arrive at their publicized political positions and why they appear to have a so called narrowly liberal orientation. What is initially striking about Benestad's book, however—and this reflects a phenomenon which I think is becoming more widespread—is the vivid realization by meticulous and open scholars of the importance and brilliance of John Paul II. Nothing comes so close to the rationale for Leo Strauss's "secret writing" as the circumspect and careful way many have had to talk of John Paul II in ostensibly Catholic universities and media, in seminaries and convents. The universities are generally hostile to the intellectual and social foundations of the pope's thought, unless, of course, they can be washed clean in socialist and anti-war rhetoric, a rhetoric which reminds us of nothing so much as the outlines of what the revival of classical political theory has worried about in recent decades.[45] No one, in my view, should graduate from a Catholic university without a thorough, sympathetic, intelligent grounding in Karol Wojtyla's thought, a thought which is in itself profoundly interesting and deeply Christian in its philosophic basis.[46]

Allan Bloom has pretty much accounted for the problem in the American universities themselves. Bloom himself indicated the reason we are getting quite different younger intellectuals—they have read his translation of *The Republic*—trained in the tradition of Strauss, Arendt, and Voegelin, who sense where the problems lie.[47] This very tradition can even take us, if we are willing to do the intellectual work, right back to where we left off before Augustine and Aquinas, Maritain, Gilson, Pieper, Dawson, Chesterton and the rest were dropped from our cultural vision. I even have the impression that Ralph McInerny at Notre Dame has refounded *Commonweal* under its original inspiration but with a different name, that is *Crisis*. McInerny's book on *St. Thomas Aquinas* (Notre Dame: University of Notre Dame Press 1982) is in any case a hint of many good things yet in the traditions.

The Problem, Not the Solution

John Paul II should be read with that care and appreciation which Strauss teaches us to read great books. The great books are themselves a reminder that Mortimer Adler on Aristotle, on the proofs for the existence of God, on education, and on the angels ought not be missed either. If so read, younger thinkers can begin to form a sense for what is wrong with Catholic ecclesiastical and academic movements. My suspicions are that the middle generations, for the most part, are already lost intellectually. They are the problem, since they are in positions of ecclesiastical and academic power. In any case, these movements in the religious sphere have become ostensibly political and have led us to many strange positions in the public order. However, these public stances can only seem strange if we have a sense of the classic and medieval philosophy upon which the truth of man is still based. Having lost this grounding today, it is absolutely logical that, in the name of religion, we deal with ideas which, in their accurate description, are aspects of what Strauss called "the modern project."[48] The essential teaching of this project is that religion is primarily a this-worldly phenomenon, to be accounted for in its manifestations by exclusively Modernist philosophic principles. Until his early death, we had a particularly brilliant guide in all of this in Bishop Roger Heckel, S.J. of Strasbourg, formerly Secretary of the Pontifical Commission on Justice and Peace. Heckel's several small booklets on the subject of Catholic social philosophy, as Benestad recognized, represented a way in which Catholic intelligence could again reappear in its full force in the intellectual and civil order.[49]

To my mind, the single most brilliant piece by John Paul II, the one that zeros in best on the heart of the intellectual issues of our era, is the address he delivered at the Angelicum in Rome on Aquinas.[50] It is almost impossible to overemphasize, as Harry Jaffa noted in his beautiful eulogy for Leo Strauss, that the relation of reason and revelation is one of the very key issues for deciding the health and destiny of modern man and society.[51] We Christians in particular are in trouble because no one can find us, as it were.[52] Almost everywhere Christianity appears before the world sounding very much like this same "modern project," which itself founded the contemporary world and which lies at the heart of its many problems, from ecological doomsday to anthropocentric humanism, from the lack of "civic courage" which Solzhenitsyn noted, to genetic engineering and the reappearance of Platonic idealism in the practical order, the very opposite of the project's intentions.[53] For the most part, in recent years it is not the Christians who are in the foreground of recovering those perennial things upon which we can base our truth.

Revival of Political Philosophy

Brian Benestad is a scholar at the University of Scranton. He possesses a theology degree from the Gregorian University in Rome and did his doctorate, upon which this study is based, at Boston College under Father Ernest Fortin, who, along with Father Francis Canavan at Fordham, is the leading priest political philosopher in the country, not forgetting the later Fathers Charles N.R. McCoy and Joseph Costanzo. What is of particular significance in this book is its understanding that the revival of political philosophy by Hannah Arendt,

Eric Voegelin, Leo Strauss, and their respective schools is the central context in which the recent problem about the politicization of religion, including now especially Catholicism, must be understood. Though we may be astounded, we should not be overly surprised if, for example, the terms of the episcopal debates on nuclear war sound not so much like Aquinas or Augustine but, rather, like Hobbes. We should expect that expressions of "compassion" or "concern" or "options" for the poor end up with the frank advocacy of the "all-caring" state.

We should be not overly surprised, therefore, if Igor Shafarevich's *Socialist Phenomenon* turns out to sound like a handbook against what is being advocated in the convents, schools, and church colleges for solving the world's ills. These latter are solutions which, as Shafarevich coldly calculated, never work for the end for which they were proposed but invariably end in the death of man.[54] It takes a lot of intellectual history, perhaps, to grasp why this shift is possible,[55] but the fact of this phenomenon seems evident in the light of authentic political philosophy. Political philosophy must, as Strauss knew, account for the divine, even if it must admit it cannot do so adequately. The death of the race as the greatest evil, the ongoing life of the species as the highest good, the collapse of all moral and intellectual distinctions before an absolute threat of annihilation, the preference in state proposed eugenics for the good life over actual life—these were ideas in the modern project bequeathed not by Christianity, nor by the classics, but by the philosophers who rejected both classical reason and faith.[56]

Benestad rightly concentrates on Strauss, who is of profound importance and who seems little known in Catholic circles.[57] Indeed, I would argue that the lack of a Catholic presence in the debate over modern political philosophy is largely caused by the very necessity which caused Brian Benestad to write this book. That is, the very issues which he chronicles as causes of the socio-ideological line of the United States Catholic Conference are themselves essentially products of unattended strands within modern political theory. Christianity now appears as a sort of commentary on the ongoing issues whose terms and origins are defined by modern liberal and socialist thought. This result arises directly out of the terms of the modern project.

The Modern Project

The larger issue, consequently, which the pope himself consistently points out, concerns the truth of Christian revelation in its classic form, a form hammered out precisely within Christian *intelligence*. This truth itself does not depend on any political regime, however much belief ought to impel citizens to better their own actual regimes, whether they be the worst or the best in practical terms. Christianity does not appear as its own truth in the public forum in most states. This is why Strauss's concern for "regime" is so important. Nor is the classic framework of Christianity taken seriously by political philosophers, who profess to see no reason to do so, since contemporary social Christianity seems to them, on analysis, to be saying nothing different from postmodern liberalism or ideological socialism. These latter are clearly products—known products in intellectual history—of the modern project, themselves designed to replace any transcendent presence in the polis.[58] Man is seen as a product of his own making and unmaking, with humanism defined precisely in terms of the elimination from reality of anything either natural or supernatural.[59]

Revelation and Reason

Indeed, Strauss thought in his lifetime that Catholic universities were still a link through Aquinas and Augustine to classical thought.[60] Strauss, I think, held that political philosophy could not close off revelation, but he was very uncomfortable with any ordered relationship between political philosophy and revelation.[61] Perhaps Frederick Wilhelmsen was right, that in this latter view Strauss carried his argument to an extreme.[62] Religion, at the same time, needed to reject anthropocentric humanism and present itself before the legitimate questions of "the queen of the social sciences."[63] Between these legitimate questions and the peculiar answers that are found in revelation, both Jewish and Christian, there lies a more profound link than Strauss seemed to have realized. The Thomistic principle about revelation and reason has more to it than the nature of faith as gift, however fundamental this is, and on which Strauss seemed to base his objections to Catholic inspired political philosophy.[64] Revelation was also addressed to thought, not to a completely unaccountable faith with no moorings in being itself. The endeavour to link Aquinas to political philosophy has collapsed among many Catholics in recent years. Then as if to prove the problem and its origins, there are Catholics who seek to interpret Aquinas in marxist or liberal categories, such that the content of revelation is selected in terms of the modern project, which filters through itself what can and what cannot be believed.[65]

With religion itself so highly politicized it is small wonder that the revival of classical political theory has few worthy interlocutors in the Christian tradition, except perhaps the pope himself. What Benestad did in this book, really, was to account for this fact—the loss of the Catholic intellectual presence in modern political philosophy and the resulting consequences in the public order when essentially modern notions become the background for particular pronouncements of the hierarchy. For Benestad, the teaching of John Paul II refers both to a methodology, whereby the bishops can again begin to instruct primarily revealed religious truths, and to the practices that directly and necessarily flow from them. The Pope also suggested a way for political philosophy to recognize the real limits or moderation which Strauss has correctly seen to be the real meaning of Plato, Aristotle, Thucydides, and Cicero. Thus in talking to the bishops, Benestad was also talking to modern political philosophers. Strauss asked *Quid sit Deus?* at the end of *The City and Man*, a question that remains an essential problem for both philosophy and revelation.[66]

The Human Problem

The need for this particular effort on the part of both religion and political philosophy to rethink where they are can be judged, I think, from Harry Jaffa's remarks at the death of Leo Strauss in 1973:

> The establishment of the state of Israel, Strauss thought, "procured a blessing for all Jews everywhere regardless of whether they admit it or not." But it did not solve the Jewish problem. That problem was at bottom the problem rising from the challenge of revelation itself, which science had not refuted, and for which the ethics of humanity was no substitute. The Jews, whose heritage made them the highest symbols of the demand of God himself that men live on the highest level, had become symbols of that cosmopolitanism which ultimately represented the lowering of the goals of political life in the interest of the universal and homogeneous state. The Nazis had singled out the Jews as representative of international banking and international communism, the ostensibly degenerate symbols of the lowered goals of modern cosmopolitanism. But the Nazis were not Christians. Their hatred of the Jews was a hatred of the entire tradition of the West. Hitler's romantic longing for the Middle Ages was an irrational longing for a noble past purged of the reality of its struggle with reason and revelation. The Jewish problem was, in the end, the human problem.[67]

What does one do with Christianity in particular?

> Strauss did not believe that the principles of reason and revelation could ever be reduced, one to the other. Nor did he believe in the possibility of a synthesis, since any synthesis would require a higher principle than either, a principle which regulated the combination. Catholic Christianity, which found its highest expression in Thomas Aquinas, attempted such a synthesis. Strauss admitted the magnificence of Thomas's efforts, and he saw in them a great humanizing and moderating of Catholic theology. Perhaps the greatest gain from the Thomistic synthesis was that Aristotle, after being a forbidden author, eventually became a recommended one. But only in traditional Judaism did the idea of revelation, and of a tradition undivided and uncom-

promised by a syncretism, find its full expression. And
Western civilization at its highest expressed the tension
between Greek rationalism and Jewish revelation.[68]

We have here, in effect, an identification of Western culture—the one
universal culture, as Strauss identified it—with the classics and the Old Testament revelation, but with a studied absence of any specifically Christian
revelational contribution.[69] The Incarnation as the specific point of Christian
doctrine has nothing, in this view, to say directly to classical questions or, for
that matter, to Jewish revelation. Yet this very core of the Christian revelation
remains the key concept which is added to political philosophy, particularly to
those fundamental questions which Aristotle brought up in Books Eight and
Nine of the *Ethics*, when he dealt with friendship and its implications regarding
God, the person, and justice.

Rigorous Honesty

The essential intellectual task of Christian thinkers, as Benestad sensed, is that
Jaffa's pregnant sentence be rigorously and honestly rewritten, on the basis of
evidence *and* reason, of openness to being, to read: "And Western civilization
at its highest expressed the harmony of Greek rationalism, Jewish revelation,
and Christian metaphysics."[70] Christians, of course, have a basic stake in not
being read completely out of either Greek rational thought or Jewish revelation.
Nor are they to be deprived of what is distinctly theirs simply on the grounds
that it is not contained directly in Greek rationalism or Jewish law. Indeed, this
is the whole point of Christian revelation precisely, namely that genuine
newness of being, which Hannah Arendt talked about, was not merely possible
but actually happened, not in thought but in being, on which thought is based.[71]
In other words, there remain questions in Greek rationalism which are addressed by both Jewish and Christian revelation, with questions in Jewish
revelation addressed by Christian revelation. (Islamic revelation, as Strauss
understood, needed to be seen and judged by both revelations as well as by
Greek rationalism.[72]) Furthermore, Christian revelation was predominant in
Western civilization, so that Jaffa's own project proposes a very different kind
of civilization from the one we in fact knew. Hidden behind these issues is the
question of whether Greek rationalism or Jewish revelation can remain the best
in themselves without Christian revelation. This question is not merely a
speculative issue but an historical fact, something Christopher Dawson often
wrote about.[73]

Eliminating Christianity

The modern project then was constructed by the unaided powers of intellect,
though of an intellect influenced by both revelations, to eliminate Christianity
in its authentic roots from Western culture. As writers such as Gilson and

Maritain understood, this result was ultimately to jeopardize not only Greek rationalism and Jewish revelation but the human condition itself, to use Hannah Arendt's valuable phrase.[74] On the other hand, not to recognize within the undergrounds of Christianity a tendency to embrace precisely that side of the modern project which would militate against the "moderation" that Strauss and Voegelin stressed as being so significant for political philosophy, is to be blind to the brilliant Modernist effort to substitute autonomous man for revelation as the complete embracing of all being.[75] The location of the best possible state in theory, a theme beloved of Augustine, currently finds its major enthusiasm not among the Jews, who are moderated by the exigencies of a real, temporal polis, nor even within a weary rationalism, but among of so many Christians. It is they, in their cosmopolitanism, who use Church organizations to preach a typically utopian doctrine which sees the state as the primary locus for the elimination of evil. Evil has come to be defined in primarily political terms, not in personal terms which relate to the natural limits of man as seen in Aristotelian metaphysics, ethics, and politics, as well as in the *Genesis* account of the consequences of the Fall.[76]

The result of this change is that religion presents itself in the public order largely in near "heretical" terms, each facet of which represents an effort to escape the limits of what man is conceived as being in the moderation of classical political philosophy. Each point of Christian and Jewish revelation is thus replaced by an intellectual hypothesis which in reality turns on man's own limits, a turning which Aristotle, in the *Metaphysics*,[77] suggested might happen. The chosen people become the *avant-garde party*. The suffering Christ becomes suffering mankind. The newness of creation is replaced by the clonings of the genetic engineers which allow only repetition of what is presumably best. The ongoing life of the species on earth replaces the doctrines of heaven and hell which are seen as results of personally responsible acts in a significant human world.[78] Redemption is the structural reordering of society, not personal conversion to the living God. Metaphysical reality becomes not the personal *supposit* but the relational being of the public order, something understood very well by Hegel.[79] Revolution replaces grace as the primary mode of action for believers.[80]

Religious Obligations

Though at first sight Benestad's study dealt with less exalted issues like bureaucratic mechanics of an ecclesiastical organization, the central burden of his thesis in fact touched all these profound topics. He sought to account for the mode of action contemplated by the social and political statements issued by the United States Catholic Conference and the bishops in their attempts to fulfil their *religious* obligations. Benestad argued that this statement-issuing system, in its consequences, in its particular analyses of economic or political issues, was both an infringement on the tasks of the laity and a misunderstanding of the subject matter of religion itself. The decisions and pronouncements came from a very narrow base and did not often come directly from the bishops themselves or the laity. Indeed, apparently, they came from, at most, five or ten men in national ecclesiastical bureaucracies.[81] How this was ever allowed to happen and its implications, are perhaps the most serious issues raised by the Benestad book.

Benestad in his presentation did two very significant things: (1) He set down the content of the USCC statements in the light of political philosophy itself. That is, he lined up the statements from the viewpoint of content analysis, the issues covered, and the ideological drift. They turned out to be, on analysis, pretty much a pious liberalism with very little relation to the classic concerns of how bishops teach, and to what they address themselves in terms primarily based on the religious tradition. (2) He sought to broaden the base of the episcopal bureaucracies themselves so that they might reflect the real intellectual variety present in the American Catholic community. He insisted that we rethink the classic distinction between particular ethical or political positions, which are always uncertain and legitimately varied, and the primarily religious conversion of the person, and his moral integrity.

Neglect

By using a series of very narrowly based, rather ideological policy statements as the primary means for exercising their teaching authority, the bishops have neglected the basic religious topics and means to which they ought to address themselves, and have tended to present as certain that which is generally only probable. The result has been that the statements and especially the authority of the bishops seem like the outpourings of just another Washington lobby, and not a very effective one at that, as studies by Benestad himself, Mary Hanna and Timothy O'Brien have shown.[82] One of the main services of Benestad's book, is precisely this very thorough exposition of how Catholic bureaucracies operate and their very limited openness to either the problems themselves or the competence of the laity engaged in these very problems. In one sense, after Vatican II the Church in the United States has never seemed more clericalized. In the public eye, the official statements and policy analyses come from very limited sources. The bishops seem content not to recognize how this constrains their own authority and integrity.

Nuclear War

Since the book has appeared, and perhaps as a result of not heeding its general line of argument, we have also been embroiled in the nuclear war issue. Suddenly, for no apparent reason among the laity or evident change in military technology, curious statements have been made in what has traditionally been considered primarily lay terrain.[83] In a certain sense, we are seeing Hobbes introduced for the first time into religious thinking with perhaps only Archbishop Lipscomb noticing it.[84] Mercy and charity have also become politicized so that they are out of their normal places in religious thinking.[85] They have become instruments to enhance state power, as Strauss seemed to indicate when he wrote about Machiavelli's lowering the sights of moral virtue.[86] What has happened is, rather, that the exalted level fostered by charity has somehow been retained, but without charity, without the religious instruments with which to attain it. Naturally, this has left the so called compassionate state with a clear moral field and a secularized concept of even the classic Christian virtues.[87] The resulting state has been largely described in the classics as a tyranny, the worst state.

Brian Benestad sensed much of this.

> John Paul II is fully aware that the world does not want to
> hear talk about the limits of justice and the importance of
> mercy. The latter is viewed as condescending, an affront to
> the equality of all human beings.[88]

The recent religious stress on justice rather than mercy—or when charity is spoken of, it is so merely as a means to justice, which remains primary—has made us a rights claiming, litigious society. We seem involved in the modern project, rather than in a giving society, as the mainstream of Christian metaphysics always taught because of its Trinitarian background.[89] This "rights" orientation leads naturally to a primacy of political structure as the focus of religious attention. This is a philosophic problem, however, and it should be recognized as such. But, as Benestad said, "It is modern error to believe that equitable social arrangements can be worked out without attention to the moral conviction of citizens."[90] It is difficult to overestimate the importance of this observation, for it explains just why the enthusiasm for a rearrangement of social structure exists among religious minds today, so that they see little use in preaching classical doctrines of virtue, prayer and sacrifice.[91]

Speciesism

This background is, of course, quite intelligible in the context of modern political philosophy, which has gradually reduced the centrality of the individual so that he is replaced by the species as the central focus of what is right and wrong. Morality is no longer personal but political in the sense that human structures replace human acts. The classical notion of bad or corrupt regimes retained the centrality of the morality of the actors in these regimes. The member of an oligarchy did define his personal happiness as wealth. The reform of the regime could not take place without a reform of the individual oligarch. "Catholic political teaching," Benestad rightly observed,

stresses the close connection between the formation of character and the quality of the political order; it opposed reducing the purpose of political life to comfortable
self-preservation; it upholds the spiritual dimension of the
human person and argues that there is a genuine common
good distinct from the sum of individual interests.[92]

This spiritual dimension from St. Thomas, be it noted, is a view of the
common good that is not opposed to the transcendent end of the human person,
which is not political in the strict sense of the word.

Brian Benestad often turned to a theme that John Paul II stresses, that
Catholics need not go to the ideologies to find out how to act in the public order.
They have resources in their own religious tradition.

The Catholic bishops need to seek justice primarily through
evangelization and education into the rich heritage of the
Catholic social and political tradition. This will probably not
take place without a significant theological renewal, including an intelligent rereading of the great Christian classics and
the primary sources in the philosophic tradition, and especially a much deeper study of political philosophy.[93]

Benestad was more than perceptive here. We must intelligently reread, that
is, read carefully in the manner of Strauss, what it is that we have been taught
in the religious-philosophical tradition which we have systematically neglected
in our universities and seminaries.[94] This means the Fathers, especially Augustine and Aquinas.[95] We have shockingly few who have read them, and we suffer
greatly for it. Ernest Fortin has recently reread Dante, while the volume
Shakespeare as a Political Thinker suggests how we Christians can, I think, get
ourselves back into serious discussion about reason and revelation.[96]

No Real Awareness

Likewise, we must know what Christian thinkers have done with the classics,
with Plato, Aristotle, Thucydides and Cicero, as well as what we specifically
mean by modern political philosophy. In reading the discussions about nuclear
war, it almost seems as if few members of the hierarchy have any real awareness
of what is at stake intellectually in the way this issue has been argued in their
name. That is, they have little sense in light of, say, Solzhenitsyn or Strauss, of
what is being argued philosophically and how it affects revelation.[97] Similarly,
the abortion issue has been allowed more and more to be subsumed into the
nuclear issue in a way that tends to substitute real being for possible being.[98]
We are thus in desperate need of intellectual and moral education based on
Christianity and not on some disguised aspect of the modern project.

Brian Benestad has shown what is at issue. Whether he can be understood
remains to be seen. To understand is itself a problem of philosophy and political

philosophy, not some tenet of social activism, redistributionism, dogmatic pacifism, or anti-life posture. Benestad's is a book that can begin to set things aright again. That it comes from a generation which is now beginning to understand what Strauss, Voegelin, Dawson, Russell Kirk, Bloom, Jaffa, Arendt, Sokolowski, Hallowell, Kossel, Charles N.R. McCoy, Gilson, Maritain, Chesterton, Fortin, and Hitchcock have been talking about, augurs well. There are indeed many young thinkers, men and women, who understand the key issues. But it is a rare university or seminary wherein such things can be properly confronted. Until there are, I suspect, Benestad's admonition for a deeper understanding of political philosophy itself will fall on dry episcopal grounds and the ideological policy statements will continue unabated. Paradoxically the way back to a genuine theology in this era, it would seem, lies primarily through a genuine political philosophy, but not the spurious "political theology" we hear so much of. *The Pursuit of a Just Social Order*, therefore, is a most important initial step, one which clearly tells us what has gone wrong and why. Whether what Benestad has argued so well can be understood, however, depends on precisely the sort of basic philosophic intelligence that Catholics, and especially their universities and their seminaries have largely given up. If we do not somehow begin here, the end has already begun.

Chapter 21

The Uncertain Alliances of the 'New Man'

Can Religion Save the Left?

> But the Pope's (John Paul II) regressive social policies (i.e., 'divorce, contraception, abortion, sexism'), when taken in the context of his anti-racism, anti-imperialism, anti-war, and anti-exploitation activism, simply do not justify an overall rejection of the Church... How deep is the Church's commitment? How reliable is the Pope as an ally?... I can only point out that *prima facie*, profound changes *have* taken place and affirm my judgment that those changes are irreversible (Marzani 1982, p. 6-7).

> It is also painful to be confronted with the illusion, so essentially un-Christian, which is present among priests and theologians, that a new man and a new world can be created, not by calling each individual to conversion, but only by changing the social and economic structures (Ratzinger 1985, p. 190).

Liberation theology, as it is called, has become a popular, even faddish, topic in Western intellectual circles. Much testimony also suggests that marxist leadership has long been perplexed by the endurance of the religious phenomenon within its own political orbit. Likewise, it has been confused by the failure of class theory to explain this religious persistence. Marxist theorists thus have begun to take a second, more tactical, look at their long-standing opposition to religion.[99]

Meanwhile, some Christian theorists have begun to take marxism more seriously. This reconsideration has occurred precisely at a time when marxism seems to be mostly rejected as a system that can produce what it claims it can, namely, a "new man," or at least freedom and abundance for existing human beings. The words of Solzhenitsyn, on his first being expelled from his own country, almost seem to mock those who think that an alliance between

Christianity and marxism could produce anything positive. Solzhenitsyn gravely warned, even in words whose full import requires an understanding of revelation, "all the Communist parties, upon achieving power, have become completely merciless." [100] He added:

> In the Soviet Union today, Marxism has fallen so low that it
> has become an anecdote, it's simply an object of contempt.
> No serious person in our country today, not even university
> or high school students, can talk about Marxism without
> smiling, without laughing. [101]

Needless to say, a lot of hope and revision seems required to make this alliance of marxism and Christianity even minimally holy at a time when Soviet leadership seems to doubt its own performance, if not its own premises.

Logically then the marxists, for their part, seem to have concluded, "if we can't lick 'em, maybe we can get religion to join us!" But a few, both within and without the mainstreams of religion, have continued to define liberation theology in a manner essentially alien and contradictory to the central meaning of revelation, at least as this revelation has been handed down over the centuries in its intelligible and recognizable form.

An Unholy Alliance

Henri de Lubac's blunt comment is representative of those who seriously question the validity of the new political enthusiasms among the clerical classes:

> Here and there clerics, who despite their name had been
> asleep in profoundest ignorance, are dazzled by the discovery
> of the vast universe; they are quite prepared to admire every-
> thing about it without understanding it and have no critical
> resources (or what they believe to be such) except against the
> faith which nourished them. They have become blind to the
> unique contribution of Judeo-Christian revelation. [102]

In other words, within the churches, the struggle is frankly over whether political ideology will become the form of faith in the actual workings of religion. This fact too is why a seemingly "religious" controversy cannot be an indifferent question to political science.

In this dispute, however, there seems to have been a missing voice. Political philosophy, it appears, has been especially slow to come to terms with the significance of this curious phenomenon which apparently seeks to join into one flesh what has, till now, seemed like an impossible union. Several reasons might be given for this momentous inattention to political philosophy. The main one, lurking in its own background, is the perennial, yet too often submerged problem from medieval, if not Platonic, political philosophy, namely, the relation of reason to revelation.

Lowered Expectations

This topic is, of course, a topic modern political philosophy, except for a Strauss or a Voegelin, hardly seems to touch upon at all. Yet when it does not consider the issue, as shown by the present case, the problem keeps recurring in other forms. Liberation theology is nothing other than the problem of reason and revelation as seen from the vantage point of modern ideology in confrontation with the central Christian tradition. What is "new" about it is the frank lowering of theological expectations along with a simultaneous rise of political demands. As a result, the two meet in one movement which thereby unites politics and revelation under of the primacy of the former.

Political philosophy, particularly in modern academia, did not seem to recognize that neglect of this relationship between reason and revelation would not on that account cause the question to go away. This neglect has resulted in a kind of professional unpreparedness for something that should have been quite obvious. That is, that religion itself, if untrained in or unaware of the classical problems of political philosophy, would, when it turned to practical matters, too easily be tempted to embrace apparently religious-like ideals. These ideals remain somehow present in our intellectual tradition but reappear in a highly dubious form within modern ideology. The task of recognizing them for what they are ought to be a major task of political philosophy.

Throughout the modern era, in a charge which itself has definite intellectual origins, religion has been accused of merely contemplating the world, not of altering it. Under such prodding from political philosophy itself, moreover, religion, often insecure with its own mission to the transcendent, has turned to practical questions. These questions mostly lack form or structure in revelation and require the particular attention of reason for their exact formulation. Christianity in particular is, in its teaching on man's relation to his neighbour, "practically" oriented in the Aristotelian sense that something definite is to be done, not just thought. The irony is that suddenly religion has concentrated on those strands of political thought that have openly or covertly remained in the "modern project," which has subordinated religion to political goals.

Perfection Achieved

Leo Strauss pointed out that the "elevation" of politics caused by the revelational tradition remained in political philosophy even after the faith justifying this elevation was lost. He thus perceptively pointed out the reason why religion, when it seriously turned to problems within worldly life, might concentrate on those ideologies, like marxism, which retained this higher goal. This turning meant essentially that the notion of a perfect society, first introduced by Plato and reinforced in an indirect way by Christianity, could be achieved, contrary to either Platonic or Christian thought.[103]

This project was, technically, "gnostic" in modern political thought, to use Voegelin's term.[104] And this project is what has created the internal crisis within Christianity itself, since this faith cannot be based explicitly on a gnostic position, which would attribute salvation or the attainment of perfection solely to man's own powers and energies.

Political philosophers, of course, realize that a major change in any religion traditional in a society will inevitably cause problems within the polity in which that change takes place.[105] One need not take a position for or against revelation to realize the validity of this observation. What has been perhaps unexpected was the ease with which religious intellectuals seemed uncritically open to political ideology. However, a serious consideration of disciplines other than political philosophy, especially theology, as a normal part of the education of the political philosopher, would have alerted most members of the discipline to the growing problem.

Vatican II ended in 1965, in a mood which supposedly augured an era of the "laity" or non-clerical elements in the Catholic Church. This Church is strategically located in practically every political entity in the world. Two very opposite results, however, seem to have taken place in fact.

Failure of Laity

First, judging from the media and publicity involved, this period has not been an era of the growing presence of laity as spokesmen for moral purpose in public life. Rather it has been an era in which bishops, priests, nuns, and other religious people have claimed to speak in the name of moral concern and in the name of the "people." In the very name of the laity, presumably concerned with actual political life, the Church has never perhaps seemed more clericalized in the modern era.

Thus, for example, in a telling interview with activist Bishop Thomas Gumbleton, Elliot Abrams, not a Catholic, found out that the bishop himself did not draw his information about the church in Nicaragua from the bishops there. Rather, Gumbleton maintained, he had obtained his ideas from "the people," who were the "church," that is, from what the Sandinista Government said the people held.[106] The voices of religion in the public order are not then the Konrad Adenauers or the Alcide de Gasparis, pious but shrewd political laymen. Rather they are bishops and pastorals and pronouncements on every sort of temporal issue.[107] They often come from a small bureaucratic staff with no strict theological competency.[108]

Few in democratic societies would want to deny to the clerical orders any legitimate opportunity to address themselves to these topics, particularly if they show in the pronouncements why there is a higher purpose arising out of the religious tradition. But it is not as if, as was said in so many historical instances, there is today a lack of qualified laity. Quite the opposite seems to be true. Many have thus wondered whether religion really has become in practice nothing but another form of politics. Ironically, the effort to be relevant seems to have resulted in a questioning by many critics of whether religion stands for anything but contemporary relevancy.

Concern for the Transcendent

Secondly, the rise of fundamentalist religions and the decline of the main line religions have led others to suspect that many no longer see in the traditionally dominant religions a concern for the transcendent. In seeking to explain this phenomenon, many sociologists have proposed that there is a relation between loss of classical faith in the intellectual classes of the clergy and the embracing of political activism as the primary expression of religion. David Martin's rather biting observation still remains true:

> The future has become a key category in some theological
> thinking, whether Catholic or Protestant. Once theologians
> are deprived of faith, they turn to hope, and hope frustrated
> converts to politics—or back to classic Augustinian realism.
> When God ceases to be transcendent he is re-embodied in the
> community and the future, more especially the community
> which marches forward into the future.[109]

The doctrinal content of the faith, expressed in prayer, devotion, and sacrament, is thus not what seems to be most important in the actual practice of a good many of the churches. All of these things have been "transformed" into some form of political participation.[110]

Exclusivity

This analysis is not to say that classical religion in theory had no room for, or justification of, economic or political activities. There is quite a body of "social thought" that is addressed to genuine political theory.[111] What seems to be new is not that the political order has some interest for religion, but rather that religion seems bent on expressing its teachings exclusively in political or economic terms. No one has to be a theologian to understand that this implies something momentously different for our culture.

When the transcendent truths for which religion had historically stood suddenly become expressed in this-worldly terms, terms very familiar to students of political philosophy since the Enlightenment, we can only wonder who is looking after religion itself. This worry is particularly the case when religion plays a fundamental part in the philosophical effort to limit politics in the first place.[112]

Who is Minding the Store?

At the end of his essay on "The New Christianity" in 1825, Henri de Saint-Simon affirmed his belief that Christianity was "divinely instituted" but that it had lost its claim to "reason." So Saint-Simon directed himself to all the members of the Holy Alliance and concluded with these words, almost prophetic in our present context:

> Harken to the voice of God which speaks through me. Return
> to the path of Christianity; no longer regard mercenary
> armies, the nobility, the heretical priests and perverse judges,
> as your principal support, but, united in the name of Chris-
> tianity, understand how to carry out the duties which Chris-
> tianity imposes on those who possess power. Remember that
> Christianity commands you to use all your powers to increase
> as rapidly as possible the social welfare of the poor![113]

The notion of "options for the poor," the watchword of liberation theology, thus has a long history.

Further, for Saint-Simon it was the scientist and technologist who could perform this feat of removing poverty. Today that side of the issue has been largely abandoned by the advocates of liberation theology in the name of political or structural reform. By this reform they mean that poverty is not a spiritual or internal problem for each person, nor do they mean that it is a question of further development of productive and distributive capacity, but that it has to do with a certain type of political and economic organization. They have, in a sense, absolutized the classical discussion of the forms of rule.

Key Issue

Poverty, no doubt, remains the key issue. In the 1986 Jefferson Lecture for the National Endowment for the Humanities, Leszek Kolakowski remarked on this project:

> It is reasonable to hope that various forms of human suffering
> be successfully fought against—that hunger can be over-
> come and some diseases become curable, but to imagine that
> scarcity as such, scarcity *tout court*, shall be eradicated is to
> defy all historical experience, because scarcity is defined by
> wants and human wants can grow indefinitely. In all those
> hopes, we perceive the same spirit of idolatry.[114]

There is, of course, nothing here with which a Plato could not have agreed. But it does alert us to the fact that the alleviation of poverty as it is presented in liberation theology does verge on the "idolatry" to which Kolakowski referred. The very purpose of religion becomes in this system an effort to achieve a politico-economic goal, an effort that ironically does not even achieve its stated end whenever practiced.

In this context, what seems most useful is not yet another statement about the content of liberation theology, but rather a philosophical consideration about the Church's official response to it. Since the publications on liberation theology by Josef Cardinal Ratzinger, himself a major thinker in this area in his own right, what would be valuable is some reflection on the rationale of the Church's official responses, both in their context and in their relation to political philosophy.[115] Rarely in either the scholarly or popular media are the content and nature of this position adequately presented.

Throughout the modern era, a large part of political philosophy has been essentially hostile to any "intrusion" of religion into politics. There is considerable reason for this, both because religion has had political claims and modern political philosophy has proposed itself, at times, as a substitute for, or reaction to, the major things religion stood for in its own terms. Consequently, when religion suddenly began to take on the wording and even methods of at least one branch of modern political philosophy, old enemies suddenly became friendlier and old friends, both of religion and political philosophy, became suspicious of one another. Many recognized that something profound was missing from the culture in which religion had protected, in one way or another, the claim of the transcendent.

Perfect State

The fundamental issue is, it seems, the Platonic one, namely, that of the location of the perfect state. Needless to say, it is by no means unfortunate to see that this question still exists. But the question remains to be debated within the context of Plato's realization that the worst tyranny could in fact appear, especially to potential philosophers or believers, as the best state. David Martin's mention of Augustinian realism is pertinent here. For it was Augustine, within the tradition of Christian political philosophy, who introduced in such a fundamental way the questions of freedom and history. At the same time, he was the most radical opponent of any effort to identify the highest ideals and goals of mankind with any existing political order, now or in the future.

Josef Ratzinger's two instructions are essentially an effort to restate the essentials of the Augustinian-Christian position that no earthly kingdom can substitute for the ends of personal holiness and the resurrection of each person that is contained within the Christian revelation.[116] Ratzinger's recognition of the tendency to politicize all reality as a consequence of a failure to understand basic doctrinal teaching is worth considerable reflection:

> In this full presentation of Christianity, it is proper to emphasize those essential aspects that the "theologies of liberation" especially tend to misunderstand or to eliminate, namely: the transcendence and gratuity of liberation in Jesus Christ, true God and true man; the sovereignty of grace; and

the true nature of the means of salvation, especially of the Church and the sacraments. One should also keep in mind the true meaning of ethics in which the distinction between good and evil is not relativized, the real meaning of sin, the necessity for conversion, and the universality of the law of fraternal love.

One needs to be on guard against the politicization of existence which misunderstanding the entire meaning of the kingdom of God and the transcendence of the person, begins to sacralize politics and betray the religion of the people in favour of the projects of the revolution.[117]

This politicization of existence is a tendency that is also noticed in political philosophy when metaphysics is eliminated as a context within which politics exist as a but limited part of reality.

At this point, moreover, it is as well to recall the doctrine of the Fall or original sin with which political philosophy has been familiar in various secularized forms. Thus, it was this doctrine in revelation that was most challenged by and subsumed into the Enlightenment, as readers of Carl Becker's *Heavenly City of the Eighteenth Century Philosophers* will have no trouble recalling.[118] Ernest Cassirer's statement of this transformation from an original sin to social analysis remains pertinent:

God is condoned and guilt for all evil is attributed to man. But since guilt belongs to this world, not to the world beyond; since it does not exist before the empirical, historical existence of mankind, but arises out of this existence, we must therefore seek redemption only in this world. No help from above can bring us deliverance. We must bring it about ourselves and be answerable for it. With this conclusion Rousseau finds the new approach to the problem of evil which he follows in his political writings undeviatingly to its logical consequences. Rousseau's ethical and political theory places responsibility where it had never been looked for prior to his time. Its historical significance and systematic value lie in the fact that it creates a new subject of "imputability". This subject is not individual man but society.[119]

This is the source, of course, for the notion of "social sin" to which Ratzinger pays so much attention and this is why he sees it as such a fundamental problem for Christianity.[120]

Original Sin

In *The Ratzinger Report*, the topic of original sin and its pertinence to political philosophy and liberation theology was noted:

Some theologians have made their own the schema of an enlightenment à la Rousseau, with the dogma that lies at the base of modern culture—capitalist or marxist—that of the man good by nature who is corrupted only by false education and by social structures in need of reform...

His (Ratzinger's) reply:

If Providence will some day free me of my obligations, I should like to devote myself precisely to the theme of 'original sin' and the necessity of a rediscovery of its authentic reality. In fact, if it is no longer understood that man is in a state of alienation (that is not only economic and social and, consequently, one that is not resolvable by his efforts alone), one no longer understands the necessity of Christ the Redeemer. The whole structure of the faith is threatened by this.[121]

The relation of political philosophy and revelation is very clear here. The utopianism of modern political thought depends on the denial of any doctrine of original sin. No gnostic reconstruction of the polity could ever by itself accomplish the major alleviation of human ills, let alone achieve that higher end beyond politics which revelation proposes to mankind. The "idolatry" of liberation theology consists precisely in toying with the possibility of this notion that social structures are the location of the problem of human order.[122]

No Accident

The fact that collective goals within history are presented as a substitute for this specific Christian doctrine is no accident. Ratzinger's statement of this recalls not only Augustine, but also the end of the *Republic*, wherein it was again possible to speak of rewards and punishments because they constituted an unsolved political problem.

The vigilant and active expectation of the coming of the Kingdom is also the expectation of a finally perfect justice for the living and the dead, for people of all times and places, a justice which Jesus Christ, installed as supreme judge, will establish. This promise, which surpasses all human possibilities, directly concerns our life in this world. For true justice must include everyone; it must bring the answer to the immense load of suffering borne by all generations. In fact, without the resurrection of the dead and the Lord's judgment, there is no justice in the full sense of the term. The promise of the resurrection is freely made to meet the desire for true justice dwelling in the human heart.[123]

This passage is, of course, directly doctrinal in Christian terms.

Salvation and Reason

In the general press, however, what is most often cited in this area are issues that are seen as political, economic, or social in nature. The whole meaning of the Instructions of Ratzinger is to suggest that these temporal issues are very important and fall within a tradition of social thought within Christianity. This thought depends primarily on reason for its content. Still, for the Christian mind, these issues are subordinate to the central importance of the salvation of each individual person in whatever society he might live. Salvation is not necessarily or philosophically opposed to what this person does in his civil society or in his personal relations. But this aspect is not what is central to his life. Here, Christian revelation is related to the Aristotelian notion of happiness and is directed to a question that has arisen outside Christianity.

The justification and attraction of ideology in the modern world has been the claim to abolish poverty by identifying and eliminating its causes. Concern for the poor and chastisement of the abuses of the rich are familiar in both the Old Testament (the *Book of Amos*) and the New Testament (the *Epistle of James*). Parables like the Good Samaritan, moreover, are part of Western culture, the need to help the neighbour in actual distress, whoever he may be (*Luke*, 10:29-37). However, the classic and Christian traditions were not immediately concerned with "eliminating" poverty—"the poor would always be with you" (*Matthew*, 26:11). Rather they were concerned to enhance the condition of the poor as being free of the more insidious dangers and moral environment that riches can provide.

The classic concern in political philosophy with greed and envy, with their political manifestations in democracy and oligarchy, was first of all addressed by the religious tradition. This attention was made not in terms of producing more wealth, but in terms of a change in the inner life of the poor or, as in the Platonic analysis, in terms of control of our passions. The poor were not at any intrinsic disadvantage when it came to the transcendent destiny of each person. In fact, they had some advantage—"Woe to you rich!" (*Luke*, 6:24; 18:24-27).

No doubt, following Aristotle, St. Thomas, and through him, the modern tradition of social thought from Pope Leo XIII in the last part of the 19th century, the notion has been accepted that the practice of normal virtue for most people requires a certain minimum of material goods. This doctrine, however, was itself subject to a good deal of cultural variation. The whole content of the question was transformed with the scientific and industrial revolutions when the moral and technological mechanisms of wealth production resulted in a potential for the normal member of society superior to anything enjoyed before 1800 even by kings and the very rich.

This very condition and its potential universality have provided, under the general discussion of socialism or the welfare state, the context of debate in the 19th and 20th centuries. Furthermore, as Josef Ratzinger observed:

112

It is widely known, even in still illiterate sectors of the world, that, thanks to the amazing advances in science and technology, mankind still growing in numbers, is capable of assuring each human being the minimum of goods required by his dignity as a person.[124]

The question, however, becomes: how is this to be achieved? Liberation theology proposes that a marxist analysis will achieve this end so that interpreting Christianity in this light is "scientific," regardless of the evidence of marxism's potential to accomplish what it claims.

Clarifying Ideology

Ratzinger's analysis of the validity of this "scientific" claim is worth considerable reflection:

But the term "scientific" exerts an almost mythical fascination even though everything called "scientific" is not necessarily scientific at all. That is why the borrowing of a method of approach to reality should be preceded by a careful epistemological critique. This preliminary critical study is missing from more than one "theology of liberation..."

It is true that Marxist thought, ever since its origins, and even more so lately, has become divided and has given birth to various currents, which diverge significantly from one another. To the extent that they remain fully Marxist, these currents continue to be based on certain fundamental tenets that are not compatible with the Christian conception of humanity and society. In this context, certain formulas are not neutral, but keep the meaning they had in the original Marxist doctrine. This is the case with "class struggle." This expression remains pregnant with the interpretation that Marx gave it, so it cannot be taken as the equivalent of "severe social conflict," in an empirical sense...

Let us recall the fact that atheism and the denial of the human person, his liberty and his rights, are at the core of the Marxist theory. This theory, then, contains errors which directly threaten the truths of the faith regarding the eternal destiny of individual persons.[125]

This passage suggests not only a constant attention to the meaning of ideology but also how this ideology relates to the content of revelation, which is the primary concern of the Church to clarify.

There is, likewise, a refreshing sense of pragmatism in the Ratzinger document. While there are theological and philosophical issues contained within liberation theology's accommodation with a marxist position, what seems to dominate Ratzinger's discussion is a kind of straightforward observation about where the marxist systems actually lead:

> The overthrow by means of revolutionary violence of structures that generate violence is not *ipso facto* the beginning of a just regime. A major fact of our time ought to evoke the reflection of all those who would sincerely work for the true liberation of their brothers: Millions of our own contemporaries legitimately yearn to recover the basic freedoms they were deprived of by totalitarian and atheistic regimes that came to power by violent and revolutionary means, precisely in the name of the liberation of the people. This shame of our time cannot be ignored; while claiming to bring them freedom, these regimes keep whole nations in conditions of servitude, which are unworthy of mankind. Those who, perhaps inadvertently, make themselves accomplices of similar enslavements betray the very poor they mean to help. The class struggle as a road toward a classless society is a myth, which slows reform and aggravates poverty and injustice.[126]

This is, no doubt, the best and most effective position to take in judging a claim or system designed to improving human well-being.

Forceful Criticisms

The Instructions of Josef Ratzinger show signs, at least, of a better awareness of the most forceful criticisms of Catholic social thought, namely, its inattentiveness to, and lack of development of, innovation and entrepreneurship in the area of poverty relief.[127] Peter Bauer's essay on "Ecclesiastical Economics," dealing directly with the Encyclicals of Paul VI, is perhaps the most direct of these critiques.[128]

Bauer maintained that the apparently distributionist ethic espoused in these documents promoted envy. The ethic did not understand the centrality of newer production and the ways to achieve it for poverty alleviation. Kenneth Minogue has repeated this position with specific reference to the Ratzinger Instructions, while simultaneously stressing the Instruction's unique importance.[129]

Primary Emphasis

The second Instruction, to be sure, does not show any profound understanding of the notion of productive capacity and its spiritual causes. However, there is attention to unemployment in terms of job creation.

> The fact that unemployment keeps large sectors of the population and notably the young in a situation of marginalization is intolerable. For this reason, the creation of

jobs is a primary social task facing individuals and private
enterprise, as well as the state. As a general rule, in this as in
other matters, the state has a subsidiary function, but often it
can be called upon to intervene directly, as in the case of
international agreements between different states.[130]

The primary emphasis in these documents as well as in John Paul II's Encyclical, *Laborem Exercens*, however, remains the prior importance of the human person and the conditions of moral, material, and political life. These positions contribute to a reasonable, though not perfect world. Ratzinger especially has understood the dangers of the utopian tradition for any kind of reasonable order.

In conclusion, the Ratzinger Instructions are fertile reconsiderations in the light of the Judaeo-Christian tradition of certain central problems of political philosophy. Their significance lies not merely in their awareness of the nature and limits of the classical positions in political thought, but of how these positions can effect religion when they are adopted in its name. They represent a fundamental effort of the Church to state clearly and simply what it is. This position is taken in the context of liberty. That is, "the quest for freedom and the aspiration for liberation...have their first source in the Christian heritage... Without this reference to the Gospel, the history of the recent centuries in the West cannot be understood."[131] The controversy over liberation theology, therefore, ought to serve as a belated reconsideration of the problem of reason and revelation within contemporary political philosophy and of political philosophy within contemporary religion.

Chapter 22

Leisure and Poverty

If any two ideas could serve to distinguish the Judaeo-Christian tradition from classical Greek and Roman thought, they would be leisure, with its highest act in contemplation, and poverty, the concrete source of active concern for a noble cause. Furthermore, within specifically modern thought, the notion of leisure and the idea of poverty are significant benchmarks which distinguish ideology from realist philosophy and genuine religion. Indeed, it can be argued legitimately that the so called "mission of alleviating the poor" itself has in much radical social philosophy become, paradoxically, that which specifically substitutes for the divinity; this holds whether what is proposed as a means for this alleviation actually works or not for the purpose at hand. Belief in God has come to be seen as a *cause* of poverty because it is said to distract mankind from doing the necessary things to produce wealth. Meanwhile, the suffering masses have themselves, in the minds of many an intellectual, become a kind of substitute for God.

We cannot understand the deep passions stirred by poverty in contemporary thought if we do not sense something of the peculiar manner in which this issue has become a programmatic means to replace God with "humanity" conceived as an image of the poor. The collective image of the poor is said to be the only morally concrete object worthy of human devotion and organization. This supposedly high ethical purpose, however, is itself isolated from the real means to develop and enhance human productivity and distribution. In this sense, a kind of substitute religious or ideological passion takes the place of what might actually improve the lot of the real poor. Much of the divisiveness in modern political and religious thought arises because of this way of conceiving poverty. And behind this consideration, and never really apart from it, lies the religious question of the nature of God and His dealings with actual human beings. Can even the collectivity of mankind substitute for God as an object worthy of absolute devotion? This is the question that is posed by the way modern ideology formulates the issue of poverty.

Weakened Understanding

Unfortunately, too, the word "leisure," which comes from the same Greek root from which we get the English word "school," has come to mean something unimportant or frivolous. This weakened understanding of a key Greek concept is itself a subtle product of a kind of modern thought that has persistently sought to undermine certain fundamental propositions found in classical and Judaeo-Christian theory. The word, leisure, as Josef Pieper recalled in his famous book, *Leisure: The Basis of Culture*, is one that takes us to the heart of our meaning and dignity.[132] Far from being a word that refers to what occurs after the important things are done, like work or business, leisure means rather the deepest reflections on the most noble things, including the highest being. However important other activities might be, without leisure, men could not achieve their truest selves. For it is leisure which relates them to something beyond themselves. People cannot find any equivalent in any human economic or political activity, although these are quite important in their own right.

Leisure, therefore, concerns what human life is about in its highest forms. The alleviation of poverty, as well as all other normal human activities, are part of human wholeness. But they are intended both to be themselves and to lead to leisure in its contemplative acts of knowing and loving the highest being. Whenever even a legitimate human enterprise or activity comes to replace this highest activity, there is some fundamental disorder in the human enterprise. Jude Dougherty stated the issue well:

> For many, belief and theology are no longer the central features of religious life. Almost without notice, religion has degenerated into a man-centered enterprise of moral concern and healing. It should never be forgotten that the primary aim in making life comfortable for others is to enable them, too, to reach the interior life.[133]

Intrinsic and Instrumental

The statement of the right relation between work, activity, politics, and contemplation remains the essential task of a leisured life. It is the necessary presupposition of any social philosophy or economic theory in its relation to religious values. The key points remain that a man-centred social theory can substitute for God, while the whole purpose of economic progress is to enable men and women to develop a richer contemplative and interior life.

In a sense, "leisure" is opposed in conception to "work" and to pleasure. If one of the happy results of modern public life has been to elevate the worth of human labour, this legitimate understanding still cannot mean that work is the same thing as truth or contemplation. Work is what it is. It is to lead to thought, not to substitute for it. This relationship is true, just as thought is to aid work to be more itself, to be more human in both orientation and in its burden. Aristotle carefully distinguished the activities necessary merely to keep alive—economic activities in his sense—from those devoted to pleasure and those which were "for their own sakes," to use his expression. Aristotle thus distinguished working, doing, and thinking. Each of these activities was good but needed to be understood and ordered properly. Keeping alive was, no doubt the precondition of every sort of human activity. But if keeping alive became itself the highest good, so that all other activities were sacrificed to it, men became worse than the beasts in Aristotle's view.

Worse than the Beasts

Moreover, a society that did not work or know how to use the laws of nature would be unable to provide for itself the conditions of any higher sort of life. Yet, a life devoted to work or craft or production and distribution would be a most constricting one if it prevented any higher sort of activity. The dignity of the worker was thus not intended to imply that human life, even for the worker, had no other purpose than an economic one, even though an economic purpose was a good purpose as such. In this sense, the existence of technology and science in the modern sense not only created the possibility of freeing all mankind from the drudgery of necessity, but it also greatly enhanced the possibility of eliminating slavery in the ancient sense. This eventuality is something Aristotle himself saw might happen.

What is perhaps new is the possibility of well fed slaves, whatever they be called. We refer here to states that completely control their populations, even though they be relatively well fed and provided for. Indeed, the opposition of freedom and poverty is one of the unfortunate developments in modern thought. The best way to eliminate poverty lies through freedom, but tyranny can sometimes produce a kind of material abundance. The worst thing then is not to be poor. Rather it is not to be free to know and follow the truth. This is why even the poor escape from modern tyrannies whenever they can. It is also why modern technology and science have made tyranny so much more effective in the modern world.

The "Vice" of Poverty

A considerable amount of attention has been paid in religious circles to the highly enigmatic phrase, "preferential options for the poor."[134] This unusual phrase, as we saw, can have a number of meanings, some distinctly ideological and not at all in the interests of the poor themselves. The phrase, when carefully distinguished, is perfectly usable. The New Testament suggests that the poor will always be with us. Evidently, this affirmation did not mean that the rich were bad. Neither did it mean that we should not make every effort to increase the wealth of families and societies. Aristotle, however, maintained, along with Aquinas and the modern popes, that most people, even to be minimally virtuous, needed a certain sufficiency of property or wealth. From this point of view we should expect to find a considerable amount of vice in very poor societies. The romanticization of poverty prevents many people from seeing the dire moral conditions many of the poor live in because of vices not always attributable to their status.

Religious literature also speaks of "the poor in spirit." There are, in fact, examples, even in the Old and New Testaments, of rich men who are also good and who are not asked to become materially poor. The essential question is rather what they do with their wealth. It is not simply assumed that this wealth was acquired by foul means. Poor men, as the classics understood, could be quite greedy and envious. In the parable of the talents in the New Testament, the man who buried his coins was chastised, whereas those who invested or traded their greater wealth were praised. This parable suggests that wealth is to be used to increase wealth, that certain ideas on savings obstruct this growth process and are to be rejected.

Aristotle was quite willing to grant that the poor have characteristic vices that disrupt their regimes. Usually because of these objective vices, they lead to worse regimes. However much we might want to aid the poor, the abiding question must always be, "do our proposals actually improve the lot of the poor or do they invariably lead to something worse?" The piety of our good intentions does not, in this sense, excuse us from answering this difficult question. Poverty in freedom is preferable to riches in tyranny. And generally freedom is the real condition of economic growth.

The Irrelevance of Wealth

The Judaeo-Christian tradition did recognize in riches an atmosphere that might not easily be conducive to a moral life, even while certain rich and powerful men and women could be saints. The vow of poverty for monks and nuns, moreover, was in part a silent witness to the danger of riches. Essentially, however, this vow was intended to witness to devotion to God alone. In themselves neither wealth nor poverty could automatically guarantee virtue or ensure vice. The criterion of virtue and vice depended on what each person chose to do with his wealth or his poverty in terms of human order. Wealth could be used nobly; poverty could foster bitterness and hatred. But there were many poor people who were holy and dignified even in their poverty. They did not *have* to be narrow or spiteful simply because they were poor.

Yet practically speaking, most people ought not to have too much, nor especially, too little. The middle class state and the widespread distribution of property were more modern adaptations of the same idea. This "too much" or "too little," however, depended dramatically on man's intellectual and artistic capacity to increase the natural gifts of the world in the service of man's estate. But he must do so without, at the same time, jeopardizing the rational and revelational insights into the nature of human virtue and vice. It is hard to claim that the incidence of virtue and vice in the modern world, with all its comparative advantages in material terms, is any greater than in very much poorer societies in the past.

The Good Samaritan Merchant

However, to continue a New Testament idea, we ought not to give a cup of water to our neighbour if the water is polluted. Consider then a man who learns what causes water poisoning or food deterioration, and who, by engineering dams or adding chemicals, provides vast quantities of good water. He must also be looked upon as providing this higher sort of service to the neighbour, even when the service comes to be routine as in many parts of the world. The account of the good Samaritan can, in this sense, be applied to scientists and engineers, as well as jobbers and merchants. Likewise, the man who learns to mass produce, at a reasonable price, a blanket or a cloak or a loaf of bread, with machines, computers and synthetics, must be seen as directly serving the poor in particular. It is true that we ought to provide for our own neighbour in need. But the ideal social arrangement is still for everyone to provide for himself and his family from what he does in exchange with everyone else doing the same thing. The market is, in this sense, an extension of concrete charity and practical reason. It enables legitimate concerns to achieve their purpose.

The expression "option for the poor" can also have overtones of political power, which conceives itself as the chief owner and provider of dependent people whose condition is needed to justify this very power. This dependency is how the poor can inadvertently become justifications for tyrannical regimes and ideologies claiming to speak in their name. The argument, in this sense, is not whether we should aid the poor, but rather *what* aids them, and at what cost in terms of more basic human dignities. The concern for the poor is, as such, quite vital and necessary. Yet once poverty is in fact replaced with an ongoing, economically productive system, it does not follow automatically that men, without virtue, will be better off in any higher human sense. Wealth makes good things possible. It also makes more substantial vices possible. The question of poverty can never replace the question of virtue.

Greater Tyranny

This awareness of the dependency of poverty and wealth on virtue brings us back to the subject of leisure. The vast scientific and technological apparatus of the modern world must in some sense be praised for making possible the increased capacity to alleviate the poor. We no longer live in a world in which many of us do not know how poverty is to be relieved. We live rather in a world of politics and ideology. What we choose in this regard will decide whether we use the appropriate means to increase wealth and freedom in the pursuit of true human worth. We need not do this, which is why the tyrannies of our century are so much greater than those of previous ages.

The limits of wealth are decided by what the human family, by what human capacities are for. Wealth ought to be created by active human beings to provide for themselves in an ever more efficient and abundant manner. This provision can be made, but it need not. So freedom remains central to any discussion of wealth and what lies beyond it. The fact that we can and ought to use our intelligence in this manner, and that our conception of the world is such that this ought to be done is, in one sense, the heritage of our classical and Judaeo-Christian inheritance. There are many religions and philosophies that do not really allow or encourage this growth and improvement. Even in the question of poverty, the ultimate truth of things remains the central issue. It does make a difference what we hold to be true.

Beyond the Material

Things of beauty, of knowledge, of human organization, therefore, are the ends and purposes of our wealth producing capacities. In so far as we do not see any transcendent purposes in human life for which all else exists, we will not rightly marshal the various capacities we possess from our nature. The tradition that encourages us to look beyond our material things, is also the one that looks on these same material things and sees that they are good and intended for human purposes. The leisure we finally arrive at when we learn how to produce and distribute wealth, ought to witness to the fact that we are more than producers of wealth. This openness is why, too, we ought to have beautiful buildings and artifacts that transcend our individual lives on this earth. It is also why we ought to recognize that even the lives of the poorest contain touches of a personal destiny that will be valid, no matter what their economic condition on earth.

To conclude, the relation of leisure and poverty links the whole of each human life, and the lives of all of us, to a pursuit both of a generous and abundant life during our time on earth and to an acknowledgement of a truth that lies beyond. We are told that we are of more worth than even the beauty of the lilies of the field. Yet this does not prevent us from cross-breeding ever more beautiful lilies which, too, will soon pass away. The reality of the transcendent also is found by us human beings through the transience of things and through our efforts to do something noble while we are here. Poverty is a sign both of our inadequacy and of our capacity. Leisure is a sign that, when we have achieved an economic and temporal abundance, our destiny, the thing for which we ultimately exist, comes into clearer focus.

Chapter 23

The U.S. Bishops' Pastoral on Economics and Social Justice

Are you surprised that the same civilization
which believed in the Trinity discovered steam?
(G.K. Chesterton)

The number of articles, conferences, addresses, and discussions generated by the various drafts of the U.S. bishops' pastoral letter on the economy now approaches infinity. Hardly a journal, university, think-tank, or high school has left the matter untouched. One can speculate on the "missionary" fervour with which some of this appears to be pursued. But there seems to have been no way for the final draft, which the bishops themselves insisted on drawing up, to have been anything but anticlimactic—something the cynics had suspected would happen all along. A number of bishops recognized that there were serious flaws of both tactics and teaching within the initial drafts, and sometimes fundamental misunderstandings of Church teaching and the U.S. economy. Those who praised the draft mostly came from a liberal or socialist agenda. Indeed, on a point by point analysis, this sort of agenda seems to be the main focus of the draft. And even though there was widespread consultation preceding the draft, the writers do not seem to have incorporated much of its fruits, or to have recognized the one-sidedness of what they wrote, its relation to earlier Catholic teachings, or to standard economic concepts.

The classic Thomist principle in affairs of practical ethics and speculative philosophy, moreover, was that revelation needed to understand reason, particularly when the topic under discussion, like economics, arose from reason. Few if any of the hierarchy responsible for the drafts seem to have had any real intellectual background in the disciplines in question or in the practice of business or political economy. I have often speculated about what sort of bishops the German hierarchy, say, would have chosen to do a similar draft. Whatever the validity of this point, the practical result of the drafts has been a rapid estrangement of the Catholic hierarchy from those actually responsible for economic thought and institutions. The broader background, however, requires that we begin to grasp the ambiguous nature of what is called "social justice" from the point of view of political philosophy, as well as the actual nature of man. Only then will we be able to encourage a free, productive, reasonable economy in which the long-range intentions of the bishops and everyone else about a more adequate world might actually be achieved.

1776: Year Zero

April 7, 1776, was a Sunday, Easter Sunday, in fact. James Boswell had noted that Samuel Johnson habitually went to St. Paul's in London on that day. Boswell was likewise struck that "there was always something peculiarly mild and placid in his manner at this holy festival, the commemoration of the most holy event in the history of the world." After St. Paul's, Boswell and Johnson carried on some varied conversation, finally to have coffee together, after which they then proceeded to the afternoon service at St. Clement's. On the way to St. Clement's, Boswell, noticing some beggars in the street, remarked to Johnson: "I suppose there was no civilized country in the world, where misery of want in the lowest class of people was prevented." To this, Johnson answered: "I believe, Sir, there is not; but it is better that some should be unhappy, than that none should be happy, which would be the case in a general state of equality." Such are remarkable words, for we have many a philosopher who would tear down the world rather than allow some to be "unhappy," be that unhappiness their own fault or anyone else's.

The case against general "equality" theory, the redistribution case, lies at the origin of mankind's gradual, unequal learning to be less than miserable. Misery, it will be recalled, was the original human condition, so that the proposition that mankind ought to be in every case less than miserable means, in practice, that on the egalitarian premise no one would ever have anything but misery. Ironically 1776, this same year in which Boswell and Johnson discoursed on the problem of misery, also saw a significant minority of mankind, in a very certain place, in England itself, begin to learn how all men, at different rates, might confront misery. This they did not by equality of distribution, which would have prevented the project from even beginning, but by abundance of production. For 1776 was the year of the steam engine, the year *Wealth of Nations* was published and the American Declaration signed, each in some way contributory to this process by which poverty could be overcome, at least for those willing to learn.

Norman Macrae, in a famous essay in *The Economist*, pointed out that between the year 1 A.D. and 1776, men had available to them much the same income (approximately $100 per year), energy sources, travel means, and life expectancy. However, Macrae went on,

> Between 1776-1975 world population increased sixfold, real
> GWP (gross world product) eightyfold, the distance a man

could travel in a day between a hundred and a thousandfold...the amount of energy that can be released from a pound of matter over 50 millionfold (with more to come) and the range and volume of information technology several billionfold.[135]

The Real Story

The percentage of mankind in 1776 living at the poverty level was about 99 percent. Today, there are about twice the number of people at this poverty baseline as in 1776. Yet at least one-third of mankind is presently beyond this level, many far beyond it. The ideological rhetoric of our time concentrates on what is left to do, whereas the real story which needs to be understood if we are to perform this remaining momentous task, requires an accurate account of how productivity and innovation have been discovered and increased in the past two hundred years. The first question we must ask ourselves now is, why is not everyone poor as in the years before 1776? For even then Samuel Johnson was quite aware that an egalitarian distribution of wealth, noble as it might sound in theory, would quite simply make everyone miserable because there was not enough to go around in the first place.

The answer to the question about whether the countries of the world can prevent the misery of the lowest classes is itself contingent upon the answer to the question about what ideas, religious values, institutions, and rewards have proved capable of producing abundant wealth where it has in fact been produced, which is clearly not everywhere. The truth is that wealth is not produced and distributed in just any old way or with just any old theory of the world. The creation of wealth is itself dependent on certain ideas we have about the family, property, profit, freedom, and invention. We must also recognize quite frankly that often very exalted and noble sounding ideals about poverty and its cure will not work. As in science so in economics, we cannot learn what works from some abstract, *a priori* philosophical premise, but we must learn it primarily from hard won experience. But this same experience must fall into an intelligible conception both of human nature and of the world. The incessantly talked about crisis of poverty, which requires considerably more intellectual discussion than it usually receives, is not essentially about whether societies can learn how to be rich. Many nations are already learning this so that the empirical lesson of how this is to be done is available to those whose agenda really is the alleviation of poverty. The more urgent question is whether a faulty ideological analysis of why the poor are poor, generally based on the redistributionist premise which holds that the poor are poor *because* the rich are rich, will through political or even religious action prevent those systems and ideas from coming into play which might indeed eliminate or considerably mitigate relative poverty.

Faculty of Reason

Yet we often wonder, because of our failure to possess what we think we ought to have been given in the first place, about how well the world was "made." What, in short, is revealed to us about *what is*? We must gradually, painfully, unevenly, over a long generation of ages, learn both how to produce wealth and how to maintain a system of freedom in which we might reveal our moral wants and preferences. We are really looking for a system of sustained wealth production which maintains and encourages those values and institutions conformable to human nature and reasonable order. Ultimately, these principles allow us to concentrate on what is not economic or material. Aquinas, at the beginning of the *De Regimine*, remarked that men are not like the animals who have instinct and nature to provide for their needs. Men are given only their faculty of reason by which they must learn for themselves how to do all these things which they admittedly come to need, come to want. Indeed, man is so situated in the world that he can produce from it not only a bare minimum of necessary things for his survival but an astonishing abundance—provided he patiently learns how. It is this fact of abundance which at first sight makes the redistributionist thesis seem plausible in the abstract, though in its workings it ends up by setting men against men, rather than by putting them in an exchange and co-operative system. Yet from another aspect, man was given the compliment of having to find out gradually for himself how to develop a more suitable life in this physical world. The discovery and effecting of this better way, in one sense, are what both virtue and history are about.

Asking the Right Questions

In this regard, I am reminded of a Mel Lazrus cartoon of Miss Peach, in which the topic of the day in the kindergarten class was: "Arthur Answers the Eternal Questions."[136] One little boy, with a properly haughty look, inquired of a thoroughly complacent Arthur: "Two questions, Arthur: (A) 'Can a person use up his brain?' and (B) 'How can he tell when he has?' " To these unsettling questions, Arthur answered sequentially: "To Question (A) 'Yes', and to Question (B) 'When he starts asking questions like that.' " Civilizations, no doubt, have given up pursuing the right questions and have shown signs of having used up their spiritual reserves. The "eternal question" is not, "Can we use up our brain?" Aristotle, after all, defined our mind as precisely "capax omnium," as that faculty which makes us capable of all things, the spiritual power in touch with all being. The question is: how do we use our intelligence correctly to discover what we are, both in some transcendent or contemplative sense, and in relation to our limited being and happiness on this earth?

    Almost immediately, in Book One of *The Ethics*, after Aristotle had defined man's activities as being pursued for the purpose of obtaining happiness, he rejected the view that our happiness consists in wealth, either in its making or

126

use. On the other hand, Aristotle, sensible man that he was, perhaps beyond all others, was not prepared to condemn wealth out of hand. In fact, he acknowledged that "happiness seems to require a modicum of external prosperity." (1099b1) The virtue of liberality, in Book Four, described how we stood in relation to our wealth, whether we dominated it for higher human purposes, or whether it dominated us. What it has taken the modern era to demonstrate, for those prepared to listen, is how this modicum of prosperity can be made available to everyone by his own activities. But what Aristotle can still teach us is that this relative abundance still does not and cannot obviate the necessity of virtue in its use.

Ultimate Wealth

At the very beginning of Aristotle's *Ethics*, moreover, man is defined graphically as that being in the universe composed of hands and a brain. Indeed, the ultimate wealth in the physical universe is exactly this human mind, rightly developed and used; that is, in its connection to the world through the human hand. Without this brain and hand, all physical things are merely things, not things capable of human use and civilization. The human mind is what discovers what is, what is new, what fits the human purpose. This purpose finally derives not simply from the world but from the unique destiny of each man. Man's own being-in-the-world, his capacities, the world itself, are not "results" of man's own powers but are rather "gifts," whose full meaning and perfection depend on man's learning and relearning about his own purposes and talents; they can in man's freedom be used against his own best interests, against even his transcendent purpose.

A proper theological and philosophical view of the world and man's place in it is necessary, then, to man's capability and willingness to use his mind and hands. The crucial parable of human talents in the New Testament, the notion that such talents can be used to produce fivefold or tenfold or can be simply buried and not used, that man is at fault not to develop what he is given—this remains the symbolic context in which to discuss penury or abundance. The most productive people often inhabit the lands with least resources. Intelligence, sacrifice, work, and energy seem to be what makes the difference. The primary reason why the world does not always seem to serve men adequately is related not to the world, but to man's own ideas about what he is in the world, as well as about his own virtue. Or, to put it in another way, the cause of poverty, once man has learned how not to be poor, is ideological, and is based on those ideas which explain wealth primarily by the exploitation of man by man rather than by the requirements of the creation of wealth in freedom.

A Paradox

To put this point more paradoxically, not unlike Samuel Johnson on leaving St. Paul's on Easter Sunday 1776, a knowledge of the single most significant event in the history of the world will alone free us from the temptation to locate what is most important to us in the politics or economics of this world. The first liberation is from a pseudo-metaphysics—today almost invariably presented in the political terms of "justice" or the economic terms of "distribution"—that knows, implicitly or explicitly, nothing but the world. In this regard, John Paul II spoke to some Peruvian bishops on the Feast of St. Francis of Assisi and while recounting to them the serious economic problems their people faced, acknowledged that there was no "justice" in such circumstances. Yet, he went on to remark to them, that even though a worse situation seems ever apparent, the less a gradual solution seems to work, "the more seductive can options of an ideological slant appear, which have recourse to ways of a materialistic stamp, to the class struggle, to violence, to power games, which do not take into account the fundamental rights of man."[137] John Paul then recalled his central advice, given at Puebla and often repeated, that religion finds the remedies for such problems in her own spiritual resources and teachings, in their fullness, not in ideological, political means. This is a constant, but gentle reminder that the resources of faith and intelligence, wherein all the relevant values and issues are included, can and will be the only workable solution.

Many thinkers are no doubt rightly concerned that neither the developed nations of the world nor the poor any longer hear that full spiritual and human message that is directed to each human person, calling him to some transcendent purpose regardless of the political order he might inhabit. P.T. Bauer, in his *Reality and Rhetoric*, put it this way: "It is paradoxical that the clergy are preoccupied with material conditions and progress at a time when the failure of material prosperity to advance and secure happiness, satisfaction and tranquillity is everywhere evident."[138] What is suggested here is that the solution to the remaining problems of misery is not to be accomplished by a theory of equality which deprives the poor of their transcendent truth, while at the same time removing them from those ideas and systems that will work for the more worldly task of producing abundance. The well-known sociological phenomenon of a clerical or intellectual class turning to this world as a result of its own loss of faith in the transcendent is not today nearly as striking as the turning by the same groups to an ideological view of the world which does not and cannot achieve those goals of prosperity and abundance that would really meet actual misery. And this latter goal was said to be the cause of turning to the world in the first place.

Reason and Revelation

In 1978 Jean Cardinal Villot, then Vatican Secretary of State, wrote a brief letter on "The Christian Practice of Economics," to a conference of French businessmen and industrialists. "The Gospel clarifies and frees the moral conscience," Villot wrote. "It also assures to human activity its rectitude and its full creativity. It does more, without identifying terrestrial progress with the increase of the Kingdom of Christ, it shows the bonds between the two."[139] This position argues that there exist layers of human purpose and good which are not exhausted by economic efficiency, however good such efficiency might in itself be. On the other hand, it also holds that the light of the higher ends or goals enables those who think about economics and deal with its realities to be better at economics and production. A harmony exists between reason, with its unanswered problems, and *revelation*, which directs its arguments to this very reason. This harmony is in turn actively locked into the concrete questions and experiences that arise in human affairs, and should forestall the temptation to confuse its elements. Instead it should lead us to follow lines of thought that enhance what human value is about. In the modern era, indeed, the main problem of the theological sciences seems to have become the effort to define their worth in terms of worldly success. Economics, in turn, has looked coldly on the religious enterprises because of their inability or unwillingness to learn about the well-springs of human productivity.

The view that religion is in fact detrimental to economic progress was articulated perhaps most pointedly by Frank Knight in a famous article, "Ethics and Economic Reform," in 1939. Knight doubted that Christianity in particular had much to contribute to economic reform. He rightly observed that "the teachings of Christianity gave little or no direct guidance for the change and improvement of social organization, and in fact gave clear *prima facie* evidence of not having been formulated for that end."[140] This comment is basically true. Christianity is not first and foremost about how to organize the world politically or economically. As I have suggested elsewhere, it is precisely the genius of Christianity not to have made this claim.[141] These enterprises must be learned, even in Christian terms, by themselves, according to their own dynamic.

Knight, however, even doubted an "indirect" Christian influence that would contribute anything of value to economic improvement. This view was to deny the very assumption that Cardinal Villot took as almost self-evident, the harmony of reason and revelation. Knight concluded:

> The question whether any proposed measure is in harmony
> with the "spirit" of Christianity commonly admits of no clear
> answer or at least none of a sort which will be accepted by
> Christians as a solution for practical political issues. Indeed,
> evil rather than good seems likely to result from any appeal
> to Christian religious or moral teaching in connection with

problems of social action. Stated in positive form, our contention is that social problems require intellectual analysis in impersonal terms but that Christianity is exclusively an emotional and personal morality; and this, while unquestionably essential, does not go beyond providing or helping to provide the moral interest, motive or "drive" toward finding solutions for problems. This is not only a very different thing from furnishing the solutions or even indicating the direction in which they are to be sought, but the teaching that it does furnish solutions has results which are positively evil and decidedly serious.[142]

Such a view would argue that religious motives might, perhaps, provide some reason for studying economics or starting a business, but they would give little or no help, and might in fact injure the project if they were to presume to teach how to do these things.

Liberal Charity

Something of this point was made recently by Raoul Audouin of the Centre Libéral Spiritualiste in Paris. In an interview with *La Croix*, Audouin was asked whether liberalism was "charitable." "Christians in this area ought often to revise their notion of charity," Audouin felt.

And they ought to understand that in practice, it is of much greater value to work more and show how to produce better, than to give freely. The true virtue of a Christian who has money, is not to give it away—except as in the case, perhaps, of the rich young man of the Gospel, he wishes to leave everything—but it is to invest—that is to say, to furnish to workers the tools to produce more efficaciously.[143]

The relation of rich to poor then must be seen in the proper intellectual context. Wealth is not primarily "taken," as in the distributionist world-view, but created. The poor are poor not because the rich are rich but because the poor have not yet learned, or in ideological regimes are not yet allowed to learn, how to be not poor. The testimony of the free and productive societies in modern history is that almost anyone can learn to improve his lot if he exists in a society that permits property, innovation, profit, family, savings, and the application of technology. Where these are not allowed or encouraged, people will remain poor or become poor—sometimes, as Solzhenitsyn testifies, precisely to control a population. In modern political philosophy "the poor" can function as a moral substitute for God or as an instrument to control a population. Not to realize the possibility of either use is, in the end, also to betray the poor.

Civil Order

The phrase "human nature" or "the nature of man," in the Greek classics usually meant what man, by himself, could be expected to do without benefit of a polity or interior virtue. The description of the consequences of original sin in the revelational tradition corresponded fairly well with Thucydides' or Plato's or Aristotle's description of what human nature "did" when left to itself. There was, moreover, a correspondence between the regimes or civil orders with the internal way that men defined their happiness in particular. An "oligarchy," for example, was not just the rule by a few rich men, but rather the rule of those, rich or poor, who thought that riches best defined the human good, so that the order of polity corresponded to its requirements. This regime was quite different from Aristotle's idea that a modicum of affluence was necessary for virtue. Likewise, a "democracy" in the Greek sense was the rule of the poor, of those who did what they pleased, who had no interior principle of rule. The democracy allowed anyone to live in its environs, even the philosopher, because there was no truth or order in what anyone did anyhow. All political systems had their own forms of "justice," which were philosophically defined and constitutionally implemented.

It was the most profound task of political philosophy to inquire about the reason for differing regimes and, behind them, for their differing interior understandings of what constitutes human worth. This enterprise necessarily recognized that less than ideal regimes were often best in practical circumstances. Indeed, the philosopher or the cleric was often seen to be in conflict with the politician because of the imperial attractiveness of the best regime. In recent discussions, the term "social justice" has come into use as that idea which directs or demands that a perfect order come into being. Of this idea, Ernest Fortin has written:

> Here I would simply caution against an excessive reliance on the newfangled and highly ambiguous notion of social justice, that typical nineteenth-century hybrid out of which nobody has yet been able to make much sense. We should all have been spared a good deal of muddleheadedness if Taparelli, who coined the expression in the 1840s, had bothered to tell us what he meant by it.[144]

The proper context, as the Greeks understood in their idea of "general justice," is virtue and moral character, no matter what the regime. This approach will counteract the anti-justice elements contained in the idea of "social justice" when it means a redistribution of goods unrelated to the requirements of their production.

Individuality and Exchange

Initially, I intended to begin this essay with a discussion of the relation of the just price to the market price. The concept of "just price" implied two things. The first was that the decision of what was to be produced at what cost was to be decided by numerous free individuals actively pursuing their own and their family's interests. This decision was not primarily "self-interest" in the pejorative sense, yet it did not deny that such an interest was evident. In some sense, acting for one's self was a basic good. The second idea was that the just price implied that the notion of an "unjust" price was to be considered, one arising from both private and governmental sources. Generally speaking, however, the complex system of market exchange with free entry into the market and the offering of a price came fairly close to what might be called just. Further, it provided an incentive to produce and to distribute the product to those who made their livings by the process—the majority of people in market economics.

In considering the moral validity of a market system which is especially geared to the needs and contributions of the large majority of the people in exchange market economics, it is of great importance to stress the reason why the market price approximates the just price. Yves Simon, in his *Philosophy of Democratic Government*, has made a unique contribution to this matter. "Is the just price equal to the cost of production?" Simon asked.

> There is a strong appearance that it is. Once more, justice in exchange is nothing else than the equality of the exchanged values. Does not equality demand that the sum surrendered by the purchaser be no greater than the total cost of the commodity purchased?
>
> If producers sold their products at a price equal to the cost of production, they would set a fine example of disinterestedness, but society would not be very well served, for there would be no provision for two social needs of the most essential character, viz., *capitalization and free distribution.*[145]

As Simon went on to point out, both of these are better done and more vital to society when they are not functions of the state, for both imply that the decisions and the initiatives of society pertain more directly to the values and lives of the people in their unique individuality.

Not Socialist

It is in this context that I wish to recall G.K. Chesterton's essay of 1908, "Why I Am Not a Socialist," since it serves to concentrate our minds on the essential point of human nature and social philosophy with regard to the kind of world we want, if we could have it. Chesterton suggested that if we examine the socialist utopias, that is, if we consider the kind of world that the egalitarian and redistribution philosophies picture, they invariably come up with a world lacking in the most essential virtues—liberality, generosity, giving, and receiving from our own goods, from our own freedom.[146]

Chesterton rightly worried about a world in which there could in principle be no hospitality, no genuine giving and taking, in which the "care" of the system substituted for the activities of the people, who should be able to take care of their own.

Unworkable Systems

What is at stake, it seems to me, in all of the discussion of poverty and the anguish at what is left to be done, is a real sense of enabling others to learn how to produce and live their own lives. There is a kind of danger which I think is very rampant in our society which "wants" people to care for, which wants poverty as a sort of justification for massive, unworkable, indeed unproductive systems that seem in theory to justify themselves by their claim to take care of enormous human problems, but which really create something even more dangerous and unworkable. Our picture of the world needs to be examined quite carefully from time to time to see whether those teachings of gift and intelligence which came from the classical and revelational traditions are still operative in our world-view.

In short, there is a great danger that we will give up most of what is worthwhile in our lives if we do not think rightly about the poor and what they can do for themselves. We seem more concerned about our guilt over the poor, or our compassion for them, than for the poor themselves. The first element of "social justice" is adequate understanding of human nature. And for this, we still can do no better than the classics from our rational and revelational traditions. In the end, the relation of the Trinity to steam should not surprise us, no less than the converse relation of misery to equality and distribution.

Unique Contribution of the Church

What the bishops' statements on the U.S. economy need to become is not a liberal or socialist "critique" of ideas or methods. This critique has already been made in practice but is not understood or incorporated in the document. Many of these ideas have proved that they do not work. What is needed is rather a contribution by the Church of what is uniquely productive and growth-causing in the United States system. This is what the world needs to know, particularly the Church. By failing to accomplish this, the drafts have further exposed free economic and political systems to ideological exploitation over the poverty issue. This result worsens the problem and further jeopardizes the freedom to which the poor themselves should have right of access. When the "war" pastoral came out several years ago, the French and German hierarchies in particular issued their own very different statements on this issue. These responses served to counterbalance the extremes of the U.S. position. It would, perhaps, be useful for the German, English, French, and Japanese bishops, among others, to analyze the economic order. However, the real irony here is that it is from the United States that many of the new ideas of economic growth, distribution, and freedom have come. In failing to comprehend this major phenomenon, the drafts have, in fact, given little hope to the real poor of the world for an escape from their condition in freedom.

Chapter 24

Religion and Capitalism:
On the Spiritual Origins
of Wealth

> The next economics should again have a theory of value. It may base itself on the postulate that productivity—that is, knowledge applied to resources through work—is the source of all economic value (Drucker 1981, p. 17-18).

> The Soviet economy needs forced labor because it is extremely wasteful of manpower. Subordinated in its entirety to the regime's political goals, the economy does not allow managers the independent authority to make even the simplest cost savings... The presence of such a vast reserve of forced laborers having no rights sets the tenor of the whole economy and sharply limits the concessions the Soviet authorities are obliged to make to motivate the non-prison work force. Problems in finding workers do not necessitate fundamental reforms because they can always be solved by increasing the number of people in confinement (Satter 1982).

At an American Fourth of July celebration in 1982 held under the huge arch on the waterfront of the Mississippi River in St. Louis, and attended by almost two million people, comedian Bob Hope looked over the crowd solemnly and quipped, "This is the most people I've seen in one spot since the government decided to give away cheese."[147] Hope, of course, did not speculate on why a government might have cheese to "give" away, nor on how much this cheese actually cost the taxpayer though it appeared to be "free." Nor did he explain what it means when a *government* "gives" something away. But Bob Hope's instincts about economics were right, for a "free" scarce item will draw huge crowds until there is no more cheese or until everyone has had so much of the product that not even a government could "give it away."

In a discussion of how to break into the Japanese distribution system, Kenichi Ohmae concluded:

> The success of Nestle, Coca-Cola, Caterpillar, and others and
> the failure of some Japanese companies in the "open" U.S.
> market, points out the old business truth. Good products are
> what really count, along with well executed strategies. There
> will always be barriers to entering a market. Losers complain
> about them, but we should watch the winners, who quietly
> and determinedly cross them.[148]

A free economy will have winners and losers. The losers will cease their efforts or else they will be encouraged by their experience to reform themselves until they too are winners. A system with no winners or losers is, in actuality no doubt, a system with losers alone. Static systems are controlled systems; not every method works. One cannot imagine the things that will work before they are tried. When the government is the sole employer, forced labour becomes the logical and necessary solution to failures of rational planning in the controlled system. We require rather a system of production that responds to human needs and wants on the basis of the freedom and initiative of each individual. We want an economic system, in short, in which something new can happen, in which a closed theory is not forced upon mankind. The only "moral" alternative ought not to be conceived as a planned, bureaucratically controlled distribution system founded on political allocation of goods, services, and burdens.

In an article about World Cup soccer, the late San Francisco columnist Charles McCabe recounted how, in 1954 when West Germany defeated Hungary, one expert said that the German victory "was considered to have had an uplifting effect on the spirits of the downtrodden German people, and it came at the dawn of the economic miracle that lifted the country from the ashes of defeat." [149] This suggests that there might be some indefinable thing, some attitude about the world and its openness to human effort that may be needed to produce winners.[150] McCabe went on, "The famous Liverpool coach, Bill Shankley, was asked by a younger reporter if he really thought soccer was a matter of life and death. Shankley answered devoutly, 'Son, it's far more important than that.' " Whether the World Cup defeat of West Germany by Italy portended a change in the relation of Mercedes-Benz to Ferrari can, perhaps, be left to one side, but the Italian Premier said that "This great event...will help bring Italians closer to one another."[151] I suspect, however, that a sense that there is something more important than life or death is likewise needed to give men incentive to put something into the world itself. There are, in other words, certain spiritual attitudes and principles which must be present for the production of wealth, for indicating how wealth can come forth from human effort to reach human needs and goals, In Peter Drucker's phrase, "knowledge" can "be applied to resources through work."

Reasons For Poverty

We could begin by asking ourselves again why are the poor, in fact, poor. At first sight this seems like an obviously spiritual, compassionate question, the most common answer to which is that the poor are poor *because* someone else is rich, someone else is "exploiting" them. They are poor, because of someone else's moral failure, someone else's *sin*, in religious terms. This answer, however, is a supposition that deprives the poor of much of their own dignity and prevents them from ever realizing their own role in the production of wealth.

The just resolution of poverty is replete with a moral mission of a kind that is "justified" by the ethical worth of "the poor" as such. Their poverty becomes a blanket justification to "act" for their good, whether such action actually does them good or not. To "restore" justice, to set things straight, to find out why things went wrong—this is high moral and religious rhetoric, often dangerously close to another kind of "exploitation" of the poor, the kind that would use them by imposing on them certain ideological positions in lieu of any real aid. This "option for the poor," with no specific indication of what the options are or do, seems also to have the capacity of putting a "spiritual" aspect on what is at first sight merely material. In this way, the aura of sanctity is given to materialist ideology.

On the other hand, the proper question to be asked is *not*, "why are the poor poor?" Rather, as we have said, it must be, "why is not everyone equally poor?" Clearly, wealth is not something that just "happens." It arises from the relation between man's efforts to dwell in and work on the earth, and what he does on and in this world. In this sense the first "spiritual" question that occurs is whether the world exists at all. If the world is a philosophic illusion, as many still hold, there seems to be no reason to do anything in it or for it. Moreover, if the world is evil, if matter is corrupt, as the Manicheans and gnostics of all ages, including our own, held, then we ought not to have anything to do with it if we would be authentic. We need, in other words, a view of man and the world which would allow us to act in it to be, as it were, more ourselves, without our very activity corrupting either the world or ourselves. We need an incomplete world open to our intelligence, and to the work of our hands which can give us actual contact with it, but in a way that requires us to discover its rules and laws so that we do not simply "impose" our private thoughts on it, no matter what.

Giving, Not Sharing

The most important fact we can know about a person is how he thinks. Our visions are more important than our actions if only because what we do follows our visions in some strange way. In this, I take my guide from G.K. Chesterton. "A man's argument," he remarked in 1908, "shows what he is really up to."[152]

Chesterton proposed, and Shafarevich has repeated much more grimly in our day, that we look carefully at the ideals of socialism in addition to what it does in practice.[153] This approach is the opposite of the normal priority of practice and theory. What does socialism's "vision" consist of? Chesterton wrote:

> Socialist Idealism does not attract me very much, even as Idealism. The glimpses it gives of our future happiness depress me very much. They do not remind me of any actual happiness, of any happy day I have ever myself spent... Almost all Socialist Utopias make happiness...chiefly consist in the pleasures of sharing... This, I say, is the commonest sentiment in socialist writing. Socialists are collectivists in their proposals. But they are communist in their idealism.
>
> Now, there is a real pleasure in sharing... But it is not the only pleasure, nor the only altruistic pleasure, nor (I think) the highest or most human of altruistic pleasures. I greatly prefer the pleasure of giving and receiving.[154]

The key question is, what kind of a world do we want to have?

Chesterton was a distributionist, an "anti-capitalist" in the sense of anti-monopoly. He wanted everyone to own property, to have his own tools, land, talents, initiative, and home.[155] The passage above, on the ideal of giving and receiving rather than sharing serves to illustrate the vital importance of our wishes, of our vision of man and the universe in our understanding of what our economy ought to be about. For Chesterton, everyone ought to be able to give and receive, to have something so that he could be a real source of initiative, not merely an object of sharing what cheese the state might "freely" hand out from its badly planned surpluses.

Scripture Themes

Paradise has been variously described as a place wherein nature ministered directly and benevolently to human needs and wants. We still call such places as Tahiti "island paradises," on the supposition that nature is so beautiful and abundant there that men need do but little to collect what they desire. Nature presents no challenge. Various utopias and classless societies are speculative secularizations of Paradise or the Garden of Eden into which Adam and Eve were placed. They may be treated as "myths" but they have had enormous ramifications in social theory. In *Genesis*, the Fall took place precisely in Paradise, a profoundly significant consideration. The Greek myth of Prometheus hinted that men wanted a dignity to be achieved precisely *against* Zeus, that what men did by themselves was more important to them than what was done for them by non-human agencies. Freedom from the law overruled freedom or obedience to the law.

Economic and political literature is filled with accounts of "trouble in Paradise." Saint Augustine thought that human problems and evils were not ultimately located in nature or social arrangements or property, family, or governance, but in the will itself; that wherever there is man, there is the possibility of corruption, no matter what the institutional arrangement. The opposite was likewise possible; goodness may be found in the worst of economic or political regimes. This century has produced not only more literature on utopia, but especially a literature of anti-utopia, such as *1984*, *Darkness at Noon*, and *Brave New World*. Indeed, as Shafarevich and Solzhenitsyn, not to mention *Mein Kampf* and Cambodia, remind us, the anti-utopias are no longer "novels," but "histories," powerful precisely to the degree to which they recount what happens to individual human beings in a Gulag in our time, wherever it be located.

Why do we not live in Paradise? Is there something wrong with God, perhaps? With nature? What is our relation to world and time that we are given something significant to do yet, in doing it, we do not ourselves become gods or substitutes for them? Scriptures also tells us that the poor will always be with us, almost as if to say that the absolute removal of poverty does not necessarily decide our destiny. It almost suggests that poverty is mostly a question of comparison with our neighbours. We need a vision of the world in which the poor can be saved without necessarily condemning the not so poor. Scripture does not, furthermore, provide a programme for the ways to produce or distribute goods, however much or little its admonitions and values might contribute to wealth or poverty. This observation must mean that the primary purpose of revelation is not the proper construction of worldly society. The latter, as the Greeks had already suggested, we are to discover by ourselves. If faith pursuing its own objectives incites us to do what we ought to do anyhow, so much the better, but religion ought not to be burdened with what it is not given to achieve. Revelation in this sense frees economics, politics, and culture of the burden of being religious ultimates. They are serious, but not so serious.

Money, St. Paul said, was the root of all evil. In a passage reminiscent of Plato's Guardians Mathew (19:16-22) recounted how a rich young man turned sadly away after being invited to sell his possessions and follow Christ.[156] Yet Scripture tells us not to steal, while it assumes that we use our talents to gain at least a minimal interest, if not a rather profitable increase of our goods. Envy is not a virtue; those who have produced more may justly possess what they have. The fact that we are greedy and covetous means that we must control our desires and discipline ourselves. It does not mean that desired things should not exist or be produced. Scripture teaches us how easily things can go awry if we are not strong willed, which is also the teaching of the Greeks and Romans.

Economics is said to be the dismal science, for man does not live by bread alone. To speak or, better, to work on behalf of the poor may be a noble service, if indeed such effort *does* actually help the poor and does not merely replace a material poverty by a spiritual poverty, or worse, an abundant tyranny. How can the poor cease to be poor? Mainly the poor ought to help themselves not to be poor, but that requires a certain confidence in human nature. It is not, in any case, simply a matter of taking from the rich whose very possession of wealth is itself unjust, according to certain theories. The poor are unimpressed with those who cannot help them to cease to be poor. They rightly resent spiritual "exploitation" by the people who use poverty to justify their ideology. When there is no concentrated wealth or capital, everyone is poorer, especially the poor.

The relation of religion to wealth is no neutral subject, while the possibility that certain religious doctrines and practices actually cause wealth or poverty seems incontrovertible. One's religion or philosophy is directly related to one's ability to produce and distribute wealth and, more importantly, the manner in which this is accomplished. Liberality and charity, alms and benefices, presuppose a background of capital. A religion that places all property in the hands of the state has secret ambitions of being a state religion. We have a deep need to give, and we ought to be able to receive from others. When there is no "mine" and "thine," as Aristotle taught, the "ours" also generally disappears. If *everything* belongs to the state, the chances are very good that so will *everyone*. Christian monasticism was deliberately designed to prevent those who opted for the "ours" from destroying the "mine" and "thine" of the majority of the people.[157]

Reconsiderations of Capitalism

To be "against" capitalism has long been the curious bias of the intellectual and, increasingly, of the cleric. Yet religion is a very real aspect of Western and American history. A good number, if not all, the early Americans came to this continent for religious reasons, to found a polity that did not contradict their faith. The general prosperity of the American economy at every stage, along with the principles of the Constitution, have allowed religion, if it chose, to build schools, churches, hospitals, clubs, and other institutions on the basis of free giving in a manner unique in the world. On this basis alone, we could expect that religion would be a great defender of the American productive system. To some extent it has been. But in recent years, often influenced by European ideological presuppositions, some Christians have embraced various anti-capitalist attitudes, primarily, it is claimed, in the name of a religious commitment to aid the poor. This change happened at a time when many actual poor were immigrating into the American economy precisely to escape their poverty. Michael Novak argues that there has been surprisingly little effort made to understand the exact nature of the American (or any other) economic productive enterprise in its relation to Christian doctrines and practices.[158]

In this regard, one could argue that Jewish and Christian intellectuals are moving in almost opposite directions in this area, or better stated, many Christian intellectuals are going the way of the old-line Jewish socialists. Half a century ago, it was the Jewish intellectual who was the utopian, the Christian largely the realist. Today, the formerly socialist Jews form the vanguard of neoconservatism, while many Christian intellectuals, as if such an option were the most logical and religious thing in the world, have embraced marxism, no doubt of a utopian kind, since the existing ideology has little to recommend it. Irving Kristol's *Two Cheers for Capitalism*, arising as it does from a disappointment with the actual practice of existing socialism, seems to embrace capitalism as the lesser of evils, hence two cheers, not three. The Old Testament emphasized creation and prosperity, but this part of the Christian heritage was never adequately developed. Now a positive spiritual basis for the economic system seems to be demanded. Thinkers like Michael Novak, Paul Johnson and George Gilder are trying to provide this foundation, with some considerable success.

At the speculative level, however, I think Leo Strauss, whose significance is hardly recognized in most Christian circles, has begun the intellectual work that must take place before the churches can realize what is at issue, even for themselves. Strauss sensed that there may be something deviant about modern life with its attempt to produce virtue by multiplying things, and to set civilization exclusively upon manufactured goods produced by self-interest.[159]

Has the relation of wealth, religion, and politics been adequately presented? What are the consequences of the possible failure to understand why people can and do produce wealth, and wealth production's relation to the family especially? The most dangerous result would be an attempt to explain wealth and poverty by the nearest and simplest—and most powerful—ideology. This explanation would surely, as Strauss also saw, break the proper relation of religion and political economy so that religious values would be presented for accomplishment by systems and ideas that cannot achieve what religion stands for. At the same time, it would undermine the variety of values needed to ground man's worth in the world. In the worst case, religion would become a tool whereby an ideological system is imposed on a people to justify its sacrifices, whether of continued poverty or loss of freedom.

In recent years, there have been a number of original attempts to rethink the contribution of religion to capitalism and of the way religion might help or hinder human wealth and productivity. Probably the most profound of these analyses was that begun by the Soviet mathematician, Igor Shafarevich, in which he argued that socialism, which is so often looked on in religious circles as *the* cure for the world's ills, is a recurrent system in all races and cultures. It involves certain notions with regard to the abolition of property, family, and religion, ideas that are always anti-human in their manifestations, and can never be humanized.[160] While I will not explore this position in any detail, it has the advantage of having arisen out of the experience of living under socialism and an intellectual history which seeks to ground the argument in scientific discourse. Shafarevich, like Chesterton, insisted upon looking at the ideas that are embraced and where they lead when they are put into practice. Unavoidably, they lead to a pseudo-metaphysics and a theology which evidently, to be consistent, must reject the kind of world that actually exists.

Development and Religion

The whole moral crux of these issues centres on development and its relation to a culture that exhibits ideas and beliefs at variance with those that might foster development. Is development, or aid to the poor, merely a transfer of technology and methods, or does this very transfer presuppose changes in the belief systems themselves? The most radical positions favour a solution which would realign "structure" to conform to socialist models. Moreover, since the "poor" hold the "moral" criterion for judging secular systems today, the real issue hinges paradoxically on the belief patterns of those who need to be helped most. William Pfaff has argued the point well:

> The religious values, moral assumptions, and social structures of these societies are at best alien, and sometimes hostile, to the values and practices of industrialism. This situation cannot be changed by the injection of money, machines, or technical instructors. For these societies to "develop" in the sense in which that term is used at United Nations conferences would require a radical and destructive remaking of life and society, and, often, a reinterpretation of the meaning of existence itself, as it has been understood by the people who live in these civilizations. What often is put forward as a simple transfer of resources, techniques, and information is, in fact, a revolutionary enterprise of the most momentous consequences.[161]

Is prosperity itself an "exportable" item, as I like to put it? "Exploitation theory," in my view the idea that the poor are poor because somebody is stealing from them, is by far the easier intellectual solution. It avoids the issue of whether ideas and religion make any difference and whether we should not begin here, in beliefs, if we really wish to confront the idea of poverty and its causes. To put the matter another way, however sobering the first and most important way to aid the poor is to be more serious about metaphysics and religion. The value of being neutral, however tolerant or benign it appears, is beside the point.

In this context let me briefly recount some of the main arguments which seek to correlate religion and capitalism. Or democratic capitalism, as Michael Novak prefers to call it, since socialism, to protect its own flanks as it were, insists on calling itself "democratic socialism." The endeavour to make "socialism" the only or preferred public expression of the Judaeo-Christian tradition is over a century and a half old, if we exclude the communalistic tendencies in various medieval heresies. This latter endeavour to "socialize" Christianity betrays in itself little new, except, perhaps, a realization on the part of marxist movements that religion, contrary to their own theories, could in fact be used for marxist purposes. What is disturbing is not so much the attraction of socialism, something that itself dates at least from Plato, but rather how little the actual experience of socialist systems, particularly their failures, seems to affect Socialist theory. "It has often been remarked," Shafarevich noted, "that to reveal contradictions in socialist teachings in no way reduces their attractive force, and socialist idealists are not in the least scared of contradictions."[162] This is another way of arguing for a realist metaphysics of being by which we can judge such ideology in the first place. Classical religion, to its credit, understood this.

Moral Values of Capitalism

The key to the moral basis of capitalism, according to Paul Johnson, is the uniqueness of each individual and his capacity for free choice. "What social system is most conducive to developing the informed conscience which will enable man's free will to make the right choices?" Johnson asked.[163] First, he suggested that the common man has developed, with the aid of freehold property, more rapidly than in any other system. The horror stories about the ills of early capitalism often blind us to the realities and we do not compare them with what men were leaving behind. The spiritual doctrine of human uniqueness and free will enabled human beings to break out of the various state collectivities eventually and to establish themselves as legal persons. This independence grounds society.[164] "The factory system, however harsh it may have been," Johnson observed,

> proved to be the road to freedom for millions of agricultural workers. Not only did it offer them an escape from rural poverty, which was deeper and more degrading than anything experienced in the cities; it also allowed them to move from status to contract, from a stationary place in a static society, with tied cottages and semi-conscript labour, to a mobile place in a dynamic one...
>
> One might say that capitalism, far from dehumanizing man, allowed him at last to assume the full individuality which Christianity had always accorded him as the possessor of a distinctive moral conscience and an immortal soul... For most of history the great majority of ordinary people have been treated by the authorities as if they were a congealed mass, without distinctive personalities, let alone individual

> rights and aspirations. For democracy to evolve, it was first
> necessary for society to recognize that it was composed of
> millions of individuals, not undifferentiated groups classified
> merely by occupation and social status.[165]

Far from understanding individualism in an extreme, utilitarian form, Johnson sees it rather as a personalism that requires for its existence a proper external order. The root of spiritual action is therefore placed in the individual person, in his radical capacity to choose and to correct his own errors. "A true moral system must contain a self-correcting mechanism: for Christianity it is the conscience of the individual. The strength of the system lies in its just estimate of man as a fallible creature with immortal longings."[166] Johnson is concerned that the state should not be allowed to become the primary arbiter of individual existence and worth. This approach considers society merely as a relation, not a super being who "knows" what the individual person wants.

George Gilder made perhaps the most persuasive case for the connection of religion to democratic capitalism. Again this relationship is not conceived as an exercise in how religion "must" have a particular economic or political "form" but rather looks to the values and principles operative in a religion and how they are best effected in the public world. Gilder directly attacked the extreme individualist, self-interest explanation of capitalism. This position he shares with papal social tradition. He argued that he is not a "neo-conservative" or a libertarian in this sense. For Gilder, it is the family, a unit of sacrifice, future, and giving that causes men and women to be innovative and to save. This foundation is the basis of any productive system, and alone gives value and the strength to look beyond immediate interests.[167] The moral consequences of extreme liberalism have led to the modern welfare state, whose collectivist-individualist premises, which shut down intermediate groupings, are chiefly responsible for our moral crises.

Thus the ecological and "limits of growth" schools of philosophic pessimism are not products of scientific analysis but indicate rather loss of nerve and vision. Gilder looked at this situation in relation to the family and other institutions of sacrifice that look beyond immediate rewards. The delivery of man to the state and to bureaucracies is the result of certain absolutist theories of human rights and human welfare which seem, at first sight, to express religious values. Natural or political "catastrophe" has paradoxically become one of the chief ways to justify control by the state. "The crucial rules of creative thought," Gilder wrote,

> can be summed up as faith, love, openness, conflict, and
> falsifiability. The crucial rules of economic innovation and
> progress are faith, altruism, investment, competition, and
> bankruptcy, which are also the rules of capitalism. The
> reason capitalism succeeds is that its laws accord with the
> laws of the mind. It is capable of fulfilling human needs

because it is founded on giving, which depends on sensitivity
to the needs of others. It is open to faith and experiment
because it is also open to competition and bankruptcy.
Capitalism accumulates the capital gains not only of its
successes but also of its failures, capitalized in new
knowledge. It is the only appropriate system for a world in
which all certitude is sham.[168]

This analysis is not only an attempt to broaden the notion of self-interest, which
is seen as incomplete in itself, but to put it on a positive moral and spiritual
basis. On a theological level, it is the effort to ask in economic terms about the
relationship of justice to charity, in the context of the Thomist principle that
grace does not contradict nature. Self-interest, in other words, need not be
wrong but is itself a true interest, a true beginning to something beyond it—to
giving, not sharing.

Gilder sought to challenge directly not only socialist tendencies in current
religious thought, but the neo-conservative side as well, which he saw as having
certain premises in common with or logically conducive to socialism. On the
other hand, Gilder also challenged religious thought for not understanding the
premises of its own creeds, when these occur in a worldly context:

Capitalism is said to be based on self-interest and consumerism, which finally erode the moral preconditions of the
system itself. It is said to be founded on forms of technological progress and bureaucracy that finally subvert democracy
and enterprise. It is said to function through crude economic
incentives rather than through love and altruism. To sum up,
it is said to be founded on greed rather than on giving.

The fact is, however, that capitalism thrives on religious
faith and decays without it. Capitalist progress is based on
risks that cannot be demonstrated to pay off in any one
lifetime. Thus, it relies on faith in the future and in
Providence. The workers under capitalism are motivated not
by crude economic rewards but by love of family. The
entrepreneurs succeed to the extent that they are sensitive to
the needs of others, to the extent that others succeed.
Altruism is the essence of the positive-sum game of
capitalism.[169]

The need for an economic and moral theory which does not by the very terms
of its theoretical structure, set people off against one another, which allows for
competition, change, and self-correction based on personal, not state, decisions,
finds solid basis in Gilder's approach. The ideas of risk, innovation, and growth
require intellectual and religious foundations, without which a society cannot
change or improve. The productivity of the modern economic and political
order has received inadequate treatment in modern religious literature, so that

one of the main reasons for a "socialist" option in religious culture seems in many cases to be either ignorance or lethargy, when it is not simply ideological commitment.[170]

Michael Novak in his book, *The Spirit of Democratic Capitalism*, was perhaps less philosophical than either Johnson or Gilder. Novak was much more concerned with the religious "contribution," if I might put it that way, to the *lack* of economic progress, especially in Latin America and the Third World. He saw this failure to be based on certain misapplied spiritual premises, in particular in a failure to grasp the nature of productivity. The Spanish possessions brought immense riches to Europe, but they soon enriched England and France and the Italian cities because the Spanish had confused wealth with gold.

Novak argued that there are three systems that have served to encourage the changes and the rational context that lead to production—an economic system, a political system, and a moral-cultural system. Each of these by itself can and has produced aberrations. The separation of these systems or powers is made along pragmatic lines. Politics can correct abuses of self-interest, while culture can give depth to both politics and economics but only if it is not totally identified with them. Novak always insisted on including the freedom that derives from the self-correcting mechanisms of separate sources of power which make any one society complete. Christopher Dawson argued in *Religion and the Rise of Western Culture*, still a most important background book for the considerations of economics, religion, politics and culture, that the dynamism unique to Western culture was rooted in the diversity of spiritual and political centres. Novak argued that the separation of economics, politics, religion, and university make an even more basic dynamism. The economic and productive side of growth did not happen until the economic and the political, as well as the religious and cultural, were distinguished and separated, not by a "wall," but by purpose and function.

On the theme of "giving" in Gilder and Chesterton, Novak wrote:

> The problem for a system of economy is how to unleash human creativity and productivity while coping realistically with human sinfulness... According to socialist theory, the rich get richer and the poor get poorer. The implication is that the poverty of the poor is caused by the wealth of the wealthy. The theory of democratic capitalism is quite different. It holds that economic activity creates wealth, and that the broader the stimulation of economic activism the great the wealth created. It does not hold that economic activists are equal in talent, judgment, exertion, or luck, nor does it expect equal outcomes. Yet it does hold that economic activism, whether on the part of a few or on the part of many, benefits not only its agents but the entire community.

> A system of political economy imitates the demands of
> *caritas* by reaching out, creating, investing, producing, and
> distributing, raising the material base of the common good.
> It respects individuals as individuals. It makes communal life
> more active, intense, voluntary, and multiple.[171]

Novak argued that theological and philosophical issues gain in importance in such a system, for there is freedom to argue within their own spheres and not in misplaced corners of economics or politics, which is what has happened in the culturally politicized systems of our era. Meanwhile, the excesses of politics and economics are checked by one another, as well as by the cultural system, which itself needs proper counterbalancing. Universities left to themselves can be as tyrannical as churches or corporations, if they have no broader societal context. George Gilder would, perhaps, be more concerned than Michael Novak about the relation of ideas to the actual moral climate. Novak's concern in this area did not blind him to the problems Gilder saw, but Novak would not want to see this spiritual element become a question of politics or economics, if at all possible.

Conclusion

At first sight, these discussions about the spiritual origins and religious context of wealth may seem obscure, if not esoteric. They arise, however, at a time when socialism is spiritually exhausted, when its historical record offers no hope for the ideological expectations so often uncritically pinned on it, especially by religion. On the other hand, the religious community itself, often considerably behind advanced intellectual currents, has not given a coherent account of wealth production and distribution which would justify its much vaunted "concern for the poor." The poor themselves should be the first ones to be wary of monks bearing only theories instead of gifts. The old-time missionary was much closer to the heart of what actually developed. The ideological systems into which Christian social thought often seems to be falling betray little real concern for what might actually help the poor to help themselves.[172] The failure to account for liberty as well as justice or peace is, as Michael Novak suggested, a most revealing lapse in contemporary religious institutions; and when "liberation" is in fact used, it almost always has ideological meanings, not concrete political or economic ones.

The key intellectual and cultural issue concerning the relation of wealth to religion has become a basic one for anyone seriously concerned about human freedom and growth. I believe it is being faced almost for the first time by Johnson, Gilder, Novak, Pfaff, Colin Clark, and others. Jacques Maritain, in his *Reflections on America*, had, in the 1950s, raised the question of the spiritual grounds of the American productive system. That initiative produced, disastrously as it turned out for main line Christianity and more especially for the

Third World leaders trained in its newer radical movements, practically no result, and no effort to think what productivity might be about. Many of the religious, educational, and cultural leaders became convinced that they should promote various species of socialism, state or otherwise, to aid the weak and poor. Instead, they often laced them under the newer forms of left absolutism which were generated in the latter part of the twentieth century, systems that do not work.

Ultimately, I suspect, this will have dangerous effects on religion and prevent its true meaning from adequately reaching modern society, rich or poor. John Paul II understands some of this, which seems paradoxically to be the root of much of the opposition to him.[173] There is nothing new in the ideological ease with which Christians seem to agree with the left, when the left translates its own ideas into spiritual, Christian sounding terms. What is new is that there is a clear alternative to both liberal and socialist positions. There is a need to suggest how democratic capitalism is not merely an incarnation of old-fashioned individualism or absolute libertarianism. In this sense, the rediscovery of the relation of Western metaphysics to modern productivity is a key step if the poor are to become richer, while not at the same time enslaved into a new kind of tyranny in the name of virtue, as seems to be the prospect under liberation theology. Man still does not live by bread alone, even in a productive economic system. The recent reflections on democratic capitalism, I think, suggest that the key item in its own possibility for success is for religion to rediscover itself, especially its sense of spiritual transcendence. If we are to save the economic, political, and cultural orders, we need to cease to politicize religious dogmas and return to their original understanding. This return would be the most effective way to aid the poor.

Chapter 25

John Paul II's
Sollicitudo Rei Socialis:
On the Limits of Social Concern

Introduction

What is known specifically as the "social doctrine" of the Church consists of a long series of public, official documents, beginning with Leo XIII at the end of the 19th Century.[174] Each of these statements rests not only on the earlier ones, from Leo XIII, to Benedict XV, Pius XI, Pius XII, John XXIII, Paul VI, Vatican II, to John Paul II, but also on the previous history of Christianity right back to its very authoritative origins in the New Testament. This history includes the concrete record of Christian life under the manifold political and economic regimes which have existed during the intervening centuries.

Likewise, this social doctrine will acknowledge its intellectual debt to its own great thinkers from Augustine to Aquinas, and their inheritors. The philosophical and political experience of society, ancient, medieval, and modern will, no doubt, be incorporated within this social doctrine. Revelation itself does not claim to be the original or primary source for specifically political or economic questions. These have to be formulated generally on the basis of reason and experience.

Ultimate Destiny

Christianity conceives itself to be responsible mainly for man's ultimate destiny which transcends all worldly regimes. This destiny to be sure relates to how each person judges and acts within this life in the light of what is found in reason and revelation. The effort to "save one's soul," as it was traditionally put, does not in principle work against the true good of existing political and economic truths—provided that they are, real truths. E.F. Schumacher has put the point succinctly:

> It is a grave error to accuse a man who pursues self-knowledge of "turning his back on society." The opposite would be more nearly true: that a man who fails to pursue

> self-knowledge is and remains a danger to society, for he will
> tend to misunderstand everything that other people say or do,
> and remain blissfully unaware of the significance of many of
> the things he does himself.[175]

The by now hackneyed accusation that religion teaches man to be concerned with the next life to the neglect of this one has receded. Often in recent decades it has given way to the worry that, on the contrary, religion itself has nothing to teach or concern itself with except this-worldly economic and social problems. The pressing danger of contemporary culture seems to be rather a practical loss within religion itself of a concern about the transcendent.

Transcendence

In any case, one aspect of the true social good for which religion remains essentially responsible is precisely the good of man's highest end, by way of instruction about prayer and sacrament and about how the highest end is to be attained. The most practical thing religion can do for the social order is to insist on fostering its own purposes by its own means. But these means are not as such specifically political or economic. John Paul II's first and most famous statement of this view was in his speech at Puebla, in Mexico, in 1979.[176] This is why the essential social good and legal principle that the Christian Church most insists on, in any civil order, is its freedom to teach each existing person what God's redemption means and how it is to be achieved (#33).[177]

On Social Concern

The latest social document of the Church is John Paul II's *On Social Concern*, (*Sollicitudo Rei Socials*) which was published on December 30, 1987, twenty years after Paul VI's *Populorum Progressio*. Possibly because of his previous encyclicals *Redemptor Hominis* (1979), *Dives in Misericordia* (1980), *Dominem et Vivicantem* (1986), and *Laborem Exercens* (1981), plus innumerable addresses on the spiritual life, the Holy Father did not think it necessary to repeat this more transcendent and spiritual aspect of Catholic thought. *Sollicitudo Rei Socialis*, by comparison, seems, if anything, rather lacking in emphasis on the importance of man's ultimate destiny for any ordering of this world.

Near the end of Leo XIII's *Rerum Novarum* (1891), for example, we read:

> Let our associations, then, look first and before all to God;
> let religious instruction have therein a foremost place, each
> one being carefully taught what is his duty to God, what to
> believe, what to hope for, and how to work out his salvation;
> and let all be warned and fortified with especial solicitude
> against wrong opinions and false teaching. Let the working
> man be urged and led to the worship of God, to the earnest

> practice of Religion, and, among other things, to the
> sanctification of Sundays and festivals. Let him learn to
> reverence and love Holy Church the common Mother of us
> all; and so to obey the precepts and frequent the Sacraments
> of the Church, those Sacraments being the means ordained
> by God for obtaining forgiveness of sin and for leading a holy
> life (#42)

Rerum Novarum, no doubt, was directed to an audience within the specifically Catholic community, whereas most social documents since John XXIII's *Pacem in Terris* (1963), including *Sollicitudo Rei Socialis*, have been addressed to everyone of "good will." This broader object will necessitate, to some extent, not talking about religious ends or means which will not be common to everyone.

Life on Earth

A more or less parallel passage in *Sollicitudo Rei Socialis* reads:

> The Church well knows that no temporal achievement is to
> be identified with the Kingdom of God, but that all such
> achievements simply reflect and in a sense anticipate the
> glory of the Kingdom, the Kingdom which we await at the
> end of history, when the Lord will come again. But that
> expectation can never be an excuse for lack of concern for
> people in their concrete personal situations and in their
> social, national, and international life, since the former is
> conditioned by the latter, especially today (#48).[178]

The subject matter of social doctrine is ever the same: namely, how the Christian religion relates to man in this world, the proper presence of man while he is mortal (#48). The man who is to seek salvation is the same man who lives in existing polities.

Many of the specific charges in the New Testament to determine how man is to stand eternally before God, however, have to do with his direct actions toward others, his neighbours, as they are called, during his own lifetime while still on earth among his fellows. *Sollicitudo Rei Socialis* seems to be directed to this context of the responsibilities of Christians towards this life. What is uniquely Christian is the claim that revelation properly understood will also affect, perhaps indirectly, the right ordering of the world. This position was the one Thomas Aquinas articulated in so masterly a fashion and one which the modern Church has consciously tried to follow (#I-II, 91, 4).

The Less Advantaged

The spirit of *Sollicitudo Rei Socialis* is certainly one of genuine concern for problems of living men and women, especially those who are less advantaged.

Needless to say, however, every modern political system or ideology purports to possess the same spirit in some form or other. Marxism, nationalism, fascism, liberalism, whatever, all insist that they are acting for the good of all men, especially the less advantaged. In some sense, John Paul II's own position requires the reader to ask whether the attitude and suggestions he makes will in fact accomplish what he seems most to want; is it, in other words, any longer sufficient to ignore the question of "what succeeds in alleviating poverty and what does not?" John Paul II maintained here that he was not proposing a kind of third economic or political system (#41). He did not claim to found a movement in politics or a school in economics which could solve hitherto neglected problems.

John Paul II, moreover, claimed that the Christian faith is not itself just another "ideology." Normally in modern terminology, ideology has come to mean the exclusively human formulation of the proper order of man's life and society. It is one formed independently of any revelation or natural order and is itself imposed by force or argument on social reality as the only proper way for men to act and live in this world. The Holy Father held that what the Church proposes in these areas is not an "ideology" of this sort. Instead, what it teaches is based on "the accurate formulation of the results of careful reflection on the complex realities of human existence...in the light of faith and of the Church's tradition." In this sense, *Sollicitudo Rei Socialis* is itself, presumably, subject to this same criterion of "accurate formulation" which it proposes for everyone.

Delicacy

John Paul II like Aquinas himself and subsequent popes tried, furthermore, to save what can be saved in every human government or philosophical system. While he maintained that it is part of his duty to "condemn evils and injustice" (#42), he seemed often reluctant to do more than praise what can be praised without entering into a specific chart of what is wrong. A certain delicacy of encouragement and praise is often more prudent than and preferable to overt criticism. One has the impression that John Paul II does not hesitate to criticize those who seem "adult" enough to understand his charitable spirit, but that he is slow to criticize the "little ones," however much at fault they might be (#44). On the other hand, in *Sollicitudo Rei Socialis*, there is beginning to be forged, under the rubric of "initiative" (#15), a way to speak to the major causes of why so many nations have not developed as rapidly as might have been wished. The Pope seemed to invite discussions about whether what he himself proposes is adequate or not.

Alternative Procedures

Many ways to approach the meaning and importance of this document present themselves.[179] We could search for what in the encyclical was not found in earlier discussions. Contrariwise, we could look at what was in previous documents which is left out of this one.[180] Moreover, we might look at the authorities, or lack of them, cited in the document's footnotes. We could examine the secular trends and phrases that the document chooses to emphasize, the terminology, and the nuances of its usage.

In this document, we find all the intellectual buzz-words of certain political viewpoints—hegemony, liberation, ecology, exploitation, excessive profit, gapism, social sin, North-South, financial and social mechanisms, limited resources, preferential option for the poor, imperialism, distributionism, human rights, and culture. Almost every one of these concepts can have modern overtones which are distinctly detrimental to the ends the Pope proposes, sometimes even to the basic truths and practices of the Catholic faith itself. What is confusing, however, is that within the document, there is very little if any apparent awareness of the inherent dangers of these ideas in their origins or present popular understandings. A certain lack of intellectual rigour some-how seems evident in this document. There are in it, it seems, even mild versions of the disastrous "seamless garment" by which effective action about abortion problems have been neutralized in the United States (#26). There are also traces of the new international communications order which is such a threat to any objective pursuit of news and truth (#22).

Social Sin

We might analyse how ideas and issues dealt with in political philosophy itself are interpreted by this document. The most pressing of these is the discussion of social sin or sinful structures, which the encyclical tries to use (#36). Then again, we could look at the overall picture of the world and the mood that this encyclical conveys. In this latter sense, though, John Paul II tried to maintain an optimistic posture. But the fact remains that this encyclical appears to be a rather negative sounding document on the whole, with little of the openness, and factual basis for it, that can be found in other analyses of the same phenomena (#47).[181] The Holy Father mentioned the relation of development to the Enlightenment notion of inevitable "progress" at a time when development depends, by all our experience, on the initiative and efforts of individual peoples and nations to choose to do what is known to succeed in development (#27).

Originality and Ideology

No doubt the very first difficulty that arises in this encyclical is its conscious effort to base itself on *Populorum Progressio*. We read that this encyclical of Paul VI "captured the attention of public opinion by reason of its originality" (#5). Memories differ, to be sure, but in retrospect, *Populorum Progressio* was certainly the most criticized of all recent papal documents and this precisely because of its dubious ideological overtones. In reading this present document, no indication is given that there were serious problems caused by *Populorum Progressio*. Even Paul VI, to some extent at least, seemed to have been aware of them when he wrote *Octogesima Adveniens* (1971) and *Evangelii Nunciandi* (1975).

Perhaps the most incisive criticism of *Populorum Progressio* came from the leading development economist P. T. Bauer, himself a Catholic, who wrote:

> *Populorum Progressio* and *Octogesima Adveniens* are documents which are immoral on several levels. To begin with they are incompetent, and they are immoral because they are incompetent. Their lack of reflection and ideological commitment leads to proposals and promotes policies directly at variance with the declared sentiments and objectives of the papal documents.[182]

Bauer may or may not have been right, of course, but he put forward serious, well-reasoned arguments against positions taken in *Populorum Progressio* and repeated in the present document.

Sollicitudo Rei Socialis has failed to come to grips with any of Bauer's basic arguments, or with the immense literature supporting his line of thought about development and how it is attained. This lack cannot but leave one uneasy about the thoroughness with which the present document was prepared, or with the means whereby its declared objectives might be attained. There are no footnotes in this document except to previous papal documents and to one United Nations publication, which latter reference (footnote #36), on unemployment figures, seems at best selective and contentious. Indeed, its employment figures are totally inaccurate when compared to the actual number of jobs that have been created in recent years. This critical line of argument seems simply unknown or ignored without evidence by the Holy Father and his advisors.[183] The failure to give any serious attention to positions that would better support exactly what the Pope wants is, for many, unsettling, to say the least.

Quiet Corrections

No doubt, it can be argued that John Paul II was rather more subtle, that he chose *Populorum Progressio* to comment on for his own reasons. In choosing specific themes found in Paul VI's encyclical, he thereby sought to correct quietly the exaggerations and dangers in the earlier statement. For instance, there is, almost for the first time in more recent papal thought, a reluctance in *Sollicitudo Rei Socialis* to speak as if the state were the sole or primary instrument for development, though the principle of subsidiarity had been practically invented by earlier papal encyclicals. Almost all evidence in recent times shows that the state in fact can be and often is, in precisely those nations the Pope was most concerned about, the primary reason for underdevelopment itself.

No one denies, of course, that the state can and ought to have a positive function, and classical Aristotelian-Thomist theory gives ample justification for this. But modern ideological theories about state control of economic development and distribution have in practice almost invariably failed. Even when partially successful in terms of relative GNP, these same theories led to a bureaucratic statism which was hardly an advantage for the citizens of that country. Though John XXIII's *Pacem in Terris* tried to do so, no papal encyclical has really adequately come to terms with the requirement for a limited state in the modern world if we are to achieve both freedom and development. If we want to look for the main causes why development has not taken place at the speed that the Holy Father seems to expect, we should look carefully at the theories of state espoused by many economically backward countries since the Second World War.

Economic Development

In one sense, the twentieth anniversary of *Populorum Progressio* would have been a splendid opportunity to have written a very different kind of encyclical. This different document would have been addressed to "development" but would have been more in tune with the facts and conditions of growth that have proven successful. Though he speaks indirectly of his familiar theme, the Third Millennium, in *Sollicitudo Rei Socialis*, John Paul II somehow does not step back and take a long-range look at the incredible advances that have taken place not only in the past two hundred years but even in the past twenty years, the ostensible period of his immediate concern (#47). John Paul wants to be confident and optimistic, and certainly that seems to be his basic character. "In the context of the sad experiences of recent years and of the mainly negative picture of the present moment, the Church must strongly affirm the possibility of overcoming the obstacles which, by excess or by defect, stand in the way of development" (#47). Yet if we look carefully at the "sad experiences" and the "negative picture" which the Holy Father paints, we cannot avoid worrying about a misunderstanding of what has been and is going on in the world (#13).

The Pope's main concern is with the famous "gap" theory, to which he often returns (#14), but there seems little appreciation of the fact that differing rates of economic growth are the reality, a fact which he should be the first to appreciate. He likewise talks of excessive profits. But he does not talk of profits themselves, of what they are and how they contribute to families and to growth (#38). "The sources of work seem to be shrinking," we are told (#18), whereas the astounding fact is the number of new jobs that have been created in modern times and more particularly in the last twenty years. Little attention is given to this latter but much more significant fact. John Paul II talks about abuse of property, but not, as *Rerum Novarum* did, of its contribution to liberty and development, to family independence and economic initiative (#42). He talks of ecology but seems unaware of the ideological dangers to family rights from this particular source, or of the facts of the so called "limits of resources" problems (#34).[184]

East and West

The Holy Father's social encyclical might best be compared with Solzhenitsyn's 1978 address at Harvard, "A World Split Apart." Solzhenitsyn too had much to say about the decadence of the West, about its intellectual acceptance of autonomous humanism, about the many worlds into which the earth is split.[185] The Holy Father apparently takes the position that the blocs into which the world is currently divided are somehow the direct cause of the problems of poverty to which he devotes this anguished document, rather than the results of real ideological dangers which must be attended to if any possibility for freedom or growth is to prevail. While Solzhenitsyn will agree that there is much materialism or "consumerism" in the West, he makes it clear that there is a substantive issue between the blocs which cannot be ignored.

Solzhenitsyn is not unaware of the Hobbesian problem that has gripped so much Christian thinking in discussions about the dangers of war. This is the position that life is the only thing that counts so that threat of war becomes the instrument to relativize all other and more important values.[186] The development of the world for the sake of the poor must not be indifferent to the fact that we can have a well fed, prosperous world which is tyrannical. We find little if any of this worry in *Sollicitudo Rei Socialis*. The Holy Father has recognized this danger in other contexts and would be expected from his own experience to know that liberty can be suppressed in marxist societies, even where there is, relative to poorer countries, a fairly high living standard.

It is quite understandable for the Pope to call attention to continuing poverty questions in this document. It is also reasonable for him to disclaim, at the same time, responsibility for offering any concrete proposals for its alleviation, on the grounds of the difference between religious or moral authority and economic and political responsibility. But the fact is that enormous development has taken place in modern times and continues to take place. To plead on moral grounds for development and its conditions and not to pay more attention to what has led concretely to development seems to undermine the moral urgency of this treatment.

The problem is not whether we can develop but whether we will accept the means to do so. There is more attention paid in this document to initiative than in any previous papal teaching. This fact shows that some attention has been give to recent analyses. But still the document is dominated by "gapism" and distribution orientations. The signs of understanding wealth production and how it is achieved in practice are few and far between. Indeed, this encyclical's discussion of initiative seems to appear out of context in the structure of the whole presentation, almost as if the parts are unrelated to each other.

An Unsettling Question

In a sense, the most important paragraph in *Sollicitudo Rei Socialis* is the following:

> It is also through these contributions that some Third World countries, despite the burden of many negative factors, have succeeded in reaching a certain self-sufficiency in food, or a degree of industrialization which makes it possible to live with dignity and to guarantee the sources of employment for an active population (#26).

This paragraph (along with #44 on initiative) stands in almost total isolation; this fact seems inexplicable in terms of the general discussion of the encyclical itself. If this document were really intelligently concerned with actual ways to help the poor, it would have begun with this fact of development and of its modern 200 year history.[187] The actual record is much more positive and hopeful than anything in this present document would suggest.

Several years ago, in a passage that could be similarly cited from many other authors, Thomas Sowell wrote:

> Because poverty is one of those things that is simply the absence of something else—wealth, in this case—special care is necessary in analyzing it. Other concepts that are simply the absence of something else—baldness, or a vacuum, for example—refer to an absence of things that occur spontaneously in nature. Wealth does not occur spontaneously in nature. Its presence, rather than its absence, requires explanation—especially since most of today's wealthy nations were poor nations only a few centuries ago. The real question is—what confluence of circumstance produced the fortunate conditions that a relatively small part of the human species enjoys today?[188]

One of the unsettling questions today for the Catholic Church in particular is why is it that non-Christian, non-Western peoples are developing most rapidly and are not following the general ideas reflected in gapism, exploitation theory, anti-profit, or distribution theory found in the present encyclical?

Monumental Force

The force of this document would have been monumental if it had objectively analysed not poverty but wealth production. It could have shown how rapidly nations develop once they understand and do what is necessary. What the Holy

Father wants, can be achieved but only if many of the approaches and ideas supported in this encyclical are modified. They must be changed in the direction of both experience and those notions more clearly espoused in earlier papal documents. The fact is, however, that hardly any papal document has really addressed itself to the issue of wealth and wealth production, its ultimate conditions, and theoretical consequences.

There are, of course, a number of things necessary for wealth production found in the encyclical (#44): the idea that every nation should be responsible for its own development, the idea that no one should expect all growth from outside, that freedom of ideas and information is required. These views, however, were unduly qualified by the attention to native culture which ignores the fact that this same culture may itself be and often is a major obstacle to development.[189]

This problem brings up another issue that is faced only reluctantly and indirectly by the encyclical but which was a normal part of the earlier social teachings of the Church: the truths of revelation which are addressed to reason. There are, within world cultures, irrational ideas and practices which directly militate against development. It is true that development theories can be morally neutral in their own right, something Solzhenitsyn has emphasized as well as John Paul II. But the reverse is also true: local cultures may be based on philosophical or moral positions that make development impossible or difficult. To the extent that this is true we cannot have it both ways by praising both culture and development.

Materialism

A specific notion that seems misunderstood in the encyclical is the idea that wealth consists of raw materials or things rather than ideas and systems of co-operation (#33). The Holy Father, of course, is groping for this idea in his own way. Max Singer's statement seems clearly to be the approach that the Pope needs:

> Two different perceptions about the nature of productive wealth are possible. One perception is the old-fashioned and obvious one: things like fertile land, rich oil deposits, and large stocks of gold are what comprise real wealth. The alternative perception, which is the modern view of productive wealth, is that wealth is mostly intangibles, for example, the characteristics of a people—such as their culture and their education—that enable them to create wealth gradually from whatever things they have. In a word, the modern view is that most productive wealth is not "rocks" but "ideas."
>
> ...If wealth comes from things it is natural to think that the poor can only get wealthy if they get things from rich

countries. And the suspicion is very easy that rich countries' wealth came from taking things that somehow how belonged to, or should have gone to, poor countries... The modern perception of wealth, which sees it as mostly coming from ideas, has a number of happy implications; that wealth is unlimited, that it can be created everywhere at the same time, and that our wealth doesn't conflict with others' wealth but is more likely to add to it.[190]

Many rich countries are very poor in everything but brains and ideas, while other countries have a wealth of raw materials but are quite poor. Why? This phenomenon can be explained by none of the exploitation or distribution theories. Wealth is not normally produced in its modern sense by taking away something from someone else. All through this encyclical the idea of complaint and guilt pervades and confuses. It informs the moral overtone of the document and is, in truth, unnecessary, for it is not what is actually happening. No one would deny that abuses can and do take place. However, if we were to eliminate all the abuses and retain the same erroneous ideas about wealth production, the world would still be poor.

Marxist Exploitation

There is exploitation in a very radical sense, but it is almost wholly related to the political programme of the marxist bloc and its sundry theoretic statist imitators.[191] The creation of wealth means that all get more though at differing rates, not that some take away from others.

Another aspect of this issue is the emphasis in the encyclical on all countries developing at the same time and the primary economic or political attention given to the poorest. Again, at bottom, the accusation that all are not developing at the same pace is based on a mistaken view of how development occurs and of the importance of the developed and even of the "superdeveloped" for those who have least (#28). Max Singer put the opposite view well:

Modern wealth is increasingly based on ideas and organization. People and intangibles are the fundamental and crucial resources, not fields and factories... The poverty that exists is still a challenge and a call to action. But it doesn't call primarily for action against ourselves, nor demand feelings of guilt. Poverty is natural; we did not cause it. Our wealth doesn't deprive the poor countries or stand in their way, it makes it easier for them to follow the track we are making. We're part of the solution, not the problem. Moreover, the task of ending traditional poverty is the opposite of hopeless.[192]

Unfortunately, the encyclical was not written from this standpoint. Such a basis would not have pleased dogmatic socialists but their theories are not working in any case. This alternative perspective would have allowed the encyclical to be freer to address in a positive way every traditional aspect of classical papal doctrine. It could have shed light on the most successful ways to achieve the alleviation of poverty—profit, work, initiative, co-operation, property, small and medium sized organizations, virtue. The one sure way to prevent the development of the poor is to slow down or stop the continued growth of the rich.

Beauty and Bread

There is a curious and hopefully not serious passage in *Sollicitudo Rei Socialis* (#31), which hints that the Church ought to sell its worldly goods, presumably its works of beauty, to aid the poor.[193] In my view this is one of the more unfortunate passages in the whole document since it fails to understand that works of beauty are themselves *generators* of economic growth—witness the millions who come to Italy to see what the Popes had built—and that the poor need beauty *more* than bread. If the Church, which already has its own normal debt, sold its goods and distributed them to the poor—the word used was "superfluous," but in a sense all beauty is superfluous—no one actually would be helped more than momentarily. The action would rightfully be seen by the poor themselves not as an act of nobility but as the disappearance from their lives of that something higher or more noble which the Church has always stood for even for the very poor. It would teach them that man indeed lives by bread alone.

All modern development theory, furthermore, suggests that savings and delayed consumption, even for the poorest, are the primary means of development and that they can and do work. No amount of foreign aid or help will be of much avail if this internal responsibility is not in place.[194] This fact is why the central emphasis that religion might teach with respect to development is self-discipline, sacrifice, and honour. The simple moral virtues which have been a basic subject matter of traditional religious instruction turn out to be the very things most in need of being taught in the area of development. The ideologies which, in the tradition of Rousseau, seek to treat development as only a social project, exempt individuals from any responsibility whatsoever. Yet again and again modern developmental experience has proved conclusively that it is primarily in societies which encourage and allow profit, property, and initiative that development takes place. The real worry is not too many property rights, but too few, if real progress is to be made.[195]

160

Alternative Options

Perhaps a useful way to approach the important issues the encyclical raises is to state what the encyclical maintains or proposes, then to offer an alternative, another option which is both a possible and preferable means for achieving the very end that the encyclical proposes.

Structures of Sin (#36)

Of all the notions in the encyclical, "social sin" is perhaps the most dangerous from a background of Christian thought and political philosophy itself.[196] It is to be noted that the very word "sin" is one from revelation. The encyclical rightly teaches that it is not talking about "corporate guilt" (#37). That is, there is in the literature of this subject the notion of some sort of super person, over and above individual persons, which subsumes the moral responsibility of each in his corporate actions. This encyclical tries to obviate this danger by insisting that all sins are personal.

On the other hand, traditional political philosophy has distinguished regimes in moral terms of good and bad, of better and worse. This form of discussion is already found in Aristotle. It is a much better way to make this point about the relation of institutions and ethical life because it keeps more clearly the distinction between individuals as substances and societies as relations. Aristotle's discussion of "general justice" is really what the notion "social sin" tries to explain, that is, how each act can affect the common good. Aristotle would have understood that all specific actions of an oligarchical society, for example, are deformed in some sense because of their chosen end. On the other hand, he would have understood that there are things worse than oligarchies so that one must be careful how one treats habitual social orders. Bad societies can change into worse societies. This "worse case" is a primary experience of modern revolutionary movements which fail to understand change in political or economic regimes. The classic treatment of regimes as forms of government with their own moral classification is far superior and less confusing than the notion of social or corporate sin, or structures of sin, when drawing attention to ways of acting within a civil society.

Human Rights (#15, 26, 28)

The modern popes have apparently used this phrase with little attention to the original meaning of the term. We can with some care use this phrase to mean what St. Thomas meant by natural law as it is manifest in each individual action. Here it retains its objectivity. However, the term "right" is a product of modern philosophy and, unless constantly and carefully distinguished, will be understood in terms of modern political philosophy, with often disastrous consequences for the faith. Naturally, it is useful to say that governments are formed to protect our rights and that many governments do not do this, so it is easy to condemn them in the name of rights.

However, the term "right" means something quite independent of any natural order. It means just what the possessor can gain for himself. "Rights" are presupposed in relation to nothing. Their content comes from one's will or the will of the collectivity. The reason the Church is constantly under siege from modern "rights" theories, and will be so long as it continues this terminology, is because it uses the term itself as if it were a word with content from natural law. However, when people speak of a "right" to abortion or to homosexual practices, the Church is defenceless because the terminology it uses in what appear to be clear and agreed cases is really terminology which can admit any content that promotes any sort of individual or social practice. The "defence" of human rights thus ends up defending what cannot be defended. Since human rights mean that which anyone or any society chooses or intends them to mean from an autonomous will, someone can always will something that is not based, in the Church's tradition, on an objectively right order.

Consumerism and Excessive Profits (#28, 37)

In this encyclical, the term consumerism is a pejorative word which is based on the "limited earth" theory. Indulgent consumption is not wrong because of what it does to oneself but because of what it deprives others of in some kind of limited resources theory. If the Holy Father had stuck to the more classical word "greed," it would have been more appropriate if what he had in mind was only the inordinate use of material goods. The word "consumer" is a perfectly good one, and it is a pity to see it used as some sort of substitute for greed. A consumer is someone who creates a demand for a product. Products only exist if there are demands from consumers for them. In other words, we cannot have a modern productive economy without consumers. And all consumers have their own proper lives which are more than mere consumption. "Pure consumers" more closely describes persons in a non-dynamic society. The multiplicity of goods in the world is not in itself an evil but rather a good which, through the market, can draw people into work, which is something the Holy Father wants. George Gilder has written in this sense:

> During the 1980's, a huge gulf opened in the perception of the U. S. economy. On the one side stood the media, the economics profession, and much of the governmental bureaucracy. Because these forces largely shape the public's image of the world, their vision came to dominate public opinion. It was, in general, a profoundly pessimistic view: a scene of economic stagnation, declining productivity, low employment, scarce resources, soaring deficits, rampant

bankruptcies, a diminished America, a cramped and con-
flicted future, even a new great depression.

On the other side of this gulf was a force that is best
summed up as the commercial imagination: the collective
view of the particular entrepreneurs—some 16 million
strong—who will largely shape the growth and define the
future of the U. S. economy.

They continued to create new businesses at a rate of
some 600,000 a year: more than six times the average for the
stable 1950's, some three times the pace of the flourishing
1960's, and more than twenty times the ballyhooed rate of
bankruptcies. Entrepreneurs inspired a venture capital industry that achieved its first billion dollar year in 1981...
They sustained a rate of employment—nearly 58 percent of
the adult population— close to the highest peacetime levels.
They continued—entirely beyond the ken of productivity
statistics—to foster a technological revolution that is ending
the resource and energy crises of the world and increasingly
the real productivity of the U. S. economy at a pace unprece-
dented in our history.[197]

Too often, however, the Pope seems to speak of work as if it is somehow for
its own sake, no matter what the product produced (#18). Moreover, the relation
of work and leisure in its higher senses requires more analysis. To use the word
"work" of intellectual and religious pursuits creates problems.

Workers, the Pope understands, do not want to work in a vacuum. They
want to do something valuable, to be caught up in something of objective value
for everyone. This value is expressed by the price someone is willing to pay for
a product. In a world where innovators and workers can respond to the demand
for given products, they can produce them at a cost which is known as wages
and profits. Without profits no one would organize a company to produce the
product. Profit is not a bad word. The very market workings normally tend to
balance demand and prices. The word "consumerism" should be dropped and
some adequate discussion of the meaning of profit be placed in the encyclicals.[198] The only real alternative to a system of profits is a system of state
control. But modern history has again and again shown that this latter option
does not work to produce the goods and services the people need and want, at
a price that they can afford.

Scarce Resources (#34)

Quite simply, there is no danger of running out of resources. There are no finite
limits as far as we know to how much or how many different raw materials we
need. As Julian Simon wrote in this context:

> Our supplies of natural resources are not finite in any
> economic sense. Nor does past experience give reason to
> expect natural resources to become more scarce. Rather, if
> the past is any guide, natural resources will progressively
> become less scarce, and less costly, and will constitute a
> smaller proportion of our expenses in future years. And
> population growth is likely to have a long-run beneficial
> impact on the natural-resource situation.[199]

The very working out of the notion that wealth is ideas, not things, makes
obsolete this discussion of the limits of earth as a moral criterion for us to limit
growth. The limits of growth thesis is not only a major way for anti-life ideology
to enter modern society, it is a restriction on growth. Pollution, another worry
of the Pope (#34), will be met by nothing other than the same innovation that
causes the problem in the first place.

Options for the Poor (#42)

"Options for the poor" is another unfortunate phrase. In so far as it reflects the
notion that the poor exist and need to know how not to be poor, it can be
tolerated. But, as we have seen, it also can have other less desirable meanings.
It can mean that the poor are legitimate subjects of the state which is responsible
for taking care of them in state institutions. Dependent poor give states moral
justification for their controlling actions, instead of freeing people to live their
own productive lives.[200] It can mean a skewering of the economy so that
nothing is really done for the poor to enable them to learn and practise ways to
become productive. The phrase unfortunately looks on the poor as a sort of
passive lot out there of whom somebody must take care. The moral justification
for those who "take care" of the poor is thus secured, no matter whether this
concern or care really does the poor any good or not.

Yet, as Peter Berger has pointed out, if we are really interested in helping
the poor and not the governments that control them, we should incorporate them
into something that very much looks like democratic capitalism, the only
system that has actually worked for the poor.[201] Perhaps, for political reasons,
because of his even-handedness with both ideological systems, as he calls them,
the Holy Father cannot pronounce such a judgment (#20). But failure to
acknowledge what really works must appear to most onlookers to this discussion as a kind of ideology itself. George Gilder's reflection seems pertinent
here:

> Throughout history, most of mankind has lived cramped and
> impoverished lives in materially affluent countries because
> of an absence of the metaphysical capital that is most crucial
> to progress: the trust in others, the hope for the future, the

> faith in a providential God that allows freedom and prompts
> the catalytic gifts of capitalism.[202]

In this sense, social documents should pay considerably more attention to what are properly philosophical and theological issues precisely to aid the poor.

Earth Meant for All (#9, 26)

The phrase "the Earth is meant for all" is from either *Genesis* or Aristotle, or from natural law theory. Historically it refers to the classical Aristotelian discussion of why all things were best not to be in common, together with the idea that the goods of the earth were meant for all, but that private ownership or initiative would be the best way for the goods to be produced and distributed. We can say that with the advent of modern economies, a relatively short period in human history, it is now literally possible for the goods of the earth to serve the needs of all, wherever they are, provided they enter into the modern world itself. The normal and best way for everyone to receive the needed goods is through participation in the money economy as a result of goods made available through the international and national market. A good deal of attention, however, is paid to deformities in international trade (#43), but until these deformities be more specifically noted so that they can be judged properly, it is difficult to know just what these imbalances are, or who causes them. The terms "counterproductive mechanisms" (#19) and "social mechanisms" (#15) bear the same mysteriously undefined overtones. They make one wonder just what these evils are that bear so heavy a load of apparent responsibility for the condition of the poor.

Gapism and Distributionism (#9, 14)

This encyclical concentrates on the idea that what counts in moral terms is not that everyone is getting richer but that some are getting richer faster. By doing so much of the moral focus misses both the tremendous advances that are being made and the means to make them. If the image one has is of a world in which every extra dollar is suddenly required to go from the richest to the poorest, the result would be that everyone would soon be poor. The actual process of growth is the systematic and gradual entrance of individuals and peoples into the rewards and savings of the wealth producing areas.

In the course of probably four centuries beginning in 1776, everyone will have accomplished this transition from poverty to wealth, provided the ways of this growth be allowed to operate in the poorer countries. In many ways this is an astonishingly short period of time.[203] The emphasis on distribution rather than production itself both enhances and distorts the moral passion for the lot of the poor. Distribution theory is usually based on a finite resource concept rather than on one which sees distribution as a major productive enterprise requiring markets, initiative, a limited state, and willingness to work. Every indication exists that the distance between the rich and the poor normally becomes quite large when everyone grows comparatively richer.

The War Problem (#10)

No doubt the devotion of much thought, energy, and money to war preparations will make it seem that this money and effort would be better spent for the poor. On the other hand, the ideological differences are not unimportant but essential to grasp in their consequences, especially if we wish to help the poor. The Holy Father speaks of "refugees" (#25), and it is noteworthy that the refugees in the modern world go only in one direction, from unfreedom to freedom and from unproductive societies to productive ones. These distinctions are not a matter of indifference.

Practically nothing that is produced for war does not have some effect for peace, including the prevention of war itself. One does not need to think this is a necessary evil in itself. But the fact remains that research for war has been a major contribution to peace and to our abilities to aid mankind. Successful war preparation, moreover, is that which achieves its purpose of preventing war, and is thus not used. By not taking the import of the real ideological differences on this planet seriously enough, this document gives the impression that the differences are merely superficial, petulant, and of no real consequence for development. This is far from the case. The energies that force free men to protect their societies are themselves noble. War production like any other production really does not take away from the poor.

War materials simply would not exist without a really defined and apparent threat, and a conscious political will to resist it. In lieu of this, the energies that went into war may or may not have materialized. The frequent suppositions that war is the real problem, or that it is easy to ignore the real ideological differences symbolized by war efforts, do not really aid the poor in the long run. The poor will be both rich and free provided certain forms of government are put into place, provided certain notions of science, economics, and wealth are accepted. Otherwise, the poor will remain and the threats of war will remain with whatever the level of technology available, for this latter is not itself the cause of the problems.

Common Good (#38, 47)

In this document, the Holy Father urges us to take into consideration the common good of the whole world in all our economic activities, to be sure that they help the less fortunate. One can wonder in what sense this is intended. In the classic discussion of this issue, it was clear that a distinction existed between willing the common good and working for the actual achievement of it.[204] Individuals have to pursue their own works and lives in the concrete. If each person is concerned about the common good in its formal content, he will end up doing almost nothing. This encyclical seems to demand that everyone know exactly what the common good of the world entails in his individual life and that each person be responsible for achieving it. This approach not only places an impossible burden on each individual's judgement, but it fails to stress what each one can actually do. The more classical papal emphasis on property and subsidiarity was a much better way in which to discuss the common good precisely as a way to help others. Another problem of greater seriousness than this encyclical acknowledges, though it does seem aware of it, is whether the present international organizations are in fact adequate or rightly oriented to the real needs of mankind.

Conclusion

These are, in conclusion, the problems that arise with this encyclical. A number of reaffirmations in it, particularly those concerning human life and initiative, are especially valuable. Clearly the Pope knows about and mentions the problems of eugenics and totalitarianism. What is no doubt the most disappointing aspect of this encyclical is not merely the ease with which its approach and terminology can be appropriated by systems and ideas quite hostile to the higher and even worldly ends of Christianity but especially the missed opportunity to see the positive side of what has been happening. There are astonishing developments that need to be understood and, yes, praised. What is striking about the world is not its remaining poverty but its growing wealth production capacities that are almost totally in conformity with the main lines of Catholic thought at its best. To picture this development as something negative could easily take the heart out of efforts to accomplish exactly what the Holy Father has in mind.

With all of his thought about the coming Millennium, it seems strange that the Holy Father did not put this encyclical in a more open and dynamic context. On the other hand, the themes of apocalypse and terminal times in a religious sense are also pertinent, and are ones left mainly to fundamentalist Protestants to develop, ones that find very little guidance from the Magisterium. Likewise, the theme of leisure and life in a world-wide abundant society requires much comment from the more metaphysical and spiritual side of Catholic tradition. The present concentration on what is not being done leaves Christians unarmed for what will be their real future. To reconcile Josef Pieper on the higher religious and cultural ends of leisure with the Holy Father's insistence on work, for example, remains rather difficult.[205] Much more needs to be said on this topic. But Max Singer is probably closer to the truth when he suggests that the primary issue we will worry about is not wealth production for everyone but what does life mean once wealth is produced. The Holy Father is the one to whom we ought to look most for the perplexing answers to this kind of question.

The nature of his analysis of poverty prevents him from adequately addressing himself to this, ultimately, more pressing problem.

Modernity

No one should doubt, that John Paul II, like Solzhenitsyn, Leo Strauss, Eric Voegelin, and others, has understood that there is something distinctly distorted in modernity. On the other hand, that which is most valuable in the efforts of modernity, the very capacity to remove the poverty which all peoples almost up to this century have known as a normal part of their lives, is something that can be celebrated provided that it come about in liberty and law. Our century has produced some of the worst tyrannies in human history, some of which unhappily still exist. The failure of the Holy See to address itself frankly in this document to the issues so well elaborated in Pius XI's *Divini Redemptoris* has made it seem that the dangers from marxism cannot be identified or treated directly, both politically and religiously. Perhaps it can be argued, as the Holy Father seems to in the present document, that this is merely a side issue. However, the truth is that until this issue is faced more directly, the problems of development and growth will remain confusing and dangerous. We may well end up with growth and no freedom, if not no growth and no freedom either, which seems closer to the record of the socialist economies in general.

Catholic Social Teaching

Sollicitudo Rei Socialis must now be considered to belong to the corpus of what is known as Catholic social teaching.[206] It will no doubt be remembered mainly as a document which was strangely out of date and out of tune with what actually could have achieved its main objectives. It will be seen as finally recognizing that there is some basic aspect ever missing in Catholic social thinking—attention to wealth production and the political, moral, and economic structures, ideas, and virtues that cause it to come about. Yet its treatment of this very issue of wealth production will be seen as isolated and framed within other considerations that would make any wealth production and distribution largely impossible. Pessimistically, this document could be seen as retrogressive, even granting some points in it well worth considering.

Yet John Paul II is, of all the public figures of our era, the one intellectually most competent and most likely to learn if he can give enough attention to a problem to think it through. No one can be in the least critical because he is concerned about the poor. This truly great man and pope has seen more poor people than perhaps any other public figure of our time or any other time. For him not to be concerned about them would betray a hard heart that is simply not his. But this document must also be considered in its analyses and proposals. Here, in many ways, the proposals for poverty alleviation do not match the problem. Too frequently, they ignore the solutions that are now generally known. If there is any challenge presented by this document, it is not that of the Holy Father inciting the prosperous to help the poor. It is rather the already prosperous guiding the Holy Father to the known recipe for accomplishing the end he so much desires.

Chapter 26

Conclusion

The relation between what we believe and what we do is very close. These comments, stories, reflections, and analyses have all, in one way or another, been efforts to follow up ideas that have appeared about wealth, poverty, and religion. I have held, in general, that the apparent conversion of much of religion to concerns about economics and politics has not been a healthy one because of the attendant ideological formulations. But there is no cloud without a silver lining. This whole trend has enabled us to better consider the meaning of religion and how it can contribute to the well-being of mankind. A concern about poverty is not in itself a bad thing. Far from it. But neither is it a good thing if this concern be expressed, knowingly or unknowingly, in ideological terms which cannot aid the poor in a way that preserves their individual dignity and freedom.

What seems curious is that a good number of the ideas and institutions in economics and politics, which have actually contributed to economic progress and political freedom, have been appreciated in classic and Christian religious sources all along. On the other hand, the clarification of ideas for the higher public good requires that religion concern itself first with the transcendent questions of faith and how these affect individual lives at a level that is not merely political. The key teachings of religion about human worth, everlasting destiny, virtue, freedom, the value of nature, and the power of human will, also turn out to be those most required for a sane and limited social order. Such a social order can be prosperous and just, but not if it is filled with ideas about absolute claims by the state on mankind's being. In the end, religion will not be "dangerous" as long as it conceives its task as that of conforming itself to the ideologies, however expressed. It will only be dangerous when it relearns in the personal and public order what its supernatural mission is. Paradoxically, this "dangerousness" will also turn out to be religion's main contribution to public peace, prosperity, and dignity.

Appendix

Prime Minister Margaret Thatcher's Speech to the General Assembly of the Church of Scotland on Saturday, 21 May 1988

Introduction

Moderator and Members of the Assembly. I am greatly honoured to have been invited to attend the opening of this 1988 General Assembly of the Church of Scotland; and I am deeply grateful that you have now asked me to address you.

I am very much aware of the historical continuity extending over four centuries, during which the position of the Church of Scotland has been recognised in constitutional law and confirmed by successive Sovereigns. It sprang from the independence of mind and rigour of thought that have always been such powerful characteristics of the Scottish people. It has remained close to its roots and has inspired a commitment to service from *all* people.

I am therefore very sensible of the important influence which the Church of Scotland exercises in the life of the whole nation, both at the spiritual level and through the extensive caring services which are provided by your Church's department of social responsibility.

Christianity—Spiritual and Social

Perhaps it would be best if I began by speaking personally as a Christian, as well as a politician, about the way I see things. Reading recently I came across the starkly simple phrase: "Christianity is about spiritual redemption, not social reform."

Sometimes the debates on these matters have become too polarised and given the impression that the two are quite separate.

Most Christians would regard it as their personal Christian duty to help their fellow men and women. They would regard the lives of children as a precious trust. These duties come not from any secular legislation passed by Parliament, but from being a Christian.

But there are a number of people who are not Christians who would also accept those responsibilities. What then are the distinctive marks of Christianity?

They stem not from the social but from the spiritual side of our lives. I would identify three beliefs in particular.

First, that from the beginning man has been endowed by God with the fundamental right to choose between good and evil.

Second, that we were made in God's own image and therefore we are expected to use all our own power of thought and judgement in exercising that choice; and further, if we open our hearts to God, He has promised to work within us.

And third, that Our Lord Jesus Christ The Son of God, when faced with His terrible choice and lonely vigil *chose* to lay down His life that our sins may be forgiven. I remember very well a sermon on an Armistice Sunday when our Preacher said "No one took away the life of Jesus, He chose to lay it down."

I think back to many discussions in my early life when we all agreed that if you try to take the fruits of Christianity without its roots, the fruits will wither. And they will not come again unless you nurture the roots.

But we must not profess the Christian faith and go to Church simply because we want social reforms and benefits or a better standard of behaviour—but because we accept the sanctity of life, the responsibility that comes with freedom and the supreme sacrifice of Christ expressed so well in the hymn:

> *When I survey the wondrous Cross*
> *On which the Prince of glory died,*
> *My richest gain I count but loss,*
> *And pour contempt on all my pride.*

Bible Principles—Relevance to Political Life

May I also say a few words about my personal belief in the relevance of Christianity to public policy—to the things that are Caesar's?

The Old Testament lays down in *Exodus* the Ten Commandments as given to Moses, the injunction in *Leviticus* to love our neighbour as ourselves and generally the importance of observing a strict code of law. The New Testament is a record of the Incarnation, the teachings of Christ and the establishment of the Kingdom of God. Again we have the emphasis on loving our neighbour as ourselves and to "Do-as-you-would-be-done-by."

I believe that by taking together these key elements from the Old and New Testaments, we gain a view of the universe, a proper attitude to work and principles to shape economic and social life. We are told we must work and use our talents to create wealth. "If a man will not work he shall not eat" wrote St. Paul to the Thessalonians.

Indeed, abundance rather than poverty has a legitimacy which derives from the very nature of Creation.

Nevertheless, the Tenth Commandment—Thou shalt not covet—recognizes that making money and owning things could become selfish activities. But it is not the creation of wealth that is wrong but love of money for its own sake. The spiritual dimension comes in deciding what one does with the wealth. How could we respond to the many calls for help, or invest for the future, or support the wonderful artists and craftsmen whose work also glorifies God, unless we had first worked hard and used our talents to create the necessary wealth? And remember the woman with the alabaster jar of ointment.

I confess that I always had difficulty with interpreting the Biblical precept to love our neighbours "as ourselves" until I read some of the words of C.S. Lewis. He pointed out that we don't exactly love *ourselves* when we fall below the standards and beliefs we have accepted. Indeed we might even *hate* ourselves for some unworthy deed.

Political Action and Personal Responsibilities

None of this, of course, tells us exactly what kind of political and social institutions we should have. On this point, Christians will very often genuinely disagree, though it is a mark of Christian manners that they will do so with courtesy and mutual respect. What is certain, however, is that any set of social and economic arrangements which is not founded on the acceptance of individual responsibility will do nothing but harm. We are all responsible for our own actions. We cannot blame society if we disobey the law. We simply cannot delegate the exercise of mercy and generosity to others. The politicians and other secular powers should strive by their measures to bring out the good in people and to fight down the bad: but they can't create the one or abolish the other. They can only see that the laws encourage the *best* instincts and convictions of the people, instincts and convictions which I am convinced are far more deeply rooted than is often supposed.

Nowhere is this more evident than the basic ties of the family which are at the heart of our society and are the very nursery of civic virtue.

It is on the family that we in government build our own policies for welfare, education and care.

You recall that Timothy was warned by St. Paul that anyone who neglects to provide for his own house (meaning his own family) has disowned the faith and is "worse than an infidel."

We must recognize that modern society is infinitely more complex than that of Biblical times and of course new occasions teach new duties. In our generation, the only way we can ensure that no-one is left without sustenance, help or opportunity, is to have laws to provide for health and education, pensions for the elderly, succour for the sick and disabled.

But intervention by the State must never become so great that it effectively removes personal responsibility. The same applies to taxation for while you and I would work extremely hard whatever the circumstances, there are undoubtedly some who would not unless the incentive was there. And we need *their* efforts too.

Religious Education

Moderator, recently there have been great debates about religious education. I believe strongly that politicians must see that religious education has a proper place in the school curriculum.

In Scotland as in England there is an historic connection expressed in our laws between Church and State. The two connections are of a somewhat different kind, but the arrangements in both countries are designed to give symbolic expression to the same crucial truth—that the Christian religion—which, of course, embodies many of the great spiritual and moral truths of Judaism—is a fundamental part of our national heritage. I believe it is the wish of the overwhelming majority of people that this heritage should be preserved and fostered. For centuries it has been our very life blood. Indeed we are a nation whose ideals are founded on the Bible.

Also, it is quite impossible to understand our history or literature without grasping this fact. *That* is the strong practical case for ensuring that children at school are given adequate instruction in the part which the Judaic-Christian tradition has played in moulding our laws, manners and institutions. How can you make sense of Shakespeare and Sir Walter Scott, or of the constitutional conflicts of the 17th century in both Scotland and England, without some such fundamental knowledge?

But I go further than this. The truths of the Judaic-Christian tradition are infinitely precious, not only, as I believe, because they are true, but also because they provide the moral impulse which alone can lead to that peace, in the true meaning of the word, for which we all long.

Tolerance

To assert absolute moral values is not to claim perfection for ourselves. No true Christian could do that. What is more, one of the great principles of our Judaic-Christian inheritance is tolerance.

People with other faiths and cultures have always been welcomed in our land, assured of equality under the law, of proper respect and of open friendship.

There is absolutely nothing incompatible between this and our desire to maintain the essence of our own identity. There is no place for racial or religious intolerance in our creed.

Christians and Democracy

When Abraham Lincoln spoke in his famous Gettysburg speech of 1863 of "government of the people, by the people, and for the people," he gave the world a neat definition of democracy which has since been widely and enthusiastically adopted. But what he enunciated as a form of government was not in itself especially Christian, for nowhere in the Bible is the word democracy mentioned. Ideally, when Christians meet, as Christians, to take counsel together their purpose is not (or should not be) to ascertain what is the mind of the majority but what is the mind of the Holy Spirit something which may be quite different.

Nevertheless I am an enthusiast for democracy. And I take that position, not because I believe majority opinion is inevitably right or true, indeed no majority can take away God-given human rights. But because I believe it most effectively safeguards the value of the individual, and, more than any other system, restrains the abuse of power by the few. And that *is* a Christian concept.

But there is little hope for democracy if the hearts of men and women in democratic societies cannot be touched by a call to something greater than themselves. Political structures, state institutions, collective ideals are not enough. *We* Parliamentarians can legislate for the rule of *law. You* the Church can teach the life of faith.

Conclusion

For, when all is said and done, a politician's role is a humble one. I always think that the whole debate about the Church and the State has never yielded anything comparable in insight to that beautiful hymn "I vow to thee my country." It begins with a triumphant assertion of what might be described as secular patriotism, a noble thing indeed in a country like ours: "I vow to thee my country all earthly things above; entire, whole and perfect the service of my love." It goes on to speak of "another country I heard of long ago" whose King cannot be seen and whose armies cannot be counted, but "soul by soul and silently her shining bounds increase." Not group by group or party by party or even church by church—but soul by soul—and each one counts.

That, members of the Assembly, is the country which you chiefly serve. You fight your cause under the banner of an historic church. Your success matters greatly—as much to the temporal as to the spiritual welfare of the nation. May we all come nearer to that other country whose "ways are ways of gentleness and all her paths are peace."

Notes

1. *U.S. News* (10 Jan. 1983).
2. George Gilder, "The Commercial Imagination," *Public Opinion* (Oct.-Nov. 1982), p. 60.
3. Henri Pirenne, *Economic and Social History of Europe* (New York: Harvest 1933).
4. *The Compass*, More Agriculture Journal, Dayton, Ohio (Winter 1980-1), p.11.
5. Jean-François Revel, "How Well Is the Third World Governed?" *Wall Street Journal* (5 Nov. 1981). See Revel's *How Democracies Perish* (New York: Harper 1985).
6. P.T. Bauer, *Western Guilt and Third World Poverty* (Washington: Ethics and Public Policy Center 1976).
7. Theodore Schultz, "The Economics of Being Poor," *Journal of Political Economy*, #4 (1980), pp.644-5.
8. Julian Simon, *The Ultimate Resource* (Princeton: Princeton University Press 1981). See also Jacqueline Kasun, *The War Against Population* (San Francisco: Ignatius 1988), chapter 2.
9. *National Catholic Register* Review of Books (July 1982). See Christopher Derrick, *Too Many People?* (San Francisco: Ignatius 1985).
10. Yair Aharoni, *The No-Risk Society* (Chatham NJ: Chatham House 1981), p.1.
11. *The Wealth of Families*, ed. Carl Anderson (Washington: American Family Institute 1982). See series of Allan C. Carlson, *The Family in America* (Rockford, IL: Rockford Institute 1987 ff).
12. Christopher Dawson, *Essays in Order* (London: Sheed and Ward 1934).
13. Edmund Burke, *Reflections on the Revolution in France* (Chicago: Gateway 1955), p. 91.
14. *Dives in Misericordia*, (1980), #12.
15. P.T. Bauer and Barbara Ward, *Two Views on Developing Countries* (London: Institute on Economic Affairs 1966). See P.T. Bauer, *Western Guilt and Third World Poverty* (Washington: Ethics and Public Policy Centre 1976); P.T. Bauer and B. Yamey, "Economics and the Third World," *Current* (Nov. 1982), pp. 46-59.
16. Testimony before House Committee on Banking, Finance and Urban Affairs, 1982.
17. Maurice Cranston, *What Are Human Rights?* (New York: Taplinger 1975), p. 65. See also Henry Veatch, *Human Rights: Fact or Fancy?* (Baton Rouge: Louisiana State University Press 1985); James V. Schall, "Human Rights as an Ideological Project," *American Journal of Jurisprudence*, 32 (1987), pp. 47-61.

18. Stanley Jaki, "From Scientific Cosmology to Created Universe," Lecture to the Discussion Club of St. Louis, November 7, 1986. See his *The Road of Science and the Ways to God* (Chicago: University of Chicago Press 1978); *Chance or Reality* (Lanham, MD: University Press of America 1986).

19. *St. Louis Globe* (17 May 1982).

20. *National Review* (26 June 1981). See Joseph Sobran, *Single Issues* (New York: Human Life Press 1982).

21. Igor Shafarevich, *The Socialist Phenomenon* (New York: Harper 1980), p. 79.

22. Walker Percy, *Love in the Ruins* (New York: Avon 1971), pp. 144-5.

23. G.K. Chesterton, "The Book of Job," *Selected Essays* (London: Methuen 1949), p. 103.

24. Phyllis McGinley, "Subversive Reflections," *Times Three* (New York: Viking 1961), p. 196.

25. Russell Kirk, Lecture, Washington, Heritage (29 Apr.), 1982. See Russell Kirk, *Reclaiming a Patrimony* (Washington: Heritage 1982).

26. *San Francisco Chronicle* (3 June 1982).

27. Flannery O'Connor, *The Habit of Being* (New York: Viking 1979).

28. Personal correspondence.

29. Hilaire Belloc, *The Path to Rome* (Garden City, NY: Doublday Image 1956), pp. 214-16.

30. Stephen Chapman, "Killing for Christ," *New Republic* (21 Oct. 1978).

31. See C. Zowell Nanniss, *Selected Readings* (Englewood Cliffs, NJ: Prentice-Hall 1967).

32. See "How Shoplifting is Draining the Economy," *Business Week*, (15 Oct. 1979), p. 119.

33. See Ellen Wilson, *An Even Dozen* (New York: The Human Life Press 1982).

34. See Walter Block, *On Economics and the Canadian Bishops* (Vancouver: The Fraser Institute 1983), document of Canadian Bishops pp. 68-76.

35. Personal correspondence.

36. Michael Novak, "The Right to Development," *Rethinking Human Rights* (Washington: The Foundation for Economic Education 1982), II, pp. 21-8.

37. *The Monitor*, San Francisco, (25 Aug. 1983).

38. *Commentary*, (Oct. 1981).

39. John Naisbitt, *Megatrends* (New York: Warner 1982), p. 250.

40. *Commentary*, (Aug. 1983).

41. Joseph Sobran, *Crucial Issue Politics*, (New York: National Committee for Catholic Laymen 1981), p. 10.

42. See E.B.F. Midgley, *The Natural Law Tradition and the Theory of International Relations* (London: Elek 1975), John Finnis, *Natural Law and Natural Right* (New York: Oxford University Press 1980); Henry Veatch, "Natural Law: Dead or Alive?," *Literature of Liberty* (Oct.-Dec. 1978), pp. 7-31.

43. See, for example, Stuart Gudowitz, "Neo-Modernist Economic Theology," *New Oxford Review* (Dec. 1982), pp. 30-1, and Peter Steinfels, "Michael Novak and His Ultrasuper Democraticapitalism," *The Commonweal,* (14 Jan. 1983), pp. 11-16. See also the review of Novak, James V. Schall, *Fidelity* (Sept. 1982), pp. 28-9.

44. See James V. Schall, "Religious Teaching on Economics: Catholicism and the American Experience," *The Best of 'This World,'* ed. Michael Scully (Lanham MD: University Press of America, 1986), pp. 1-13; and "Christianity and the Cures of Poverty," in *Christianity and Politics* (Boston: St. Paul Editions 1981), pp. 178-212.

45. See James V. Schall, *Church, State, and Society in the Thought of John Paul II* (Chicago: Franciscan Herald Press 1982). See also Andrew Woznicki, *Karol Wojtyla's Existential Personalism* (New Britain: Mariel 1980); *The Dignity of Man As A Person: Essays on the Christian Humanism of John Paul II* (San Francisco: Society of Christ 1987).

46. George Hunston Williams, *The Mind of John Paul II* (New York: Seabury 1981); and Paul Johnson, *Pope John Paul II* and the Catholic Restoration (New York: St. Martin's 1981).

47. Allan Bloom, "Our Listless Universities," *National Review* (10 Dec. 1982). See also his translation, *The Republic* (New York: Basic Books 1968); *The Closing of the American Mind* (New York: Simon & Schuster 1987).

48. Leo Strauss, *The City and Man* (Chicago: University of Chicago Press 1964), introduction.

49. Roger Heckel, *Self-Reliance*; *The Human Person and Social Structures*; *Religious Freedom*; *General Aspects of the Social Catechesis of John Paul II* (Vatican City: Pontifical Commission on Justice and Peace 1978-80).

50. John Paul II, "Perennial Philosophy of St. Thomas for the Youth of Our Time," in *The Whole Truth About Man: John Paul II to University Faculties and Students,* ed. James Schall (Boston: St. Paul Editions 1981), pp. 209-27.

51. Harry Jaffa, "Leo Strauss: 1899-1973," in *The Conditions of Freedom* (Baltimore: The Johns Hopkins University Press 1975), pp. 3-8; See also James V. Schall, *Reason, Revelation, and the Foundations of Political Philosophy* (Baton Rouge: Louisiana State University Press 1987).

52. See James V. Schall, "On the Pertinence of a Catholic Intelligence," *Center Journal* (Fall 1982), pp. 101-18; and "Of Doctrine and Dignity:

From Heretics to Othodoxy," *Another Sort of Learning* (San Francisco: Ignatius 1988), pp. 92-111.

53. See Alexander Solzhenitsyn, "A World Split Apart," in *Solzhenitsyn at Harvard*, ed. R. Berman (Washington: Ethics and Public Policy Center 1980), pp. 3-22.

54. Shafarevich, *The Socialist Phenomenon*.

55. See Leo Strauss, *Natural Right and History* (Chicago: University of Chicago Press 1952). See also Leo Strauss, "The Three Waves of Modernity," in *Essays on Political Philosophy*, ed. H. Gilden (New York: Bobbs-Merrill 1975).

56. See Charles N.R. McCoy, *The Structure of Political Thought* (New York: McGraw-Hill 1963). Cf. also James V. Schall "Political Theory, Religion, and War," in *Catholicism-in-Crisis* (Jan. 1983), pp. 19-22.

57. See James V. Schall, "Revelation, Reason, and Politics: Catholic Reflections on Strauss," *Gregorianum*, Rome #2 and #3 (1981).

58. See Joseph Cropsey, "The United States as a Regime," in *Political Philosophy and the Issues of Politics* (Chicago: University of Chicago Press 1977), pp. 1-18. See also Frederick D. Wilhelmsen, "The Enemies of Faith Today" (Reston, VA: YAF 1981).

59. See Gerhard Niemeyer, "The Autonomous Man," *The Intercollegiate Review*, (Summer 1974), pp. 131-7. See also Schall, "Atheism and Politics," in *Christianity and Politics*, chapter 4.

60. See Leo Strauss, "The Crisis of Political Philosophy," in *The Predicament of Modern Politics*, ed. H. Spaeth (Detroit: University of Detroit Press 1964).

61. See Leo Strauss, "The Mutual Influence of Theology and Philosophy," *Independent Journal of Philosophy* (1979).

62. See Frederick Wilhelmsen, *Christianity and Political Philosophy* (Athens: University of Georgia Press 1980), chapter 8.

63. Strauss, *City and Man*, introduction.

64. See Frederick Wilhelmsen, "Faith and Reason," *Modern Age*, 23 (Winter 1979) pp. 25-32.

65. Paul Sigmund "Thomistic Natural Law amd Social Theory," *Calgary Aquinas Studies*, ed. Anthony Parel, (Toronto, Pontifical Medieval Institute 1978,) pp. 65-76.

66. Citation is found on last page of Strauss, *City and Man*.

67. Jaffa, "Strauss: 1899-1973."

68. Ibid.

69. See Strauss, *City and Man*, introduction.

70. See Jaki, *The Road of Science*.

71. Hannah Arendt, *The Human Condition* (Garden City: Doubleday Anchor 1959), pp. 155-224.

72. See Introduction to Ralph Lerner and Muhsin Mahdi, *Medieval Political Philosophy* (Ithaca: Cornell University Press 1963), pp. 1-21.

73. See Christopher Dawson, *Religion and the Rise of Western Culture* (Garden City: Doubleday Image 1959), *The Making of Europe* (New York: Meridian 1965); *Religion and Culture* (New York: Meridian 1948).

74. See Etienne Gilson, *Reason and Revelation in the Middle Ages* (New York: Scribner's 1938); Jacques Maritain, *Integral Humanism* (Notre Dame: University of Notre Dame Press 1973); Joseph Pieper, *The Silence of St. Thomas* (Chicago: Regnery 1978); Charles Norris Cochrane, *Christianity and Classical Culture* (New York: Oxford University Press 1977).

75. See Strauss, *Natural Right and History*; and Eric Voegelin, *The New Science of Politics* (Chicago: University of Chicago Press 1952); Schall, *Reason, Revelation, and the Foundation of Political Philosophy*; Henri de Lubac, *The Drama of Atheist Humanism* (New York: Meridian 1964).

76. See James V. Schall, "Old Testament and Political Theory," *Politics of Heaven and Hell: Christian Themes from Classical, Medieval, and Modern Political Philosophy* (Lanham, MD: University Press of America 1984), pp. 1-20.

77. 982b29

78. See James V. Schall, "The Neglect of Hell in Political Theory," *Politics of Heaven and Hell*, pp. 83-106; *Human Dignity and Human Numbers* (Staten Island, NY: Alba House 1975).

79. See James V. Schall, "The Reality of Society in St. Thomas," *The Politics of Heaven and Hell*, pp. 235-52; "The Recovery of Metaphysics," *Divinitas*, #2 (1979), pp. 200-19.

80. See James V. Schall, *Liberation Theology* (San Francisco: Ignatius Press 1982).

81. See Brian Benestad, *The Pursuit of a Just Social Order: Policy Statements of the U.S. Catholic Bishops (1966-80)* (Washington: Ethics and Public Policy Centre 1982), part 3.

82. Mary Hanna, *Catholics and American Politics* (Cambridge: Harvard University Press 1979); Timothy O'Brien, "Groupism in American Politics" (Ph.D. diss., Catholic University 1980). See also Peter Berger, *Different Gospels and the Social Sources of Apostasy, Erasmus Lecture* (Rockford, IL: Rockford Institute 1987).

83. See William V. O'Brien, "The Peace Debate and American Catholics," *The Washington Quarterly* (Summer 1982). See also continuation of this topic in Autumn 1982.

84. See James V. Schall, "Religion and National Security," *International Security Quarterly* (Summer 1982), pp. 135-54.

85. See above, chapter 8.

86.	See Leo Strauss, *Thoughts on Machiavelli* (Glencoe: Free Press 1958), p. 29.
87.	See above, chapter 6.
88.	Benestad, *Social Order*, p. 127.
89.	See James V. Schall, *Redeeming the Time* (New York: Sheed and Ward 1968), chapter 3.
90.	Benestad, *Social Order*, p. 128
91.	See Kirk, *Reclaiming a Patrimony*.
92.	Benestad, *Social Order*, p. 130.
93.	Ibid., p. 131. See also James V. Schall, "Doctrine Frees: On the Content of Evangelization," *Church, State, and Society*, pp. 181-96.
94.	See Christopher Derrick, *Escape from Skepticism: Liberal Education as if the Truth Mattered* (LaSalle, IL: Sherwood Sugden 1977).
95.	See Ralph McInerny, *St. Thomas Aquinas* (Notre Dame: University of Notre Dame Press 1982); Herbert Deane, *Political and Social Ideas of St. Augustine* (New York: Columbia University Press 1965).
96.	*Shakespeare as a Political Thinker* (Durham, NC: Carolina Academic Press 1981). See the review by James V. Schall, "The Supernatural Destiny of Man," *Another Sort of Learning*, pp. 82-91. See Ernest Fortin, *Political Idealism and Christianity in the Thought of St. Augustine* (Philadelphia: Villanova University Press 1971).
97.	See "Solzhenitsyn," *30 Days*. (Dec. 1988), pp. 62-6.
98.	See James V. Schall, "On Life and the Defense of Life," *Life Report*, (Baltimore), (Jan. 1983), p. 4; *Christianity and Life* (San Francisco: Ignatius 1981); John O'Connor, *In Defense of Life* (Boston: St. Paul Editions 1980).
99.	See James V. Schall, "Revolutionary Spirituality," *Christianity and Politics*, pp. 149-77.
100.	Alexander Solzhenitsyn, Speech of 9 July 1975 (Washington: AFL-CIO 1976), p. 35.
101.	Alexander Solzhenitsyn, Speech of 30 June 1975, ibid., p. 24.
102.	Henri de Lubac, *Nature and Grace* (San Francisco: Ignatius Press 1984), p. 99.
103.	See Strauss, *Thoughts on Machiavelli*, p. 177 ff.
104.	See Eric Voegelin, *Science, Politics, and Gnosticism* (Chicago: Gateway 1968).
105.	See *Studies on Religion and Politics*, ed. James V. Schall and Jermone Hanus (Lanham, MD: University Press of America 1986).
106.	Elliot Abrams and Thomas Gumbleton, "Going to the Mat for Nicaragua," *Catholicism-in-Crisis*, 4 (Apr. 1986), pp. 22-7. See also the Statement of Miguel Cardinal Obando y Bravo, Archbishop of Managua, "The Sandinistas Have 'Gagged and Bound' Us," *The Washington Post*, (12 May 1986).

107. See James V. Schall, "Political Philosophy and Catholicism," *Divus Thomas* {Piacenza} LXXXVII, #3 (1984), pp. 153-64.
108. See *The Ratzinger Report*, ed. Vittorio Messori (San Francisco: Ignatius Press 1985), pp. 55-7.
109. David Martin, "Revs and Revolution: Church Trends and Theological Fashions," *Encounter* (Jan. 1979), p. 15. See also Peter Berger, "Can the Bishops Help the Poor?" *Commentary* (Feb. 1985), pp. 31-5; Michael Nelson, "C.S. Lewis," *The New York Times* (22 Nov. 1988).
110. See Hans Urs von Balthasar, "Flight Into Community," *New Elucidations* (San Francisco: Ignatius Press 1986), pp. 104-11.
111. See the three essays of Bishop Roger Heckel, *The Human Person and Social Structures*; *The Use of the Expression 'Social Doctrine' of the Church*; and *The Theme of Liberation* (Vatican City: Pontifical Commission on Justice and Peace 1980); Charles, *The Social Teaching of Vatican II*; and Schall, *The Church, State, and Society in the Thought of John Paul II*.
112. See Schall, *The Politics of Heaven and Hell*.
113. Henri de Saint-Simon, "The New Christianity," *Social Organization, the Science of Man, and Other Writings* (New York: Harper Torchbooks 1964), p. 116.
114. Leszek Kolakowski, "The Idolatry of Politics," the Fifteenth Jefferson Lecture in the Humanities (Washington: National Endowment for the Humanities, 7 May 1986), p. 23. See also Barrington Moore, *Reflections on the Causes of Human Misery and on Certain Proposals to Eliminate Them* (Boston: Beacon 1973) Gertrude Himmelfarb, *The Idea of Poverty* (New York: Knopf 1984); and James V. Schall, "Christianity and the 'Cures' of Poverty," *Christianity and Politics*, pp. 178-212.
115. The two documents are: 1) "An Instruction on the Theology of Liberation," 6 Aug. 1984, *The Pope Speaks*, 29, # 4 (1984), pp. 289-310; and 2) "Instruction on Christian Freedom and Liberation," *The National Catholic Reporter* (25 Apr. 1986), pp. 9-12, 41-4. See also "A Certain 'Liberation'," *The Ratzinger Report*, ibid., pp. 168-90; International Theological Commission, "Human Development and Christian Salvation," in Schall, *Liberation Theology*, pp. 263-83.
116. It is interesting to note that both Josef Ratzinger and Hannah Arendt, whose *On Revolution* (New York: Viking 1965) is so important for this topic of freedom and liberation, wrote on St. Augustine: Josef Ratzinger, *Volk und Haus Gottes in Augustin's Lehre von der Kirche* (München: Karl Zink 1954); Hannah Arendt, (her doctoral dissertation), *Die Liebesbegriff bei Augustin* (Berlin: Springer 1929). "For the history of the problem of freedom, Christian tradition has indeed become the decisive factor... The idea of freedom played no role in philosophy prior

to Augustine." Hannah Arendt, *Between Past and Future* (New York: Viking 1968), p. 157.

117. Ratzinger, Instruction #1, *Volk und Haus Gottes, p. 309.*

118. Carl Becker, *The Heavenly City of the Eighteenth Century Philosophers* (New Haven: Yale University Press 1932). See also Robert Nisbet, *History of the Idea of Progress* (New York: Basic Books 1980); Ernest Cassirer, *The Philosophy of the Enlightenment* (Boston: Beacon 1955).

119. Cassirer, p. 157. See John Young, "Original Sin," *Homiletic and Personal Review*, LXXXIX (Dec. 1988), pp. 9-16.

120. Ratzinger, Instruction #2, #75, 43.

121. *The Ratzinger Report*, p. 79.

122. Ratzinger, Instruction #2, #39, 12.

123. Ibid., #2, #60, 41.

124. Ibid., #1, 291.

125. Ibid., 298-9.

126. Ibid., 307-8.

127. See Michael Novak, *Freedom With Justice* (San Francisco: Harper 1984). See also the comments of Franz Mueller, "Catholic Social Doctrine," *Review of Social Economy*, XLIV (Apr. 1986), pp. 40-5.

128. P.T. Bauer, *Reality and Rhetoric: Studies in the Economics of Development* (Cambridge: Harvard University Press 1984), p. 89.

129. "Relying on the popular conviction that it is bad for some to be gorging themselves beside swimming pools while others starve, the papal 'Instruction of Christian Freedom and Liberation' suggests a merely redistributionist conception of what ought to be done. Still, the Congregation for the Doctrine of the Faith has at least clarified the central point; namely, that in concentrating its energies on social change, the Church is in danger of sinking to the level of political partisanship, and losing its own soul. In its insistence that the Church is the custodian of the mystery of the Christian revelation, it leaves its readers in no doubt that a Church is one thing and a political movement quite another." Kenneth Minogue, "At God's Left Hand," *The Times*, London, 26 April 1986.

130. Ratzinger, Instruction #2, #85, 43-44.

131. Ibid., #2, #5, 9. In this context, it is extremely interesting to note what Hannah Arendt says about the importance of the American Revolution and its relation to the heritage of the French Revolution on the questions of both liberty and the alleviation of poverty. *On Revolution.*

132. Josef Pieper, *Leisure: The Basis of Culture* (New York: Mentor 1956).

133. Jude P. Dougherty, "The Interior Life," *Crisis*, 5 (May 1987), p. 23.

134. See above chapter 7.

135. *The Economist*, Survey (25 October 1975), p. 19.

136. *Field*, (11 Sept. 1984).

137. *L'Osservatore Romano*, English, (19 Nov. 1984).

138. Bauer, *Reality and Rhetoric*, p. 89.

139. *La Documentation Catholique* (18 Juin 1978), p. 576.

140. Frank Knight, "Ethics and Economic Reform," *Economica*, (Nov. 1939), p. 399.

141. See Schall, *Christianity and Politics*; *The Politics of Heaven and Hell*.

142. Knight, "Ethics and Economic Reform."

143. Un entretien avec Raoul Audouin, "Peut-être libéral et chrétien?," *La Croix* (2 Mai 1984), p. 12. See also Peter Berger, "Can the Bishops Help the Poor?" *Commentary* (Feb. 1985), pp. 31-5.

144. Ernest Fortin, "Catholic Social Thought and the Economy," *Catholicism-in-Crisis*, 3 (Jan. 1985), p. 43.

145. Yves Simon, *The Philosophy of Democratic Government* (Chicago: University of Chicago Press 1977), p. 245.

146. G.K. Chesterton, "Why I Am Not a Socialist," *The Chesterton Review*, VII [(4 Jan. 1908) Aug. 1981].

147. *St. Louis Globe-Democrat* (5 July 1982).

148. *The Wall Steet Journal* (28 June 1982).

149. *San Francisco Chronicle* (2 July 1982).

150. See P.T. Bauer, *Equality in the Third World and Economic Delusion* (Cambridge: Harvard University Press 1981); *Western Guilt and Third World Poverty*.

151. *San Francisco Chronicle*, (12 July 1982).

152. Chesterton, "Why I Am Not a Socialist," p. 190.

153. Shafarevich, *The Socialist Phenomenon*.

154. Chesterton, "Why I Am Not a Socialist," pp. 190-1.

155. Ibid.

156. See the author's "The Christian Guardians," *The Politics of Heaven and Hell*, pp. 67-87.

157. See the author's "Monastery and Home," *The Distinctiveness of Christianity* (San Francisco: Ignatius Press 1982), pp. 200-17.

158. See Michael Novak, *The Spirit of Democratic Capitalism* (New York: Simon & Schuster 1982) chapter 20. See also the author's "Religious Teachings on Economics: Catholicism and the American Experience," *The Best of 'This World,'* pp. 1-13.

159. See Strauss, *Natural Right and History*; *City and Man*. See also the author's "Revelation, Reason, and Politics: Catholic Reflections on Strauss," *Gregorianum*, #2 and #3 (1981).

160. Igor Schafarevich, "Socialism in Our Past and Future," *From Under the Rubble* (Chicago: Gateway 1981), pp. 26-67.

161. William Pfaff, "Economic Development," *The New Yorker* (24 Dec. 1978), p. 47. See the author's "Christianity and the 'Cures' of Poverty," *Christianity and Politics*, chapter 7.

162. Shafarevich, "Socialism," p. 65. For an advocacy view, See John C. Cort, *Christian Socialism* (Maryknoll, NY: Orbis 1988).

163. Paul Johnson, "Is There a Moral Basis for Capitalism?" *Paideia* (Spring 1980), p. 1. See Paul Johnson, "Has Capitalism a Future?" *Will Capitalism Survive?* (Washington D.C.: Ethics and Public Policy Center 1979), pp. 3-16; *Enemies of Society* (London: Weidenfeld and Nicolson 1977).

164. See the author's "The Reality of Society," *The Politics of Heaven and Hell*, pp. 235-52.

165. Johnson, "Is There," p. 3.

166. Ibid., p. 4.

167. See George Gilder, "The Family and our Economic Future," *The Wealth of Families*, pp. 27-34. See also Michael Novak, "The Family," *The Spirit of Democratic Capitalism*, chapter 8, pp. 156-70.

168. George Gilder, *Wealth and Poverty* (New York: Basic 1981), p. 265.

169. George Gilder, "Why I Am Not a Neo-Conservative," *The National Review* (5 Mar. 1982), p. 220.

170. See the author's "Catholicism, Business, and Politics," *A Judaeo-Christian View of Business* (Notre Dame: University of Notre Dame Press 1982).

171. Novak, *The Spirit*, pp. 356-7.

172. See the author's "Revolutionary Spirituality," *Christianity and Politics*, chapter 6.

173. See the author's *Church, State and Society in the Thought of John Paul II*.

174. Daughters of St. Paul, America Press, the USCC, *The Pope Speaks*, and the English edition of *L'Osservatore Romano*, all publish various individual encyclicals. The Paulist Press' *Seven Great Encyclicals* contains *Rerum Novarum, Quadragesimo Anno, Casti Connubii, Divini Illius Magristri, Divini Redemptoris, Mater et Magistra*, and *Pacem in Terris*. See James V. Schall, "Social Thinker," *The Sixth Paul* (Canfield, OH: Alba Books 1977), pp. 103-24; "On the Renewed Dynamics of Catholic Social Thought" and "Background to the Social Thought of the Church," *The Church, the State, and Society in the Thought of John Paul II*, pp. 125-44; 151-96; "From Catholic 'Social Doctrine' to the 'Kingdom of God on Earth'," *Communio*, III (Winter 1976), pp. 284-300; *Christianity and Life*; "The Altar as the Throne," in *Churches on the Wrong Road*, ed. Stanley Atkins and Theodore McConnell (Chicago: Gateway 1986), pp. 193-238; "Christianity and the 'Cures' of Poverty," *Christianity and Politics*, pp. 178-212.

175. E.F. Schumacher, *A Guide for the Perplexed* (New York: Harper Colophon 1977), p. 119.

176. John Paul II, *Address to Third Conference of Latin American Episcopate, 28 Jan. 1979, Puebla: A Pilgrimage of Faith* (Boston: St. Paul Editions 1979), pp. 93-126.

177. See Schall, "The First Right: Religious Freedom," *The Church, the State, and Society in the Thought of John Paul II*, pp. 41-58.

178. John Paul II, *On Social Concern* (Boston: St. Paul Books 1988). I will use this edition, which is the Vatican Press English translation, and its numbering.

179. Some comments on the Encyclical: [1] "It seems very odd these days to read a lengthy statement about economic development that is so oblivious to the resounding triumphs of liberal capitalism in the Third World in the years since *Populorum Progressio*." *Fortune*, (28 Mar. 1988), p. 156. [2] "How is it possible that this Pope, son of Poland, could write about the two systems (communism and capitalism) without troubling to make it utterly clear that under one religion is oppressed, freedom denied, police rule imposed, whole nations imprisoned, including his own? It seems a lapse of political sensitivity, whatever his intent." A.M. Rosenthal, *The New York Times* (15 Mar. 1988), p. A27. [3] "Obviously, in 102 pages one can find the ritual Christian affirmations. But they are swamped by a theological version of the kind of historical revisionism generally associated with modern nihilists. One prays that the Holy Father will move quickly to correct the encyclical heart-tearingly misbegotten." William F. Buckley, Jr., *The National Review*, (18 Mar. 1988), p. 18. "It has been argued that highlighting these faults of the United States or of the Western free world will only enervate our will to resist communism. It might be countered, however, that to a large degree we already have lost that will to resist evil, and for many of the reasons that the Pope highlights in this encyclical." Angela Grimm, *The Light* (Mar. 1988), p. 7.

180. Tom Bethell, for example, rightly pointed out that there are a very large and significant number of things in *Populorum Progressio*, especially those having to do with state planning and hesitation about initiative, that are not found in *Sollicitudo Rei Socialis*. "Mea Maxima Culpa," *The National Review* (15 Apr. 1988), pp. 34-6.

181. See the ongoing series in recent years of Surveys on the overall economic condition of the world found, especially those of Norman Macrae, in *The Economist* of London, as a comparison with the dominant outlook in the encyclical. For example, among others, see Nicholas Valery, "Factory of the Future," *The Economist*, Survey, (20 May 1987). It seems clear that little of this sort of thinking is even considered by the encyclical.

182. Bauer, "Ecclesiastical Economics: Envy Legitimized," *Reality and Rhetoric*, p. 89. For a more thorough analysis of *Sollicitudo Rei Socialis*, see *Aspiring to Freedom*, ed. Kenneth A. Meyers, (Grand Rapids, MI.:

Eerdmans 1988) with contributions by Peter Berger, George Weigel, Michael Novak, Roberto Suro, and Richard J. Neuhaus.

183. Let me cite at least a few works: Gilder, *Wealth and Poverty*; Herman Kahn, *World Economic Development* (New York: Morrow 1979); Simon, *The Ultimate Resource*; Julian Simon and Herman Kahn, *The Resourceful Earth* (New York: Basil Blackwell 1984); Peter Berger, *The Capitalist Revolution: Fifty Propositions about Prosperity, Equality, and Liberty* (New York: Basic Books 1986); Ronald Nash, *Poverty and Wealth: The Christian Debate over Capitalism* (Westchester, IL: Crossway 1986); Wilfred Beckerman, *Two Cheers for the Affluent Society: A Spirited Defense of Economic Growth* (New York: St. Martin's 1974); Irving Kristol, *Two Cheers for Capitalism* (New York: Basic Books 1978); Buckminster Fuller, *Utopia or Oblivion* (New York: Bantam 1969); Novak, *The Spirit of Democratic Capitalism*; Bauer, *Western Guilt and Third World Poverty*; Max Singer, *Passage to a Human World: The Dynamics of Creating Global Wealth* (Indianapolis: Hudson 1987); *Theology, Third World Development and Economic Justice*, ed. Walter Block and Donald Shaw (Vancouver: The Fraser Institute 1985); T.E. Uttey, *Capitalism: The Moral Case* (Westminster: Conservative Central Office 1980); Alejandro A. Chafuen, *Christians for Freedom*, (San Francisco: Ignatius 1980); Arnold F. McKee, *Economics and the Christian Mind* (New York: Vantage 1987).

184. See Schall, *Human Dignity and Human Numbers*; Kasun, *The War Against Regulation*, 1987.

185. *Solzhenitsyn at Harvard*, ed. Ronald Berman (Washington: Ethics and Public Policy Center 1980).

186. See the valuable discussion of this point in the French and German Bishops' *Pastorals on War, Out of Justice, Peace*, ed. James V. Schall (San Francisco: Ignatius Press 1984).

187. See Singer, *Passage*, pp. 1-61.

188. Thomas Sowell, "Second Thoughts about the Third World," *Harper's* (Nov. 1983), p. 14.

189. See the discussions of culture in Stanley L. Jaki, "On Whose Side Is History?" *Chance or Reality and Other Essays* (Lanham, MD: University Press of America 1986), pp. 233-44; Theodore Schultz, "The Economics of Being Poor," *Journal of Political Economy*, 88, #4 (1979), pp. 639-51; Bauer, "Remembrance of Studies Past," *Reality and Rhetoric*, pp. 1-18; Bloom, "Culture," *The Closing of the American Mind*, pp. 185-93.

190. Singer, *Passage*, pp. 22-3.

191. See Jean-François Revel, *How Democracies Perish* (New York: Harper 1983).

192. Singer, *Passage*, p. 292.

193. See James V. Schall, "On Building Cathedrals and Tearing Them Down," *The Praise of 'Sons of Bitches' : On the Worship of God by Fallen Men* (Slough, England: St. Paul Publications 1978), pp. 22-35.

194. See P.T. Bauer and B.S. Yamey, "Foreign Aid: Rewarding Impoverishment?" *Commentary* (Sept. 1985), pp. 38-40.

195. See the valuable work of the Center for Economic and Social Justice on the topic of property and poverty (P.O. 40849), Washington, D.C., 20016.

196. See James V. Schall, "The Reality of Society according to St. Thomas," *Politics of Heaven and Hell*, pp. 235-52.

197. George Gilder, "The Commercial Imagination," *Public Opinion* (Nov. 1982), p. 2.

198. In an Address in Verona, April 17, 1988, the Holy Father gave a much more restricted and acceptable discussion of profit where he distinguished reasonable and excessive profit, though without facing the nature of profit itself or the meaning of excessive, since the very nature of profit refers to the production of new wealth, which is presumably what the economy is supposed to do. "From this perspective (of the common good) it is clear that the sole criterion of profit is insufficient, especially when it is raised to the level of an absolute: "earning" more in order to "possess" more, not only tangible objects but also financial holdings, making it possible to enjoy new forms of property that are ever more expensive and ever more dominating. Not that aiming at profit is itself unjust; a business cannot do without it. The reasonable attempt to make a profit is, for that matter, connected with the right of "economic initiative" which I defended in the Encyclical just cited (n. 15). I merely intend to say that, in order to be just, profit must be regulated by moral criteria, in particular by those connected with the principle of solidarity." This passage, unfortunately, was not specifically in the Encyclical, and its absence seems the cause of most of the confusion about the subject of profit and its justification.

199. Simon, *Ultimate Resource*, p. 5.

200. See Michael Novak, "Why Latin America Is Poor," *The Atlantic Monthly*, (Mar. 1982), pp. 66-75; Roger A. Freeman, *Does America Neglect Its Poor?* (Stanford: Hoover 1987).

201. Peter Berger, "Can the Bishops Help the Poor?" pp. 31-5.

202. George Gilder, "The Moral Sources of Capitalism," *Imprimis* (Dec. 1980), p. 5.

203. See the discussions of this in Singer, *Passage*, pp. 275-94; Herman Kahn, *The Next 200 Years* (New York: Morrow 1976).

204. See the important discussion of Simon, *The Philosophy of Democratic Government*, pp. 36-71.

205. Josef Pieper, *Leisure: The Basis of Culture* (New York: Mentor 1952); *In Tune with the World: A Theory of Festivity* (Chicago: Franciscan Herald 1973); Hugo Rahner, *Man at Play* (New York: Herder 1976): Josef Ratzinger, *Feast of Faith* (San Francisco: Ignatius 1986); James V. Schall, *Far Too Easily Pleased: A Theology of Contemplation, Play, and Festivity* (Los Angeles: Benziger-Macmillan 1976).

206. "I recognize that Rome is impelled to keep on producing such statements (as the present encyclical) by its conception of the magisterium of the Church, a conception that I do not share. But, even given these theological and ecclesial assumptions—that is, looking at this document and indeed at the growing body of Catholic social doctrine from a Catholic point of view—I wonder what is gained from these exercises. Very possibly they actually undermine the authority of the teaching mission that they are supposed to express. I'm reminded of the reply given by Samuel Gompers to the question as to what the American labor movement wants: 'More!', he replied. I ask myself what I would want from Rome in terms of its social doctrine. Respectfully, regretfully, but with increasing assurance I find myself replying: 'Less!'," Peter Berger, "Comments on *Sollicitudo Rei Socialis*", *Aspiring to Freedom*, p. 118..

Bibliography

Abrams, Elliot and Thomas Gumbleton, "Going to the Mat for Nicaragua," *Catholicism-in-Crisis* (Apr. 1986).

Adler, Mortimer, *Ten Philosophical Mistakes* (London: Macmillan 1985).

Aharoni, Yair, *The No-Risk Society* (Chatham, NJ: Chatham House 1981).

Anderson, Carl, ed., *Wealth of Families* (Washington: American Family Institute 1982).

Arendt, Hannah, *Between Past and Future* (New York: Viking 1968).

_____, *The Human Condition* (Garden City, NY: Doubleday Anchor 1979).

_____, *Die Liebesbegriff bei Augustin* (Berlin: Springer 1929).

_____, *On Revolution* (New York: Viking 1965).

Audouin, Raoul, "Peut-être libéral et chrétien?" *La Croix* (Mai 2, 1984).

Bauer, P.T., *Equality in the Third World and Economic Delusion* (Cambridge: Harvard University Press 1981).

_____, *Reality and Rhetoric: Studies in the Economics of Development* (Cambridge: Harvard University Press 1984).

_____, *Western Guilt and Third World Poverty* (Washington: Ethics and Public Policy Center 1976).

_____ and B. Yamey, "Economics and the Third World," *Current* (Nov. 1982).

Becker, Carl, *The Heavenly City of the Eighteenth Century Philosophers* (New Haven: Yale University Press 1932).

Beckerman, Wilfred, *Two Cheers for the Affluent Society: A Spirited Defense of Economic Growth* (New York: St. Martin's 1974).

Belloc, Hilaire, *The Path to Rome* (Garden City, NY: Doubleday Image 1956).

Benestad, Brian, *The Pursuit of a Just Social Order: Policy Statements of the U.S. Catholic Bishops (1966-80)* (Washington: Ethics and Public Policy Center 1982).

Berger, Peter, "Can the Bishops Help the Poor?", *Commentary* (Feb. 1985).

_____, *The Capitalist Revolution: Fifty Propositions about Prosperity, Equality, and Liberty* (New York: Basic Books 1986).

Block, Walter, *Focus: On Economics and the Canadian Bishops* (Vancouver, BC: The Fraser Institute 1983).

_____ , Geoffrey Brennan and Kenneth Elizinga, ed., *The Morality of the Market: Religious and Economic Perspectives* (Vancouver, BC: The Fraser Institute 1985).

_____ and Irving Hexham, ed., *Religion, Economics and Social Thought* (Vancouver, BC: The Fraser Institute 1986).

_____ and Donald E. Shaw, ed., *Theology, Third World Development and Economic Justice* (Vancouver, BC: The Fraser Institute 1985).

_____ , ed., *The U.S. Bishops and their Critics: An Economic and Ethical Perspective* (Vancouver, BC: The Fraser Institute 1986).

Bloom, Allan, *The Closing of the American Mind* (New York: Simon and Schuster 1987).

_____ , "Our Listless Universities," *National Review* (10 Dec. 1982).

_____ , ed. *The Republic* (New York: Basic Books 1968).

Burke, Edmund, *Reflections on the Revolution in France* (Chicago: Gateway 1955).

Carlson, Allan C., *Family in America* (Rockford, IL: Rockford Institute 1987 ff).

Cassirer, Ernst, *The Philosophy of the Enlightenment* (Boston: Beacon 1955).

Chafuen, Alejandro A., *Christians for Freedom* (San Francisco: Ignatius Press 1986).

Chapman, Stephen, "Killing for Christ," *New Republic* (21 Oct. 1978).

Charles, Rodger, *The Social Teachings of Vatican II* (San Francisco: Ignatius Press 1982).

Chesterton, G.K., *Selected Essays* (London: Methuen 1949).

_____ , "Why I Am Not a Socialist," *The Chesterton Review*, (Aug. 1981).

_____ , *What's Wrong with the World. The Collected Works of G.K. Chesterton* (San Francisco: Ignatius Press 1986), Vol. 4.

Cochrane, Charles Norris, *Christianity and Classical Culture* (New York: Oxford University Press, 1977).

Cort, John C., *Christian Socialism* (Maryknoll: Orbis 1988).

Cranston, Maurice, *What Are Human Rights?* (New York: Taplinger 1973).

Cropsey, Joseph, *Political Philosophy and the Issues of Politics* (Chicago: University of Chicago Press 1977).

Dawson, Christopher, *Essays in Order* (London: Sheed and Ward 1934).

_____, *The Making of Europe* (New York: Meridian 1965).

_____, *Religion and Culture* (New York: Meridian 1948).

_____, *Religion and the Rise of Western Culture* (Garden City: Doubleday Image 1959).

Deane, Herbert, *Political and Social Ideas of St. Augustine* (New York: Columbia University Press 1965).

de Lubac, Henri, *The Drama of Atheist Humanism* (New York: Meridian 1964).

_____, *Nature and Grace* (San Francisco: Ignatius Press 1984).

Derrick, Derrick, *Escape from Skepticism: Liberal Education as if the Truth Really Mattered* (LaSalle, IL: Sherwood Sugden 1977).

_____, *Too Many People?* (San Francisco: Ignatius Press 1985).

Dougherty, Jude, "The Interior Life," *Crisis* (May 1987).

Drucker, Peter, "Towards the Next Economics," in *The Crisis in Economic Theory*, Daniel Bell and Irving Kristol, eds. (New York: Basic) 1981.

Ellul, Jacques, *Betrayal of the West* (New York: Seabury 1978).

Finnis, John, *Natural Law and Natural Right* (New York: Oxford University Press, 1980).

Fortin, Ernest, "Catholic Social Thought and the Economy," *Crisis* (Jan. 1985).

_____, *Dissidence et philosophie au Moyen Age: Dante et ses antécédents* (Paris: J. Vrin 1981).

_____, *Political Idealism and Christianity in the Thought of St. Augustine* (Villanova, PA: Villanova University Press 1971).

Freeman, Roger, *Does America Neglect Its Poor?* (Stanford: Hoover Institution 1987).

Fuller, Buckminster, *Utopia or Oblivion?* (New York: Bantam 1969).

Gilder, George, "the Commercial Imagination," *Public Opinion* (Oct.-Nov. 1982).

_____, "The Moral Sources of Capitalism," *Imprimis* (Dec. 1980).

_____, *Wealth and Poverty* (New York: Basic Books 1981).

_____, "Why I Am Not a Neo-Conservative," *National Review* (15 March 1982).

Gilson, Etienne, *Reason and Revelation in the Middle Ages* (New York: Scribner's 1938).

Grisez, Germain, *The Way of the Lord Jesus* (Chicago: Franciscan Herald Press 1983).

Hanna, Mary, *Catholics and American Politics* (Cambridge: Harvard University Press, 1979.

Heckel, Roger, *Self-Reliance*; *The Human Person and Social Structures*; *Religious Freedom*; *The Theme of Liberation*; *The Use of the Expression 'Social Doctrine of the Church'*; *General Aspects of the Catechises of John Paul II* (Rome: Pontifical Commission on Justice and Peace 1978-80).

Himmelfarb, Gertrude, *The Idea of Poverty* (New York: Knopf 1984).

Hitchcock, James, *What Is Secular Humanism?* (Ann Arbor, MI: Servant Publications 1982).

Jaffa, Harry, *The Conditions of Freedom* (Baltimore: The Johns Hopkins University Press 1975).

Jaki, Stanley L., *Chance or Reality?* (Lanham, MD: University Press of America 1986).

_____, *The Road of Science and the Ways to God* (Chicago: University of Chicago Press 1978).

Johnson, Paul, *Enemies of Society* (London: Weidenfeld and Nicolson 1977).

_____, "Is There a Moral Basis for Capitalism?" *Paideia* (Spring, 1980).

_____, "Has Capitalism a Future?" in *Will Capitalism Survive?* (Washington: Ethics and Public Policy Center 1979).

_____, *Modern Times* (New York: Harper Colophon 1983).

_____, *Pope John Paul II and the Catholic Restoration* (New York: St. Martin's 1981).

Kahn, Herman, *The Next Two Hundred Years* (New York: Morrow 1976).

Kasun, Jacqueline, *The War Against Population* (San Francisco: Ignatius Press 1988).

Kirk, Russell, *Reclaiming a Patrimony* (Washington: Heritage 1982).

Knight, Frank, "Ethics and Economic Reform," *Economica* (Nov. 1939).

Kolakowski, Leszek, "The Idolatry of Politics," The Fifteenth Jefferson Lecture in the Humanities (Washington: National Endowment for the Humanities 1986).

Kristol, Irving, *Two Cheers for Capitalism* (New York: Basic Books 1978).

Maritain, Jacques, *Integral Humanism* (Notre Dame: University of Notre Dame Press 1973).

Martin, David, "Revs and Revolution: Church Trends and Theological Fashions," *Encounter* (Jauary 1979).   •

Marzani, Carl, "The Vatican as a Left Ally?", *Monthly Review: The Independent Socialist Magazine*, 34 (July-August 1982).

McCann, Dennis P. *Christian Realism and Liberation Theology* (Maryknoll: Orbis 1983).

McGinley, Phyllis, *Times Three* (New York: Viking 1961).

McInerny, Ralph, *St. Thomas Aquinas* (Notre Dame: University of Notre Dame Press 1982).

McKee, Arnold F., *Economics and the Christian Mind* (New York: Vantage 1987).

Messori, Vittorio, ed., *The Ratzinger Report* (San Francisco: Ignatius Press 1985).

Midgley, E.B.F., *The Natural Law Tradition and the Theory of International Relations* (London: Elek 1975).

Minogue, Kenneth, "At God's Left Hand," *The Times*, London, (26 Apr. 1986).

Miranda, Jose, *Marx and the Bible* (Maryknoll: Orbis 1974).

Molnar, Thomas, *Politics and the State* (Chicago: Franciscan Herald Press 1982).

Moore, Barrington, *Reflections on the Causes of Human Misery and Certain Proposals to Alleviate It* (Boston: Beacon 1972).

Mueller, Franz, Catholic Social Doctrine," *Review of Social Economy* (Apr. 1986).

Myers, Kenneth A., ed. *Aspiring to Freedom*, (Grand Rapids, MI.: Eerdmans 1988).

Naisbitt, John, *Megatrends* (New York: Warner 1982).

Nash, Ronald H., *Poverty and Wealth: The Christian Debate over Capitalism* (Westchester, IL: Crossways 1986).

_____, ed., *Liberation Theology* (Milford, MI: Mott Media 1984).

Neuhaus, Richard John, *In Defense of People* (New York: Macmillan 1971).

Niemeyer, Gerhard, "The Autonomous Man," *The Intercollegiate Review* (Summer 1974).

Nisbet, Robert, *History of the Idea of Progress* (New York: Basic Books 1980).

Novak, Michael, *Freedom with Justice*. (San Francisco: Harper's 1984).

_____, "The Right to Develop," *Rethinking Human Rights* (Washington: The Foundation for Economic Education 1982), Vol. II.

_____, *The Spirit of Democratic Capitalism* (New York: Simon and Schuster 1982).

_____, "Why Latin America Is Poor," *The Atlantic Monthly* (Mar. 1982).

Obando y Bravo, Miguel Cardinal, "The Sandinistas Have 'Gagged and Bound' Us," *The Washington Post*, 12 May 1986.

O'Brien, Timothy, "Groupism in American Politics," Ph.D. Dissertation, (Catholic University, Washington 1980).

O'Brien, William V., "The Peace Debate and American Catholics," *Washington Quarterly*, (Summer 1982).

O'Connor, Flannery, *The Habit of Being* (New York: Viking 1979).

O'Connor, John, *In Defense of Life* (Boston: St. Paul Editions 1980).

Percy, Walker, *Love in the Ruins* (New York: Avon 1971).

Pfaff, William, "Economic Development," *The New Yorker*, (24 Dec. 1978).

Pieper, Josef, *Leisure: The Basis of Culture* (New York: Mentor 1956).

_____, *In Tune with the World: A Theory of Festivity* (Chicago: Franciscan Herald 1973).

_____, *The Silence of St. Thomas*. (Chicago: Regnery 1978).

Pirenne, Henri, *Economic and Social History of Europe* (New York: Harvest 1933).

Rahner, Hugo, *Men at Play* (New York: Herder 1976).

Ratzinger, Josef Cardinal, "An Instruction on the Theology of Liberation," (6 Aug. 1984), *The Pope Speaks*, #4 (1984); "Instruction on Christian Freedom and Liberation," *National Catholic Reporter*, (25 April 1986).

_____, *Feast of Faith* (San Francisco: Ignatius Press 1986).

_____, "A Certain Liberation," in *The Ratzinger Report*, Vittoria Messori, ed., (San Francisco: Ignatius Press 1985).

_____, *Haus Gottes in Augustin's Lehre von der Kirche* (München: Karl Zink 1954).

Rawls, John, *A Theory of Justice* (Cambridge: Harvard University Press 1972).

Revel, Jean-François, *How Democracies Perish* (New York: Harper 1985).

_____, "How Well Is the Third World Governed," *Wall Street Journal* (5 Nov. 1981).

Saint-Simon, Henri de, "The New Christianity," *Social Organization, the Science of Man, and Other Writings* (New York: Harper Torchbooks 1964).

Satter, David, "The System of Forced Labor in Russia," *The Wall Street Journal*, 24 June 1982.

Schall, James V., "The Altar and the Throne," in *Churches on the Wrong Road*, ed. Stanley Atkins and Theodore McConnell (Chicago: Gateway 1986).

_____, *Another Sort of Learning* (San Francisco: Ignatius Press 1988).

_____, *Church, State, and Society in the Thought of John Paul II.* (Chicago: Franciscan Herald Press 1982).

_____, *Christianity and Politics* (Boston: St. Paul Editions 1981).

_____, *Far Too Easily Pleased: A Theology of Contemplation, Play and Festivity.* (Los Angeles: Benziger-Macmillan 1976).

_____, *Human Dignity and Human Numbers* (Staten Island, NY: Alba House 1971).

_____, "Human Rights as an Ideological Project," *American Journal of Jurisprudence*, 32 (1987).

_____, *Liberation Theology* (San Francisco: Ignatius Press 1982).

_____, "On the Pertinence of Catholic Intelligence," *Center Journal* (Fall 1982).

_____, "Political Philosophy and Catholicism," *Divus Thomas*, #3 (1984).

_____, "Political Theory, Religion, and War," *Catholicism-in-Crisis* (Jan. 1983).

_____, *The Politics of Heaven and Hell: Christian Themes from Classical, Medieval, and Modern Political Philosophy* (Lanham, MD: University Press of America 1984).

_____, *The Praise of 'Sons of Bitches' : On the Worship of God by Fallen Men.* (Slough, England: St. Paul Publications 1978).

_____, *Reason, Revelation, and the Foundations of Political Philosophy* (Baton Rouge: Louisiana State University Press 1987).

_____, "The Recovery of Metaphysics," *Divinitas*, #2 (1979).

_____, *Redeeming the Time* (New York: Sheed & Ward 1968).

_____, "Religion and National Security," *International Security Quarterly* (Summer 1982).

_____, "Religious Teaching on Economics: Catholicism and the American Experience," *The Best of 'This World'* (Lanham, MD: University Press of America 1986).

_____, "Revelation, Reason, and Politics: Catholic Reflections on Strauss," *Gregorianum*, #2 and #3 (1981).

_____, *The Sixth Paul* (Canfield, OH: Alba Books 1977).

_____, Editor, *The Whole Truth about Man: John Paul II to University Faculties and Students* (Boston: St. Paul Editions 1981).

_____, and Jerome Hanus ed., *Studies in Religion and Politics* (Lanham, MD: University Press of America, 1986).

Schultz, Theodore, "The Economics of Being Poor," *Journal of Political Economy*, #4 (1980).

Schumacher, E.F.., *A Guide for the Perplexed* (New York: Harper Colophon 1977).

Shafarevich, Igor, *The Socialist Phenomenon* (New York: Harper 1980).

Shakespeare as a Political Thinker ed. John Alvis and Thomas G. West (Durham, NC: Carolina Academic Press 1981).

Sigmund, Paul, "Thomistic Natural Law and Social Theory," *Calgary Aquinas Studies*, ed. Anthony Parel (Toronto: Pontifical Medieval Institute 1978).

Simon, Julian, *The Ultimate Resource* (Princeton: Princeton University Press 1981).

_____, and Herman Kahn, *The Resourceful Earth* (New York: Basil Blackwell 1984).

Simon, Yves, *The Philosophy of Democratic Government* (Chicago: University of Chicago Press 1977).

Singer, Max, *Passage to a Human World: The Dynamics of Creating Global Wealth* (Indianapolis: Houston 1987).

Sobran, Joseph, *Single Issues* (New York: Human Life Press,1982).

Solzhenitsyn, Alexander, *Solzhenitsyn at Harvard* (Washington: Ethics and Public Policy Center 1980).

_____, AFL Speeches, 30 June 1975 and 9 July 1975 (Washington: AFL-CIO 1976).

Sowell, Thomas, "Second Thoughts about the Third World," *Harper's* (Nov. 1983).

Strauss, Leo, *The City and Man* (Chicago: University of Chicago Press 1964).

_____, *Essays on Political Philosophy* ed. H. Gilden (New York: Bobbs-Merrill 1975).

_____, "the Mutual Influence of Theology and Philosophy," *Independent Journal of Philosophy* (1979).

_____, *Natural Rights and History* (Chicago: University of Chicago Press 1952).

_____, "the Crisis of Political Philosophy," in *The Predicament of Modern Politics*, ed. H. Spaeth (Detroit: University of Detroit Press 1964).

_____, *Thoughts on Machiavelli* (Glencoe, IL, Free Press 1958).

Utley, T.E., *Capitalism: The Moral Case* (London: Conservative Central Office 1980).

Veatch, Henry, *Human Rights: Fact or Fancy?* (Baton Rouge: Louisiana State University Press 1985).

_____, "Natural Law: Dead or Alive?" *Literature of Liberty* (Oct.-Dec. 1976).

Voegelin, Eric, *The New Science of Politics* (Chicago: University of Chicago Press 1952).

_____, *Science, Politics, and Gnosticism* (Chicago: Gateway 1968).

von Balthasar, Hans Urs, *New Elucidations* (San Francisco: Ignatius Press 1986).

Walker, Michael, ed., *Freedom Democracy and Economic Welfare* (Vancouver, BC: The Fraser Institute 1988).

Weber, Max, *The Protestant Ethic and the Spirit of Capitalism* (New York: Scribner's 1958).

Wilhelmsen, Frederick D., *Christianity and Political Philosophy* (Athens: University of Georgia Press 1980).

_____, *The Enemies of Faith Today* (Reston, VA: YAF 1981).

_____, "Faith and Reason," *Modern Age* (Winter 1979).

Williams, George Hunston, *The Mind of John Paul II* (New York: Seabury 1981).

Wilson, Ellen, *An Even Dozen* (New York: Human Life Press 1981).

Woznicki, Andrew, *The Dignity of Man as a Person: Essays on the Christian Humanism of John Paul II* (San Francisco: Society of Christ 1987).

_____, *Karol Wojtyla's Existentialist Personalism* (New Britain: CT: Mariel 1980).

Young, John, "Original Sin," *Homiletic and Pastoral Review* (Dec. 1988).